BEFORE BOTOX

BEFORE BOTOX

I Knew Them When...Twenty Years of Celebrity Interviews

ARLENE PECK

ISBN: Hardcover   978-1-5245-5781-2
             Softcover   978-1-5245-5780-5
             eBook   978-1-5245-5779-9

Print information available on the last page.

Rev. date: 03/26/2019

To order additional copies of this book, contact:
Xlibris
1-888-795-4274
www.Xlibris.com
Orders@Xlibris.com
546504

CONTENTS

Introduction

Who is Arlene Peck...And Why Has She Written This Book?

One day, a friend said to me, "You have a thousand pictures of famous people who you've interviewed, partied with or somehow known on one level or another. You really ought to put this all in a book. These stories shouldn't be lost. They give a unique insight into the lives of celebrities and politicians that the public doesn't get to see. Why don't you share your experiences with everyone?"

At first, I didn't really give this conversation much thought; however, like a moth to a flame, the book idea kept returning in my mind. The more I looked through the pictures, the more the memories returned, and I began reaching in my brain for details. Readers, this wasn't easy for me. Hey, I'm always amazed when in court the lawyer asks, "Where were you on the evening of July 30th, 1997?" and immediately the person relates exactly where they were, what they were doing, and even what they were wearing. I am a woman who has difficulty remembering where I park the car at the mall. Often the security guy has to drive me around the parking lot until I spot the damn thing. People talk about finding their "G spot." I can't even find where I put my keys.

Anyway, I realized that some of these stories about these people were priceless. It's not that I had merely met or had pictures taken with famous, and sometimes infamous, people; there was more to these experiences. Somehow, there was always something that happened in my connection that made them so memorable. Normal vibes don't follow me. Life is an adventure!

In addition to meeting hundreds of well-known people over the years, I also interviewed famous celebrities and other notable figures on television for over 20 years. When I began to watch the recordings of my shows I realized that my friend may have been on to something with this book idea. I realized that the celebrities I interviewed were indeed providing "unique insight" into their lives, and our discussions ranged across a wide variety of topics. At this point, I decided to go for it and write the book!

So, how did I end up meeting so many famous people and interviewing many of them on my own television show? Well, before my television career began, I was a journalist for many years. I didn't really think about being a writer while growing up in Atlanta, GA. I studied Business Law and Real Estate in college. I worked my way up from the University of Alabama to Columbia! My writing career began in 1976 in Russia, when the KGB arrested me for smuggling prayer books. That's right! I kept a diary of my adventure. When I returned to Atlanta, I sent my tales from Russia to the local Jewish paper, which at the time was called *The Southern Israelite* (now the *Atlanta Jewish Times*). They liked my stories and asked if they could run them as a six-week series. I said, "Sure!" The reader response was positive, and I was soon contacted by the national paper, the *Jewish Post and Opinion*. The national paper published my diary and soon asked me to do a regular series. That's how I became a syndicated columnist.

I continued writing my column for over 30 years. People in the press seemed to get invited to every event, dinner, and party, so I made hundreds of contacts. Oh yes, and the syndicated national Jewish newspapers gave me a political outlet, which I enjoyed.

As a journalist in the Jewish press, I traveled to the Middle East over 25 times and covered war conflicts in Beirut and Gaza, where I spent five weeks in June of 1982. That was probably one of the best times in my life. I had the most favorable odds I would ever have—67,000 sex-starved, gorgeous Israeli soldiers and only four female correspondents. Lucky me! I returned to Gaza in 1993 for "Operation Accountability," where I entered with the Israeli Defense Force as a representative of the media.

Also, for six years in the 1970s I was the chair of a Jewish discussion group at the Atlanta Federal Penitentiary. I wrote about my experiences in my first book, *Prison Cheerleader: How a Nice Jewish Girl Went Wrong Doing Right.* The success of my program led to the formation of similar groups in other prisons.

After 15 years of wedded boredom, I had the good fortune of my husband leaving me for another woman. Because my divorce case became a landmark case in Atlanta, I became a subject in the media. Maybe because it was the first time a man left his wife for another woman and then sued his wife for her money—and got it! Although it was a painful experience, my divorce ultimately boosted my self-confidence. I discovered that instead of being a pot roast, I was, in fact, the chateaubriand. There was life after divorce!

Soon after my divorce I started writing for *Atlanta Singles Magazine, Atlanta Women's News,* and other women's magazines. In my articles I usually discussed various women's issues, particularly those that arise in dealing with men, and the various trials and tribulations—and joyous freedom!—of being divorced and single. I became an expert on things I knew nothing about: men and relationships!

I eventually started receiving invitations to speak at various organizations and events, which began my stint on the speaker's circuit. My topic was often "Older Women, Younger Men" or variations on that theme, such as "Older Women, Younger Men, and How Their Daughter Feels about Them." But over the years my younger men kept getting older...

I taught a course that I called "An Outrageous Approach to Divorce" at The Learning Annex in Atlanta. In class I gave lessons on surviving divorce and keeping a sense of humor. Finally, I started appearing as a guest on various local talk shows, and for awhile I did a regular two-minute radio spot on WCNN which aired twice a day.

I should perhaps pause here to explain that my viewpoints have sometimes been described as being to the right of Attila the Hun. Now, that's just a bit exaggerated, but I admit that I am a conservative woman who prides herself on being politically incorrect. In fact, *Lifestyles* magazine ran a four-page spread on me called "Politically Incorrect and Loving It." Perhaps I sometimes rubbed my readers and listeners the wrong way. But I usually got their attention!

So, with my syndicated columns in the Jewish press, articles in women's magazines, and various speaking, teaching, and television engagements, I was a busy woman. This was all wonderful and exciting, but in 1989 I was ready for a change in location. For so many years in Atlanta I had been somebody's wife, mother, daughter, etc., and I wanted to see what it was like striking out on my own.

So I moved to Los Angeles. I had already developed a following, and it must have reached to L.A., because it wasn't long before I began receiving speaking invitations there. After I had appeared as a guest on several television shows there, several people suggested to me that I should do my own show. At first I wondered, "Are you kidding?"

But I went for it. A friend put me in touch with Comcast, and soon my show, *Wow! It's Arlene Peck*, was born. For the show I taped 30-minute interview segments with each guest. And by the time it was over my show had run for over 20 years. Comcast still broadcasts *Wow! It's Arlene Peck* in Atlanta. Check your local listings, Atlantans! You can also see selected episodes on YouTube.

At first it was of course hard to get people to come on the show. I can't even remember the name of my first guest. But soon I started getting invited to parties, openings, and other events, where I met a lot of celebrities. I was very social, and in L.A. celebrities are everywhere. I loved being part of that scene! As my network of friends and connections grew, I was able to more easily find guests for my show. Steve Allen was probably my first "famous" guest. After Steve appeared, and as my viewing audience grew, I started getting calls from the P.R. people representing other well-known celebrities.

My guests included actors, writers, directors, comedians, attorneys, doctors, psychiatrists, and Penthouse Pets of the Month. In this book I have written about a number of my celebrity guests, including Ed Asner, Steve Allen, Martin Landau, Garry Marshall, Pat Boone, Shirley Jones, and José Canseco, to name just a few.

I have written about my dear and dearly missed friend Irv Rubin and about Theo Bikel, "The Fiddler." You'll read in this book about Dr. Carole Lieberman, "Shrink to the Stars," as well as famous women's rights attorney Gloria Allred. Carole and Gloria each appeared on my show several times.

My guests never failed to captivate the audience with their stories. Some of the guests who had particularly interesting life stories to tell, just a few of which I've related in this book, were Jack Klugman, Peter Falk, and Vidal Sassoon.

I don't know if it was as a result of my show or my articles (yes, I was still doing my column), but at one point I got a call from *The Jerry Springer Show* to appear as a guest. I had never even heard of Jerry Springer, but the show sounded like such fun. I called my daughter, Dana, and told her, "Get packed, because we are going to Chicago to be on *The Jerry Springer Show*. A driver is picking us up at the airport. We will go on a shopping spree and stay in a nice hotel." Dana answered me unequivocally, "You are not going on that show." Since I already had my own bags packed, I was furious; but we didn't go. Three days later Dana called me and said, "Quick, turn on the television, they're showing that wonderful show that you wanted to go on!" As I watched, all I could say was, "Oh my G-d." Those guests were aliens from another planet whose only purpose in life was to appear on *Jerry Springer*. They were awful, awful people. I would have truly died of embarrassment had I not listened to Dana's instinct to stay at home. For me, *Jerry Springer* was one example of how not to do an interview show!

Somebody once asked me what my goals were in doing my show. Honestly, I just wanted to have fun! I invited people who I thought would be interesting. And almost always, they were. And as the years went on I found that I was having more and more fun on my show. I hope that at least most of my guests also enjoyed themselves.

And readers, there were moments where I saw sides of a guest that I never intended to see. I remember one incident in the early days, when I still didn't know many celebrities to invite. I received a call from a public relations firm wanting to introduce me to a client of theirs who had a very unique cleaning company. I said, "Sure, send him over." At the time, I didn't know that this particular company specialized in cleaning in the nude. A few hours later my bell rang and a very athletic, California-looking guy was standing at my door with a dustpan in hand. He told me his name was Biff, and that he was the CEO of the cleaning company. We spoke for a few minutes and then my telephone rang. I answered it and began a conversation that I knew was going to be longer than just a few minutes. Biff motioned to me and asked where I kept my cleaning supplies. Preoccupied, I waved him to the kitchen pantry and went back to my call. A few minutes later, I turned around to see this tanned surfer vacuuming my living room totally in the buff. I mean naked as the day he was born! All I could think of was, "Oh my G-d, the neighbors!" I hollered for him to get away from the windows! Later in the day, the public relations company called to find out when I would be scheduling this company for a future television interview. And no, I did not ask the naked cleaning guy to be on my show. I had seen enough. Sometimes less is more.

When people ask me which guest I liked best, Garry Marshall is usually my immediate answer. His reputation as "one of the nicest guys in the business" was truly deserved. But I liked all of my guests. I didn't invite them on the show if I sensed we wouldn't have a rapport. So it's hard for me to remember many people in the "not so nice" category.

Some guests I remembered from when I was a little girl watching the movies. One actress who comes to mind is Jayne Meadows, who although well into her eighties was always immaculate in her St. John's dresses and hair and make-up done perfectly. You can read about Jayne in my story about her husband Steve Allen.

Two other actresses I remembered from my girlhood were Esther Williams, whom I met at a Beverly Hills benefit, and Ann Rutherford, who I first met at the 50th anniversary of *Gone With the Wind* (Ann played Scarlett's sister). Ann invited me to her mansion when I moved to L.A.; what a gracious hostess! When I later saw her at a celebrity event at the Beverly Wilshire Hotel, where she was being honored, I was amazed that she remembered me. So of course I asked her to be a guest on my show!

Although they were excellent guests, I don't have stories about Esther's or Ann's appearances on my show in this book. The same is true for most of my other guests; I only had time to write about some of them! Here are just some of the other guests I had on my show:

James Cromwell
Mike Farrell
Kent McCord
Billy Barty
Karen Black
Dick Van Patten
James Reynolds
Menahem Golan
Wink Martindale
Ruta Lee
Denise Brown (Nicole's sister)
Brigitte Gabriel
Stella Stevens

Michael Lerner
Valerie Harper
Peter Mark Richman
Norm Crosby
Esai Morales
Jerri Vale
Connie Stevens
Ray Bradbury
Hugh O'Brien
Dr. Wafa Sultan
Tippi Hedren
Betty Garrett

In 2009 the L.A. City Council decided to stop funding local cable access studios, and all were forced to close. And that, readers, ended my live interviews. By the time it ended, my show was one of the longest-running cable shows in the Los Angeles area. As I mentioned, *Wow! It's Arlene Peck* is still running in cities like Atlanta, where incidentally I have now returned to live, and on YouTube.

In my busy life outside of my television show I've known, and sometimes interviewed, Presidents, Prime Ministers, and Nobel Peace Prize winners. I've included in this book stories about Shimon Peres and Elie Wiesel. I've also written about some of the other famous people I've known over the years, either as a friend or just informally. These include Ted Turner, Julio Iglesias, Joan Rivers, and Arnold Schwarzenegger. You'll read about my encounters with celebrities such as these who, though they didn't appear on my television show, left me with some good stories to tell.

As I said, my friend suggested that I should write a book about my experiences after seeing on the wall of my condo the hundreds of pictures of me posing with different celebrities. I've included a number of my pictures in this book, taken either on the set of my show or in various other places. In fact, the cover of this book looks a lot like my living room wall!

Sadly, some of the people I've written about have now passed away. I really miss Steve Allen, Garry Marshall, James Avery, and Irv Rubin. Jack Klugman, Joan Rivers, Peter Falk, Casey Kasem, Art Linkletter, Vidal Sassoon, Meir Kahane, Elie Wiesel, and Shimon Peres are also no longer with us. I hope that my stories about these wonderful people will add to their legacy.

I've met so many interesting people I can't remember them all. Not all of these people were necessarily famous in the tabloid sense, but they were important figures nonetheless. A few times I wasn't aware of a person's significance at the time we were introduced. Probably the most impressive person I ever met was Edward Teller. I was president of an organization called ORT, Organization of Rehabilitation through Training, which supports Technion, the MIT of Israel. Teller was appearing as a speaker in Chicago in 1972, and though I was too young and innocent and dumb to know who he was, there I was talking with him. I remember he had dark circles under his eyes. I learned later that he was the founder of the Manhattan Project. Wow! This just shows you that so many of the people I've met either I don't remember or was too oblivious at the time to know who they were.

Finally, since the 2016 Presidential election has just completed, I feel it is timely to point out that Kenny Kingston, the "psychic to the stars," was a guest on my show about 15 years ago. At one point during the show he said, "Do you know who ought to be President? Donald Trump." I kid you not. Sadly, Kenny died in 2014, so he wasn't here to learn that his long-ago prediction ultimately came true!

So, who is Arlene Peck? Why should you care what makes her tick? Well, aside from the fact that I am fabulous and flawless, you should you know that I am a woman of adventure. In addition to my exciting career of interviewing celebrities, covering wars, and having my own talk show, I love living on the edge of excitement. Over the years you might have seen me hang-gliding, parasailing, white water rafting, skydiving, or chasing elephants and lions in Africa. But, I've never done floors or windows and don't plan to start.

Looking back, there were mistakes I made in my last book, *Prison Cheerleader*, where I didn't give proper editing credit. This book, however, has had excellent editing guidance from several people. First, Alan Fontana, who graduated from Brown with a B.A. in English and Creative Writing, helped in early draft stages.

A good friend of mine, Melody Major, read through my draft and made many helpful suggestions. But then she got a real job!

Finally, Dean Polk, a freelance editor from Atlanta, entered the picture. Dean watched the DVDs of my shows, helped me write about my interviews, and provided significant and valuable editorial assistance with all of the stories in this book. I have a lot of good qualities, but patience and humility aren't two of them. Dean showed me how to be more patient by helping me to improve the content of these stories and not just write up some recollections and send my first draft to the printer. I'm working on the humility.

My life has been one of fun, excitement, and enlightenment, due in large part to all of the wonderful and interesting people I've met over the years. So, readers, let me share with you just some of my experiences with the wide variety of celebrities I've known. I hope you'll have fun reading my stories about these individuals who, I think, are people you'll want to know more about. Feel free to laugh and cry—as I often do as I reminisce. Let's let the journey begin. Hold on to your seats. It's going to be a bumpy, exciting ride!

Steve Allen...Renaissance Man

I first met Steve Allen some time in the late eighties. I had been flying back and forth between Atlanta and Los Angeles, checking out whether I really wanted to move to L.A. Somehow I ended up at the same party as Steve. It was held at the jet set hangout, the Sunset Marquis Hotel, and was hosted by the Television Academy's *EMMY Magazine* and the Directors Guild. In those days, I was a total tourist in awe of the whole celebrity scene. Actually, I don't think I've changed too much since then; I'm just less vocal about it. However, back then I had no compulsion about going over to this famous man and asking to take a picture with him. Later, when I returned to Atlanta, I mailed him a copy of the photo along with a request to interview him when I came back to town for my newspaper.

Lunch with Steve Allen, 1989

He was a doll and wrote me a very nice letter complimenting some of my columns I had sent to him. Over the next couple of months I received press material from his office. I wrote back to this legend and certified genius that, if I were going to have to wade through his considerable material, he'd have to read my thoughts also. And I'd give him a test later. He responded that he liked my style of writing and asked when I wanted to set up an interview. When did I want to set up an interview!? I was thrilled to study at the feet of this master. I accepted his invitation. Soon afterward his secretary, actress Pat Quinn, called to tell me that we would be having lunch in Mr. Allen's office. Pat, incidentally, was "Alice" in *Alice's Restaurant.*

Eventually I flew back to California and went to Steve's office to do the interview. He had provided a beautiful catered lunch. This started a pattern that continued every time I was in town. Steve arranged every detail. Usually he had someone on his staff call me to find out what kind of lunch I would prefer to have ordered in: Thai, Chinese, or Mexican. One time Steve even invited my daughter Dana to join us for lunch.

Also, Steve and I began a correspondence that was to last for several years. Steve Allen's mind went in so many directions. Our mutual topics of interest, conversations, and letters involved politics and causes that he was involved with at the time. I sent him my "trashing men" columns, which he seemed to enjoy. He usually responded to me with ideas for books and columns.

While I still lived in Atlanta, there was a famous murder case involving a young Jewish girl named Julie Love, who disappeared in 1988. A search went on for over a year, and Steve wrote to me from time to time wanting more information. Eventually, Ms. Love's body was found. I think he had wanted to write a book about the case, but he never did so.

I wrote several columns about Steve, and still have the taped recordings from our lunches. He would set up my camera in the right spot and make sure our whole dialogue was saved for posterity. In them, he spoke about his family, his background, and what he wanted out of life. His office and desk reflected his mind, a hodgepodge of many varied things. Along the walls were books, many of which had been written either by or about him.

Later, when I moved to California from Atlanta, he always made sure that I received invitations to his concerts. Long after I met Steve Allen, I found out that he wasn't Jewish, contrary to public opinion. In fact, during one of our first meetings, I wondered what my Jewish angle would be for the syndicated columns in the Jewish newspapers that would carry our interview. It wasn't a problem.

Steve had some wonderful stories about how he played the parts of three Jewish men: Hyman Goldfarb, Benny Goodman, and George Gershwin. Once, when asked about it while he was speaking to a "Jewish group," he answered, "Yes, as a gentile I'm kind of out of work. But, as a Jew I'm gainfully employed." His obvious respect and profound understanding of the Jewish people impressed me. He spoke about how many people believed him to be Jewish. Over the years he received quite a bit of hate mail from sickos spewing anti-Semitic garbage at him.

Sometime in the late nineties Steve gave me a copy of a short story he had written called "The Day the Jews Disappeared." In the story, he described how one day the world woke up and all the Jews in the world had just vanished. Food was on tables. Cigarettes still burned in ashtrays. Everything was normal—except there were no Jewish people to be found. Everyone rushed to get the story of the disappearance of the Jews on the news. But the news

Outside my studio, 1993

directors were Jewish, and therefore missing. The hospitals were filled with people having heart attacks, strokes, etc., but the doctors, too, were missing. There were no psychologists or psychiatrists because most of them were also Jewish. Despair was worldwide, except in parts of the Middle East, where the Arabs were dancing in the streets and shooting their guns in the air. Eventually a nuclear war started. Then there was no world left.

I found the story fascinating. I wondered why he had never published it. "I was going to, but some of my Jewish friends prevailed upon me not to," Steve replied. I wondered if these were the same people who ran Jewish organizations like the Anti-Defamation League, whose sole mission in life seems to be "don't make waves."

Once I asked him, "You've been in everything. You've done everything in the world of creativity. Have you always been a legend?" He laughed and said, "Sure, at seven years old I became a legend." Then he sort of cocked his head a bit pensively and said, "Actually, I've always thought of myself as a little odd." You know, folks, more men should be so odd!

Then seriously, almost apologetically, Steve added, "I'm interested in everything. Everything I see is fascinating." He pointed to the plate with the remains of our lunch and said, "The way they put these two vegetables together is interesting. Your wristwatch is interesting…everything." Let me tell you, an attitude such as that makes for damned good company.

On my set, 1997

Steve appeared as a guest on my television show a number of times. We discussed a wide variety of topics and many of his accomplishments and experiences. Steve was perhaps best known as a comedian and talk-show host, but he was also a successful author. By the time of his death Steve had written almost fifty books. I had always heard that if Steve Allen wanted to read a book, he would sit down and write it instead. At the time of one of his appearances on my show he was about to publish his latest book, *Die Laughing*, part of a series of comic mysteries in which he and his wife Jayne Meadows are the co-protagonists who solve murder cases. I asked Steve how this series came about. He replied that his publisher had come to him with the idea of some light comic murder mysteries in which the lead characters would be Steve and his wife. Steve said, "It seemed like a cute idea. One immediately thinks of the old *Thin Man* movies with William Powell and Myrna Loy...That is the gimmick and I've had great fun with it."

On another show, around 1994, I showed our audience Steve's new book *Reflections*, which Steve described as "a collection of philosophical observations" that had occurred to him over the years. I don't know if Steve was in a philosophical or spiritual frame of mind on this show, but he went on to talk about his book on the Bible, which is appropriately titled *Steve Allen on the Bible, Religion, and Morality*. He said that one reason he wrote this book is because very few people read scholarly works. According to Steve, many in the public view the Bible as a "perfect document," the Word of God, and therefore as totally reliable and historically accurate with no internal contradictions or errors. Theologians know this isn't true, he said, but added half-jokingly that they don't admit it because they'd get fired from their jobs. Also, most Americans are unaware of the actual contents of the Bible. In the book Steve attempted to logically evaluate the Bible as a historical document as he explained many of its events, characters, and themes. Yet he also made sure to say on my show that he finds great value in Scripture and to note how meaningful the Bible still is for us today.

Steve tried to raise public awareness of historical figures and events, too. To that end he created a television series called *Meeting of Minds*, in which he as the host "interviewed" famous people from history played by actors. Just a few of the historical figures he mentioned on my show were Aristotle, Plato, Socrates, Voltaire, and Martin Luther. Wow, this guy was smart!

Steve also wrote books about comedy. On one show I asked Steve, "Can you actually teach people how to be funny?" Steve responded, "Yes and no; that's not an evasive answer, it's just that each word has to be qualified." He added that there are tricks of the comedy trade, and he included in his books many that he learned from his years of experience. But, you still may not be able to succeed as a comedian if you don't have the talent to make people laugh, just like you wouldn't be ready to do brain surgery simply by reading a book about it. Steve concluded, however, that "if you've got the gift of making people laugh, then some tips can be helpful."

On the subject of comedians, Steve said, "Some people are a little bit funny, others are very funny; but unfortunately a lot of people in the first category currently have become very successful, which is annoying." I commented that comics don't make fun of themselves anymore. Steve told a story about Jack Benny being one of the first comedians to do that, at least in a way. On his radio show, certain people, such as the announcer or Jack's wife, would make fun of him, but it was the Jack Benny character, not the real Jack Benny. The character was not very likable; he was cheap, lied about his age, etc. I told Steve that I met Jack Benny once at the Fontainebleau hotel in Miami. Steve asked me what happened, but since I had been only about five or six at the time I couldn't remember the details!

Steve was an adamant nonsmoker, emphasizing on my show several times that smoking kills 425,000 people a year in this country. He co-authored (with Bill Adler) a book on this subject called *The Passionate Nonsmoker's Bill of Rights.* In talking about this book on my show, Steve referenced the Ibsen play *Enemy of the People,* in which a doctor works in a small European community famous for its waters. Just before the town is to host a big fair, with many tourists expected to visit, the doctor warns of a dangerous organism in the waters. The city fathers told him to keep his mouth shut until after the fair. According to Steve, the tobacco industry engaged in "similar criminality and immorality."

Steve also wrote almost 5,000 songs, including "This Could Be the Start of Something Big" and the lyrics to the theme from the movie *Picnic.* And he didn't even read music! On my show Steve once said that he was a "musical illiterate. But so was the guy who wrote 'Misty.'" But my favorite of Steve's songs is called "Arlene," which he wrote especially for my television show. When he sent me the first version of this song, I promptly returned it, saying that it sounded like elevator music. He was sweet enough to write me another, which probably took him all of five minutes, and I used this one as my theme song for the remainder of my show's history. My friends couldn't get over my chutzpah to ask Steve for such a favor and then return his first effort as though it came from Macy's.

We talked about music a lot on my show. Once I made the comment that they have taken the melody out of songs. Steve responded, "Today's composers by and large don't have the sheer gift for melody." He said that melody was once important, even in jazz. He added that the early jazz composers such as Ellington wrote "highly melodic material." They wrote the songs as instrumentals but because they were "so singable, so pretty," the songs eventually had lyrics attached to them and became pop hits.

On my set again

I love jazz, at least the good jazz, the older stuff. I asked Steve, "Is Jazz dead?" He said that it wasn't, adding that there were more "fine players" today than there were in the golden age of the thirties, forties, and fifties. He felt it was encouraging that the most gifted musicians at university music schools either wanted to play serious jazz or join symphony orchestras. Steve called these musicians "true artists."

On the subject of the lack of melody in music, I had to ask Steve about rap and hip-hop. His response reflects his musical astuteness and social awareness. He said that the rhythm is good, that the songs "often swing." He acknowledged that the lyrics often make meaningful social commentary, but that some of the lyrics stray too far (e.g. "Let's kill some cops"). Steve said that "there's nothing admirable about that whatsoever. It's disgusting."

And speaking of lyrics, I asked Steve about one of the sketches he'd been doing for years, in which he straightforwardly recites the lyrics to famous songs, such as the Rolling Stones' "(I Can't Get No) Satisfaction." Steve said that when he did that sketch most listeners laughed hysterically at the inanity of some of the lyrics.

We also talked about the slim chances of a song "hitting it big." Steve mentioned that Irving Berlin, "one of America's greatest songwriters, probably still America's favorite," had maybe 50 or 60 out of 1,200 songs that made it. He said that just a few hundred of his own songs had been recorded, and that only eight or ten of those were really big hits and got replayed a lot. In the last 30-40 years, Steve said, even the "big songwriters" had maybe seven or eight songs that made it big, and that even though back in the old days songwriters such as Berlin and Cole Porter may have written more songs that became famous, most songwriters wrote many, many songs that never saw the light of day.

Knowing that Elvis had appeared on "The Steve Allen Show," I asked Steve what he thought of Elvis. Steve said that he had first seen Elvis on a show co-hosted by Jimmy and Tommy Dorsey and, "to use that old phrase, he had something." He said that although Elvis didn't have a "pure voice" he had something "much more important: a star quality, charisma, and a goofy country boy appeal." He said that Elvis was such a powerful entertainer that he became a superstar without recording very many good songs. Crosby and Sinatra were superstars, too, but they sang "glorious musical material." Elvis didn't even need that, Steve said. By the time Steve booked him for his show, Elvis had "suddenly become more controversial and therefore important." I asked, "Because of Ed Sullivan?" and Steve said that Elvis was on *his* show before he appeared on Ed Sullivan. When I asked Steve about Elvis's appearance on his show, he responded, "It went fine, we had a lot of laughs."

I asked Steve if he had ever had any bad guests on any of his talk shows, and he said that he could only remember one. It was a woman whose name he couldn't remember and who he hadn't authorized to be on the show; she came out and talked "pretty much like a teamster or a drunk in a saloon." He said that he didn't think she was ever on television again, "although today they could make her a big star" since "dirty language dominates American humor" today.

He said that Jerry Lewis was one of his funniest guests. Steve did a sketch called "Funny Phone Calls," and when Jerry was his guest he put him on a call with a caterer in Chicago. Steve said that Jerry was "hysterical for a full 12 minutes."

During our lunches and on my show, Steve told many marvelous anecdotes. He spoke about his youth. We discussed his family, his writing, Hollywood stories, jazz. He was a brilliant man; there was nothing he did not want to touch upon. Although I always loved having Steve as a guest on my show, there were times that were a little nerve-wracking. I recall occasions when he took the time to drive clear across town to the studio to tape my show. Yet, when he arrived, he was busy talking into this little recorder he always took with him. He would forget to talk to anyone else, even the crew or bystanders. Sometimes I had to really push to get him to open up. It's not that he had nothing to say. I believe that he had attained an age where he had heard it all before, had been there and done that.

I once asked Steve on my show why he uses the recorder. He said that he was very dissatisfied with his memory and used the recorder as a memory aid. When he used "the back of the proverbial envelope," he would make a few cryptic notes which he could barely read when he "put the jacket on a week later." Steve also used the recorder to write his books.

My style of interviewing can be a little too much for someone used to taking the microphone and talking about whatever they felt like. So, there were a couple of times, thank G-d not many, when I made the fatal mistake of interrupting his thoughts. Instead of jumping right back into the discussion, Steve would stop, sit back, cross his legs and arms, and just look at me—not a wonderful thing to happen with a guest if you're taping a television show. A few times I received calls after the show from viewers, giving me hell about being presumptuous enough to interview a man like Steve Allen in such a fashion. I tend to think that at those moments he knew exactly what he was doing, and did it just to be ornery and give me a hard time.

When Art Linkletter was on my show we were talking about Steve. I told Art that he was a much easier interview than Steve. Art replied, "You may not believe this, but Steve was basically an introvert. He liked to be by himself, didn't like going around to cocktail parties, but he could be a funny guy and take a pie in the face and do a lot of embarrassing things...But that wasn't him at all." Art mentioned Steve's *Meeting of Minds* series, adding that Steve was "a Renaissance Man, a man I admired deeply."

I had always thought that Steve's wife Jayne Meadows was an assertive Jewish woman. Like me, she had these strong vibes. That's why I was surprised to learn from Steve that she was born in China and lived there for the first seven years of her life; her parents were Episcopalian missionaries. One time on my show I asked Steve about whether Jayne was funny. He responded that she was "very intelligent, funny in a non-intentional way." He said that Jayne never tried to get laughs but often got "screams of laughter," especially from people who knew her. He added that, possibly as a result of her early childhood in China, her mind was "sort-of back in 1917." He said that because she was "in a sense out of tune with her times" her reactions to people and situations were "automatically comic."

Art Linkletter and I talked briefly about Jayne on my show. When I commented that Jayne was more outgoing than Steve, Art said, "Yes, she was a talker." Then he kidded me with a sly smile, saying that "she could talk to *you* and get a word in edgewise. I said, "I know, I try."

With Steve's wife Jayne Meadows, 2002

Once or twice, Steve came with Jayne in the car, but I never really had the chance to talk to her until after his death, when she consented to be a guest on my show. She was a delightful person. As tough an interview as Steve could be, she was a breeze. I found her to be outspoken and charming. She was the type of guest who had a "story" for anything you wanted to talk about.

We were a lot alike in many ways. Besides being red heads, we tended toward flamboyancy and flair. As I got to know Jayne, I liked her even better. She had what's known as personality. And, unlike so many in Hollywood whose smiles never reach their eyes when they meet you, she actually seemed to want to know how your week went.

When Steve died I remembered being so shocked. He had a fender bender but didn't think he was injured, so he didn't go to the hospital. He went to the house of his son, who later found Steve unconscious in his bathroom, and paramedics were unable to revive him. It was eventually determined that the traffic accident had caused a blood vessel in his heart to rupture. I was unable to go to the funeral.

I have several hours of videotapes from our lunches in which Steve is talking to me about his family background. I figure I'll keep these in case somebody ever wants to make a documentary about Steve. Call me! He was a Renaissance Man worth remembering.

With Steve in Beverly Hills, 1995

Jackie Zeman...Forever Nurse Bobbie

I get a warm fuzzy when I have people on the show who I really like. And this is how I felt as I introduced Jackie Zeman, a lady I love. Jackie has been on *General Hospital* for what seems like a zillion years. I watched her show with my kids, and when I was waiting for them to come home from school; now my kids have their own kids who are watching the show! People who have been watching Jackie as Nurse Bobbie all these years know what a kind person that character is. Jackie herself is just as kind, "such a sweet person," as I said on my show.

Shortly after I moved to L.A., I walked into the Beverly Center Mall, recognized Jackie, and exclaimed, "Oh my God, you are Jackie Zeman, Nurse Bobbie!" She smiled and said, "Yes, I am." I proceeded with the "excited fan act," telling her that she was my favorite character. I continued to say that I had just started my own television show and that one day I wanted her to appear as a guest. She said, "That is lovely," and that was that.

Years later, I was invited to an event, and Jackie was sitting next to me. I did a "double take" and said, "You are Jackie Zeman," and reminded her of our previous conversation about my loving her on *General Hospital*. At this point in my life as talk show host, I had the nerve to invite big celebrities to appear on my show. As I had promised years earlier, I extended the invitation to her; Jackie was very gracious and said that she would love to appear as a guest.

Jackie arrived looking gorgeous. During my introduction I said, "I don't care if you hate soap operas, everybody knows Jackie Zeman slash Nurse Bobbie from *General Hospital*." When I told the audience that she was born in

New Jersey, I added, "You know, I was born in Atlanta, but people think I was born in Jersey!" Jackie said that when I speak she can hear both places—Southern and Yankee, I guess! She added that my voice is a "wonderful mesh" of the two.

I told the audience that I had considered kidnapping Jackie that day at the Beverly Center Mall. Jackie said, "Yes, it was about 12 years ago," and then added, "Look at the run you've had; I mean, my goodness, isn't that incredible!" What a great compliment!

I told her that when we ran into each other at the recent event and I asked her to appear as my guest, I had been surprised that she remembered me! And Jackie responded, "Well, you're a memorable person! You stand out. Very glamorous." Then I told her how my mother always said that if I had been a twin she would have drowned the other one because she could only handle one of me. Jackie laughed and said, "You have an effervescent personality and a good sense of humor. You should be doing a situation comedy." Maybe some day!

During both of her appearances on my show we spent much of the time talking about the humanitarian causes Jackie supports, some of which are ones that people probably don't know very much about. For example, Jackie helps promote public awareness of organ donorship. She said she was inspired to join this cause by a storyline on *General Hospital*. When her "TV daughter" died, she donated her heart to her cousin who needed a transplant. Jackie said she started learning about donorship then, and that she received a lot of correspondence from fans who had either received organs or knew someone close to them whose organ helped save someone's life.

On my set with Jackie Zeman

Jackie has been a spokesperson for the cystic fibrosis foundation. Her good friends have a daughter who has had the disease since she was very young. Jackie hosts an annual fundraiser that sells out every year, not only raising a lot of money but helping to enhance awareness of this horrible disease.

The cause for which Jackie was most passionate for many years was the Gabriel Project, which helped provide life-saving heart surgery to children from Africa. She told us how she got involved with this wonderful charity. She said that around 1990 she began receiving letters from middle school students in New Jersey. The kids told her about the project. One of their teachers founded the organization. They started small, receiving 10 and 20 dollar donations and hosting events such as read-a-thons and bowl-a-thons. Over the years the organization grew, as did Jackie's involvement.

Dinner with Jackie in L.A., around 2009

Every July Bobbie went to Dar El Salam, Tanzania to pick up a child (or two or three, depending on the funding available) and a parent. The children had been approved for surgery by the doctors in Africa. Jackie escorted them back to New Jersey for the surgery at the Deborah Heart and Lung Center. She showed us pictures of some of the kids the project had helped. But that year the organization was having funding problems, and Jackie was traveling to schools around the country trying to raise additional funds.

Jackie is also a jewelry designer. She said she has been doing it since she was little and loves it. She told us how some people believe that there's karma and a message attached to jewelry. That's why people pass down their diamonds from generation to generation. And we both commented on the lasting quality of jewelry.

When Jackie appeared on my show in 2007, it just happened to be the 30th anniversary of her role as Nurse Bobbie! I mentioned my amazement that some soap opera stars seem to have been on their shows forever. We talked about Erika Slezak, who plays Vickie on *One Life to Live,* which was Jackie's first soap opera. Jackie said that this "marvelous, wonderful actress" was still on that show.

Jackie told a funny story about an old trick soap opera stars sometimes use in order to "get more close-ups." They use microphone booms when shooting soaps. If you talk softer, they have to bring the boom closer to pick up the sound, which means they also have to bring the camera closer to tighten up the shot so the boom won't get in the picture. She said Chris Robinson, who played Rick Webber on *General Hospital*, taught her that! Jackie said it's possible to do "tricks" like that in soap operas, because they have to get through 80 or 90 pages of script each day, and usually have time for only one take before they have to move on.

I asked Jackie about the kids she had worked with over the years, suspecting that some of them might have dysfunctional family situations. She said most of the kids are bright, smart, happy, and well-adjusted, adding that most of them go to "regular school" on days they're not shooting.

We talked about the international popularity of soap operas. In some countries, though, the shows don't air for months or even years after they're shown in the U.S. I told a story about being in Korea (or somewhere) on the way to Hong Kong with my teenage daughter. I was surprised to see a bunch of soldiers at the airport bar watching *General Hospital*! But they're six months or so behind over there, so my daughter, a huge fan of the show, was saying things like, "Oh no, she's not going to end up with him," and the soldiers were hanging on to her every word!

Jackie said that when Rick Springfield was on the show—the first time—he would go home to Australia and tell his parents he had been on *General Hospital*, but they had to watch for almost a year until they finally got to his episodes. Jackie added that it's also strange seeing your show "dubbed." She was once in Italy and looked up at a TV to see herself on the screen, with another voice speaking her dialogue in Italian!

Like me, Jackie has two lovely daughters, Cassidy and Lacey. She showed us a picture. Jackie is a wonderful mother. She said that she has done some movies, but when her kids were younger she turned down some roles because she "wasn't going to be the absentee mom." Jackie wasn't going to leave her kids for four to six weeks to go shoot a film. She wanted to be present to raise her children.

I asked Jackie if she ever felt any guilt when she did have to be away. She responded that she wanted to be a good example for her girls, to help them grow up to be productive, well-educated, and with a career, but she also wanted to be present for them. She told us a recent story about her daughters. Cassidy had just gotten her driver's license. When Jackie watched Cassidy and her sister drive down the driveway for first time, she felt like it was as much a rite of passage for her as it was for them. She added that now that her kids were older she was opening herself up to more opportunities. Jackie felt like she was entering an "exciting, new chapter" in her life.

On another subject, I told Jackie and the audience my perception that a lot of people in the gay community like my show. People would come up to me and say, "I love your shoes. Girlfriend, your shoes were fabulous on that last show!" Thinking I needed to find out what shoes I had been wearing, I would respond, "Thank you. Who was my guest?" and they'd say, "I don't remember, but your shoes were great!" Jackie told us that her teenage son on General Hospital is a gay character. He had "come out" recently on the show. She said that she and her TV son heard from a lot of men, some of them in their thirties, who said they loved how the issue was handled in the show. The men said that it put them right back in that time when they were telling their own mothers that they were gay.

We talked about the importance of having a positive outlook. Jackie looked like a "soap opera person" when she gave me a big smile and said, "I believe if you are happy and have a positive attitude, it will show in your face." I mentioned that I had on my refrigerator a postcard with a picture of a woman fanning herself and the caption, "So many men, so little time." I guess that was my version of positive attitude! I also told her about a sign on my bedroom door that said, "It's good to be queen." Actually, to this day, I have many signs throughout my home. I love the one that says, "Never, never give up" and the one that says, "Take these four words out of the English language: fair, equitable, oughta, and should."

Before the parade with Jackie and our parade car

Jackie got me in a parade one time. We sat in our "float car," me as a syndicated columnist, and her as Nurse

Bobbie. When I watched the tape of the parade, I was proud to see my "float wave."

Jackie has been a great friend of mine for years now. She was always the first person who came to see me in the hospital whenever I was there. And that, Readers, is only one of the many reasons Jackie is someone I love.

Out and about with Nurse Bobbie

After shooting my show

Garry Marshall...The Loveliest Man of All

It seems like it took forever to get Garry Marshall to come on my show. I gushed when he appeared; Garry is a legend. When I opened my show with Garry, I asked the audience, "How can I say to a man who has been married to the same woman for 45 years that I adore him? I'm absolutely in love with this man!" Continuing with my praise, I said that someone had recently asked me to name the nicest celebrity who had ever been on my show, and I responded "Garry Marshall," even though he'd never been a guest! He'd been promising for years to come on the show, and I knew he would some day and would be the nicest. I added, "I'm not kidding you, folks, that is the emiss."

Garry wasn't sure if viewers knew what "emiss" meant. I said flippantly, "Oh, people know that." And he said, "Well, I'm Italian, and for the Italian people, 'emiss' means honest, the truth." Then he added, "Just to help my people!"

I said, feigning surprise, "You're Italian? I keep forgetting you're not Jewish! Who's more Jewish than Penny Marshall?" Garry laughed at my reference to his sister and said that their birth name was Masciarelli.

I told the audience that during the years I was trying to get Garry on my show I used to threaten to kidnap him and bring him on. He commented, "I don't like kidnapping, it hurts." I said that I'd use feathers.

For the screen credit under Garry's name we decided to put "Entertainment Icon." This man was everything in the film and television industry: writer, director, producer, and actor. In his early days in television Garry was a writer for *The Tonight Show*, *The Danny Thomas Show*, *The Lucy Show* and *The Dick Van Dyke Show*. In the 1970s he adapted Neil Simon's play *The Odd Couple* for television and also created *Happy Days, Laverne and Shirley,* and *Mork and Mindy.* During a span of over thirty years he directed eighteen films, including *The Flamingo Kid, Pretty Woman, Beaches, Runaway Bride,* and *The Princess Diaries.* His last film, *Mother's Day,* was released in April 2016.

Garry was also the owner of the Falcon Theater, which is a darling playhouse in Burbank. I told Garry that all the shows I had seen at the Falcon had been great. We talked about opening nights at his theater, when Garry always provided a complimentary buffet for all the ticketholders. There were meatballs, little hot dogs, and lots of chips.

I commented on the "big stars" I had seen perform there. Garry said that the theater had also helped some "unknowns" to become stars. He talked about a few of the young actors who had been "discovered" acting in his plays and had gone on to TV, movie, and Broadway roles. For example, Ana Ortiz, who was in Garry's play *Wrong Turn at Lungfish,* was offered a role in *Ugly Betty.* And the kid who played Chachi in the *Happy Days* play at the Falcon was cast as Frankie Valli in the Broadway production of *Jersey Boys.* Garry looked into the camera and said, "If you wanna be somebody, they'll discover you at the Falcon! But not on opening night, because everybody just comes for the meatballs." I said, "Well they come for you too. You're there at the Falcon every night."

"Garry invented the word nepotism," Jack Klugman told me when he was on my show. Garry used his friends in his movies and gets them to come to the Falcon to work or see the shows. Jack said that he and some others call them "FOGs," Friends of Garry. Then, of course, Jack and I had gone on to talk about what a great guy Garry was. So I kidded Garry about being the king of nepotism, and he laughed and said, "It's not illegal, I found out. You can't be put in jail for nepotism."

With Garry Marshall and Jack Klugman, 2007

I asked Garry K. Marshall what the "K" in his name stood for. He said, "K is for Kent," and then joked, "My mother went for fancy." But he added that his mother named him and his siblings so you would smile when you said their names. And then he pronounced their names, "Pen-ee," "Gar-ee," and "Ron-ee," smiling as he made the "ee" sound.

I commented how nice that was and told my own naming story. I had married a Yankee, and those people destroy names (Howard is Howie, Richard is Richie, etc.). Therefore, I made sure that when I picked my kids' names they would be nice, easy ones that couldn't be ruined with a nickname. At that point Garry cracked, "Yehuda?" That was funny. But no; I named my kids Keith, Dana, and Marla.

I explained that I had been worried when my daughter Dana had her own daughter. What name would she choose? Garry was still going with the Jewish names; he said, "Yetta? I always liked the name Yetta." I explained that Dana had named her daughter Ivy. Garry told us that his new grandchild was named Sienna LaGambina, adding, "You wanna get any more Italian than that? She's five months old and she'll probably be a singer, who knows?" Garry said that he had six grandchildren, and I topped him with seven. Garry said that was amazing "for two young people, under 40." Hah!

Garry was married to his wife Barbara for over 50 years. She was a nurse; as Garry said, she never got into show business. Garry was very proud of his children. He told us about Lori, his oldest, who is a writer. His middle daughter Kate "runs the Falcon," and his son Scott is a director. At the time Scott was up in Michigan shooting a film with Ann-Margret, Cedric the Entertainer, and Christina Ricci. I told a story about walking out of my condo one night and noticing that they were shooting a movie with the whole cast and crew. Garry was there. I said "Hey, maybe I'll do an interview." He said "No, do my son. I'm just here visiting." It was Scott who was actually shooting that movie!

We talked about Scott's movie *Keeping Up With the Steins*. I remembered that Garry had been naked with Darryl Hannah in the film, and it made me think of Jack Nicholson and Kathy Bates in *About Schmidt*. So I guess I was sort of questioning the idea of old people being naked in movies! Garry laughed and said, "Hey, it's my son's show, I do what he says." I thought it was a hilarious picture. Garry said, "It was about bar mitzvahs, but everybody could understand it."

Garry had mentioned Ann-Margret, so I commented how gorgeous she still was, and that certain women seem to have that total sex appeal, even when they get older. Garry interjected, "My sister Penny is one, but go ahead." I wasn't sure if he was joking! When I mentioned that Lainie Kazan had been on my show, Garry said, "I love Lainie, she was in *Beaches*!" I commented that she's a gorgeous woman who has that sex appeal, like me! Garry, looking at the camera, said, "Zaftig is the word, in her language" as he pointed at me. Readers, in case you don't know, that term refers to a woman with a full, rounded figure!

Garry graduated from Northwestern University. I commented about his generosity to Northwestern, where he funded several buildings. He joked, "All my children went to Northwestern and none are in jail; you gotta give back!" And he told us that the Marjorie Ward Marshall Dance Center at Northwestern is named after his mother.

I brought up the topic of the strange people in L.A. I had gotten a phone call from a woman I barely knew inviting me to "Wilbur's barbeque" for his birthday. "Who is Wilbur?" I asked. "My dog," she responded. Garry said, "So Wilbur had a barbeque? You had to go on your hands and knees?"

I said that, in Atlanta, if you want to fix somebody up, you ask about their family, what school did they go to, and other "who are they?" types of questions. But in L.A., the first question you ask is, "Is he normal?" I told Garry that he seems normal. He responded, "I'm not so normal, but I'm happy."

I had to ask Garry about *Happy Days*, with Henry Winkler as the Fonz. We talked about what a great guy Henry is—a mensch, as I called him. Garry told us that Henry was dyslexic; when they first started the show and he was having some problems reading the script, they initially thought they hadn't printed the text big enough, but then they found out he was dyslexic. Garry said that Henry has written a "wonderful series of books" about dyslexic kids. Garry also said that they all went to Milwaukee for the dedication of the "Bronze Fonz" Statue. He added that Henry had helped the actor playing the Fonz in the *Happy Days* musical, which was touring the country at the time.

Speaking of Henry Winkler, here we are at the Falcon Theater!

Garry received a "Star" on the Hollywood Walk of Fame. He tactfully told me that his star is located in front of a building that is for sale. He said, "I hope no one buys the building and covers up my star." He was serious, but who would want to cover his star? I should buy the building and make everyone kiss his star before they enter!

Despite being so talented, Garry never seemed to accept it. He told me a story about Martin Short. He said that "Marty" had a show during which he would "recognize" a celebrity sitting in the audience, as if he hadn't known that person was going to be there for the taping. It was a standard part of every show; Marty would look out in the audience and say something like "Look, it's so-and-so," and then the camera would pan to the celebrity. So, Garry called Marty Short and said, "I will come watch your show," thinking Marty could "recognize" him in the audience. Marty said, "That is great! I will have you as my guest celebrity." Garry said, "I think you can get someone who is a bigger celebrity than I am." And Marty replied, "I am not going to be able to top you on a Wednesday show!"

Garry said that it wasn't so easy getting started. He said, "Sometimes I got so lonely I would call the lady who tells the time, just to hear her voice." I told him that he had come a long way since those days.

Backstage at the Falcon (Jack Klugman and Penny Marshall in background!)

As we were winding up, I asked Garry to quickly sum up his philosophy on life. He said, "We should laugh. People come on your show and they laugh. Without laughs the world is too hard to live in. So laugh today and you'll have a great day tomorrow." I was thrilled to hear this very funny man say that people come on my show and laugh!

Not many people know what a great author Garry was. Garry gave me a signed copy of his book *Wake Me When It's Funny.* Inside he wrote, "Thanks for being a good friend and talented host. I wish you 'Happy Days' ahead!" And as a P.S. he added "You are a 'Pretty Woman.'" This is probably the best book signature I've ever received!

Garry Marshall was just a lovely man. When he died in July 2016 I was surprised to learn that he was 81 years old, because he had such a boyish enthusiasm about him. And he had that infectious smile. As he said as we were wrapping up my show, he just wanted to give the world a few laughs. Boy, did he ever.

Helping others came naturally to Garry. Many actors went on to greater fame from the Falcon Theater, as I mentioned earlier. Julia Roberts became a star after she appeared in *Pretty Woman*. Garry "discovered" Henry Winkler when he cast him as The Fonz in *Happy Days*. And of course there was Hector Elizondo, Garry's "lucky charm," who appeared in all eighteen of Garry's films!

And Garry even helped little old me. Garry was one of the people who I wanted to ask to write something for my book jacket, but procrastination prevented that from happening. But I will be forever grateful to Garry for doing a nice video clip for me on the occasion of my last show, when Martin Landau was my guest. In the clip, which I played on the show, Garry said

Hi, Arlene. I know this your last show and I just wanted to wish you well . . . I've been on your show and I've watched your show . . . I can't be there but I'm there in spirit. Thanks for all those memories and all those wonderful, wonderful shows you've done . . . Talk to you soon. Come to the Falcon Theater!

Everybody loved Garry. For me, Garry was the loveliest man of all.

After taping my show, 2008

Irv Rubin...Suicide? I Don't Think So

The news said that Irv Rubin had killed himself. Shortly later, the news said that Irv Rubin was brain dead. Then, I heard on the radio that Irv Rubin had died. Irv was a friend, and I knew his mentality. Nothing about the story made sense.

For those of you who are unfamiliar with the case of Irv Rubin, I will tell you about him. He was the head of the Jewish Defense League (JDL). His predecessor, Rabbi Meir Kahane, founded the organization in the '60s. I knew both men, and their styles were completely different. Sometimes you had to strain to hear Kahane, but not so with Irv Rubin. Irv was most comfortable with a bullhorn trying to create a disturbance. If there was a Nazi or skinhead demonstration occurring somewhere, whether in Idaho or Germany, Irv would have been right in the middle of it, organizing his own counter-demonstration.

Irv Rubin was very earthy, crass, and educated. He would call me at all hours of the night about some political issue that he'd been upset about. One time he was asking me what I thought about him going on Jerry Springer with the head of the Nazi party. I said that I couldn't believe you would go on that show, especially with a Nazi guy. (Not that I hadn't previously entertained the idea of appearing on Jerry Springer myself, as I mentioned elsewhere. But I listened to my daughter's advice and declined Mr. Springer's invitation.) But Irv did it anyway. They ended up getting in a fight, and Irv broke his finger badly enough that he had to have an operation. I gave him hell for being a damn fool.

Irv could be noisy and disruptive, yet articulate and bright. I like what he did, even though I didn't necessarily agree with his style.

Irv appeared several times on my show. When I introduced him for one of his appearances, in 1998, I said that I could probably simply say "here's Irv" and he would just start talking. The year 1998 marked the 30th anniversary of the JDL's founding and the 50th anniversary of the formation of the state of Israel. I described Irv as an "activist extraordinaire" who took over the chairmanship of the JDL from Meir Kahane.

Irv was involved in fighting anti-Semitism throughout most of his life. We first discussed the concept of "peace for pieces," or "pieces for peace." Irv claimed that the United Nations and the current U.S. administration had tried to compel Israel to withdraw to the "Auschwitz borders." He said that he didn't agree with the apparent U.S. conception of Israel as an obstacle to peace and expressed frustration that the U.S. was always demanding that Israel must give up land for peace. We discussed how Israel is already so very small. I pointed out that Israel is about the size of New Hampshire.

Irv felt that we faced an implacable foe in radical Islam. He noted that the Palestinian Authority (PA) still advocates "destruction of the Zionist entity," that is, the state of Israel. I shared my perspective that the PLO gets all the good press, with Israel appearing like the occupying power. I added that Arafat had done nothing to curb terrorism. Palestinians were teaching their children to hate Jewish people.

Irv was frustrated with the lack of support for Israel from American Jews, noting that "they hem and haw" about the two-state solution. He was tired of hearing sophisticated Jewish liberals saying that two states should be OK. Irv said no, that's not OK: "Palestine already exists, and it's called Jordan." Irv did not feel that Israel should conquer Jordan though. He concluded, "Israel is a good nation in a bad neighborhood."

We discussed the fact that Israel is surrounded by 22 hostile nations. You need eight million Jews for a viable state, Irv said, but the Arabs and the U.S. were saying to Israel to give up more land. Irv posed the question, "Do we really believe that God gave us that state? If God's the landlord, you don't mess with the eviction notice." He expressed frustration with "all those left-wing Israelis and liberal Jews who are saying to their Arab brethren that we can share this state, we can split it in half. We can't."

Irv said that he doesn't like to dwell on the Holocaust as much as the present and future. He said that the motto of the JDL is "Never Again," a slogan that doesn't just apply to the Holocaust. He added that we have a "quiet Holocaust here in America with alienation, intermarriage, and cult-like organizations." Irv worried about the future of Jewish people, either in Israel or in parts of the Diaspora, such as the U.S. As long as we stay outside of Israel, Irv said, "Jew Hatred" will still be there. He worried about Farrakhan calling Judaism a "gutter religion," about Internet sites spewing Jewish hatred. Irv also pointed out that one reason the JDL seemed to be on the forefront of the battle on so many occasions was that so many Jewish people, and the American people in general, don't give a damn.

Irv said that Rabbi Kahane was murdered because he was a compelling Jew who asked uncomfortable questions. I reminded our audience that Rabbi Kahane's murderer was a member of the terrorist cell responsible for the 1993 World Trade Center bombing.

I asked Irv about his time in Cicero, IL, protesting against the KKK. Irv was able to get the black and Hispanic gangs to unify against the Klan. He said that the City of Cicero eventually paid the KKK $10,000 not to march. He said that it was the first time in the history of our country that a municipality had paid an organization not to demonstrate. But, Irv said, "You can't buy off the bully." He wondered what the neo-Nazis would do in such a situation. Irv believed that you couldn't give the Palestinians land and think they'd be happy.

Irv had this to say about the future of Israeli-Arab relations: "If the Israelis ever wake up and find some common sense, they must conclude that the only reason we have this land is because God gave it to us. If He didn't, we stole it from the Arabs. Once they come to that realization, they can say to all those so-called Palestinians, 'You don't want to accept Jewish sovereignty? You want to commit suicide? You think you're a Palestinian? Pack your bags, you're going to Palestine, and that's called Jordan.' Or bring them over here to the United States, or bring them to Canada, or bring them to Uganda. They can't live in the state of Israel."

Perhaps in an effort to cool off this heated discussion, I said, "Well, God knows, there's not an easy solution." Referring to the Never Again commitment, I added, "One solution is not to give up."

Irv wasn't finished. "Sure there's an easy solution," he said. "The solution is to give the Arabs back to the Arabs. Repatriate those Arabs who can't be first-class citizens in a Jewish state. That won't fly in Beverly Hills. But it has to fly in a common-sense nation called Israel."

And that was the end of that show. I closed by saying, "Why am I always exhausted when you come on my show?"

In a show from the early nineties, I asked Irv at the beginning, "What makes Irv Rubin Irv Rubin?" Irv responded, "A tremendous sense of obligation. When you see a problem, don't ignore it." He said that he's not a doctor, that he can't solve all the world's ills. But we have a problem of Jew Hatred, of anti-Semitism.

On the set with Irv Rubin, 1994

He commented that when times are bad, people in the U.S. worry that "little Johnny is going to have to go off and fight in the Golan Heights." Such fears could result in a new rise in anti-Semitism. But when times are good you don't hear that as much.

I brought up the subject of Louis Farrakhan and anti-Semitism among blacks. Irv recalled his time in Forsyth County, GA, where he had gone years earlier to battle the Klan. He remembered seeing signs that read, "Nigger, don't let the sun set on your head." Irv stressed that one thing he really hates is apathy. He firmly believed in the right to countermarch. He marched in a group of 25,000 against the KKK and white supremacy. People were throwing stones at them, and they wanted to fight back. The organizers wanted the protest to be non-violent, but he wanted to pick up every stone and throw it right back. "Violence is a very subjective thing," Irv said. Sometimes, he added, you may have to resort to violence, but only as a last resort: "When you do it is when you have no other choice."

He went on, saying that the "black community is leaderless without a rudder." He mentioned Farrakhan's associate Khalid Abdul Muhammad going on campuses and spewing Jew hatred. He recalled Jesse Jackson describing New York as "Hymietown," putting his arm around Arafat and saying he's sick and tired of Zionism. Irv wondered, "Why should black people hate Jews? What motivates that?" He reminded viewers that Michael Schwerner and Andrew Goodman had made the ultimate sacrifice. "Jewish people and their money got behind Martin Luther King," he added.

Irv said that Jews have so many potential points of solidarity with black people: fighting Nazism, white supremacy, and those ideologies that say we're a minority and should be put down. Irv pointed out that Farrakhan could do so much for black youth to motivate them, but instead he was taking money from Tom Metzger, the white supremacist leader.

Growing up in Montreal, Irv had experience dealing with anti-Semitism among the Quebecois, who had been taught by the Catholic hierarchy that Jews were responsible for deicide. Montreal was 80% French Catholic, and there was little separation of church and state at that time. Irv recalled being forced to read the New Testament. And then there was the common belief that the Jews killed Christ. He remembered hearing, "Jew, you killed my God." Every Easter was "open season" on the Jews. His father and particularly his grandfather directly experienced bigotry, hatred, and acts of aggression such as their beards being pulled. Irv recalled that his father wanted to fight back, but his grandfather said no, that is not the Jewish way. Irv said that sometimes we need to fight back. But he added that he's been heavily criticized for fighting back against people like Farrakhan.

I recalled my own experience growing up in the South. At many universities back then there was a "quota system" that limited the number of Jewish students accepted as part of a class of incoming students. Also, when I didn't participate in Christmas prayers or songs, I was singled out. I recalled my choral teacher asking, "Why is Arlene Greenberg not singing?" I stated my belief that prayer belongs in the home. Irv said that we could have a voluntary silent moment for all religions. Also, I recalled that my parents had a very "don't make waves" attitude back then, because it was so soon after the Holocaust.

But Irv did say that if we're a minority religion in a predominantly Christian country, then we have to respect their rights. But, he added, "When you and I recall the bigotry under which we grew up, there has to come a time when we stand up."

When we were discussing the stereotypes about Jews trying to dominate Hollywood, I tried to lighten the mood. I said, "Well, yes, Jewish people are very creative!" Irv at least chuckled a bit at that.

Irv believed that we need more "Sandy Koufax-type people," more people who can say to the Farrakhans and the Metzgers, "Hey, if you kick me I'm gonna kick back. Look, we're Jews, and we couldn't be prouder, and if you can't hear us we'll yell a little louder." That sounded like it came straight from a protest march, which it possibly did.

Referring back to the question with which I had opened the show, Irv said, "What makes me tick? We don't have to be so humble and cower, and so pious that people walk on us." And he added, "It's time we stand up as a collective people and say that we're not gonna take it any more . . . We have to become less humble, creative, and intellectual, and have to become more physical as a people. We have to say enough is enough. And we need Jewish leaders to teach Jewish kids what Judaism is all about."

Irv also appeared on my show in October 2001. Yes, just after 9/11. It is clear from watching the tape that we were both still in shock from that tragic event.

One of Irv's first comments was, "We've been hit. We've been hit so hard, we'll never be the same as a nation again," adding that "we've got to take stock; we can't be complacent anymore." He reminded our audience that this show was happening right after Yom Kippur, which is "our day of atonement, when we take an introspective look, see where we're going." Irv expressed fear for our loved ones and the lives of our citizens, calling the events "a tragedy beyond comprehension."

I pointed out that Israel seemed to have a suicide bombing every week. Americans don't understand what that's like.

Irv said that we have to take a hard look at who our enemy is, to take stock of what Islam really is today. He said that Islam is all about submission; they can use whatever force they have to make you submit. Ironically the majority of the Islamic following is in the third world, Irv pointed out, and many countries in the third world are very comfortable with brutalizing women and children. They have certain followers who are dedicated to destroying the Great Satan, and for them Israel is the little Satan.

We turned to the subject we had addressed on previous shows, the two-state solution. I read some excerpts from a recently published article in which the author wondered why the Palestinians were claiming any right to Jerusalem. The author pointed out that Israel really became a nation in 1312 BCE, 2,000 years before Muhammad. Arab refugees in Israel did not begin identifying themselves as "Palestinian" until 1967. Jerusalem has been the Jewish capital for over 3,300 years. It has never been a Muslim capital. When the Jordanians occupied Jerusalem, they never sought to make it their capital, and Arab leaders never came to visit. Jerusalem is mentioned over 700 times in the Torah but not once in the Koran. 600,000 Arabs fled Israel in 1948 because the leaders asked them to. But Jews left Arab countries, too. Their leaders expelled them.

We both noted that Golda Meir said that there is no such thing as Palestine. The Jewish right to Israel is that God gave us this land; the Torah is the blueprint. The Bin Ladens of the world want to destroy that land; they can't tolerate a Jewish entity in the heart of Arab territory. As Irv said, "They want the whole loaf of bread."

As to the Israeli relationship with the U.S., Irv said that "Israel has been the best friend this country has ever had. Israel has been heroic beyond belief." But we got into an argument about U.S. economic aid to Israel. Irv said that Israel should stop taking the aid or it would always be a vassal nation, a beggar nation, kowtowing to America's interests. Israel must stand on its own. I disagreed strongly, saying it's a pittance anyway, only about 3 billion. But Irv said that "America will always make us dance to their tune" if we keep taking it.

Sadly, this was the last time Irv was a guest on my show. Soon after he appeared, Irv was charged with the crime of a conspiracy to bomb a King Fahd Mosque and the office of a Lebanese-American Congressman, Rep. Darrell E. Issa.

I know that Irv and the FBI had a mutual dislike of each other. Irv's style was too vocal and abrasive for them. He used to tell me that he didn't have to go out of his way to make enemies with the FBI, because there were those in the government who were after him anyway. The mood in the country at the time of his arrest was one of political correctness. What could be more politically correct than to arrest the head of the JDL to show the "fairness" of the FBI?

So, when the FBI informants were able to entrap both Irv Rubin and his sidekick, Earl Kruger, they arrested them for planning the bombing and had the tapes to prove it. Yet according to Rubin's attorney, his voice was on only two of the eleven tapes. I could see Irv going to the fateful meeting at Jerry's Deli and going along with what the informants were promising to do, just to see what they had on their minds. Yet, I still do not believe that he had any intention of following through on what he was charged with.

I never believed that Irv would do something so stupid as to engage in this conspiracy. Nor did he ever have it in him to plan the blowing up of a building or an individual. There is no way that I would believe he was guilty of the charges that put him in prison, just as I've never believed he would kill himself. He had a lot of characteristics, but self-doubt was not one of them.

In November 2002 Irv died in prison. As I mentioned earlier, the official verdict was that Irv had committed suicide. The prison said that a number of guards had seen him slash his throat with a disposable razor and then jump 18 feet over a railing. Yet in a place that has video cameras all over the place, supposedly there was no video of the incident.

There is no way in hell he would commit suicide. Nor would he do this act in the violent manner suggested by the news. I know Irv would not have killed himself the day before his anticipated court date, because there was a chance he might have been acquitted. It doesn't make any sense. None.

Irv took his Judaism seriously; suicide is against the religion that he fervently practiced. Also, he loved his family and wouldn't have considered doing anything without leaving a note at least. He was just too close to his boys to do something that would destroy them in such a manner.

Most of all, the Irv Rubin who I knew, who I had on my television show and argued politics with, had a good heart and was a good man.

Irv Rubin was too strong to die. Whether by suicide, as was widely reported, or through more insidious means, as many others, including me, believe, we'll perhaps never know.

On my set again with Irv, and dog!

Elvis Presley...I Swear To G-d!!

When the idea came into my head of putting my encounter with Elvis Presley into this book, my first thought was, "I don't have any pictures to prove it." But, I swear to G-d, it really did happen!

Around my senior year in high school—if I could even remember the exact year I wouldn't tell—I had a brand new, silver-blue Cadillac convertible, and a quartet of girlfriends who used to cat around with me in it. One evening Elvis was appearing at the Roxy Theatre in Atlanta, Georgia, which was my childhood home.

In Los Angeles, it's commonplace to see stars wherever you go. But, in that nameless year in Atlanta, Elvis Presley's appearance was a major event. Not to me of course—I was too cool to get overly excited about such a thing. In fact, I was probably the only teenager in America who thought he was a redneck yokel; but I did like his music.

My girlfriends plotted for an entire week on how we would get to meet Elvis, and that's why, that particular day, we were hanging around his hotel. I have to say, my car with five really, really, cute Southern girls sitting in it was certainly a man magnet! Shortly after I parked the car, a couple of redneck types came out of the hotel. My friends were "in the know" about Elvis and they knew these guys were in the band—Elvis's band!

It wasn't too difficult to strike up a conversation with them. One of them, I think the piano player, said, "Well, looky, looky, what have we got here! Do y'all know where we can catch a cab to the place where Elvis is going to be playing tonight? We're strangers here, and we shore would like some pretty little girls like you to show us some of that Hotlanta hospitality that we keep hearing about."

They leered into the convertible for a few more minutes. Even then, I didn't particularly like really Southern boys, but these guys were from Elvis's band! My friends quickly offered these three Elvis guys a ride before they could change their minds. G-d knows how we squished them in the car, but we did, and I know they loved it. It was a short ride over to the Roxy. Once we arrived, one of the guys got out of the car and said, "I don't know if I can get you all in." Then, I was sure he looked straight at me and said, "But since you drove us over, come backstage tonight. I'll get you in somehow."

I wasn't sure if I'd actually do that since I had a date, a sort of blind date. Three hours before he picked me up, I began to dress. I picked out a tight red chiffon dress that flared out at the bottom with matching lace that hung out beneath the bottom of the dress. Then, I put on red shantung high heels and sparkly matching earrings. I could easily pass for nineteen instead of sixteen, which I actually was! I knew I was totally cool as I waited for my blind date to arrive.

Could I pass for 19?

Many of you ladies can probably identify with this experience. A guy would call you up and say, "Remember me from last summer?" And you'd think he was the cute guy from the pool, but then he would turn out to be that geek you would have never gone out with? Well, that's the guy I had a date with that night. So, when Harold picked me up at my home, the Elvis backstage invitation was suddenly very much on my mind. But as it turned out this geeky guy had bought tickets to the show! The concert was the biggest thing in town, probably for the whole year.

By the time Harold found parking and we walked in, the place was packed. I definitely stood out, as everyone else my age was wearing jeans and sneakers. We entered the Roxy and found our seats, and I began to formulate my plan. The plan wasn't nice, particularly to Harold, but I really thought I'd get back to my seat before the show started and none would be the wiser.

I excused myself to go to the restroom and headed toward the backstage entrance. I found myself surrounded by teenagers like myself, trying to get backstage. But I didn't look like any of them—I was dressed nicely. When I said, "Excuse me, excuse me, I have to get past you," people made a path for me. I blinked and suddenly I was backstage, being escorted by an usher who thought I was part of the show…yeah right!

There was excitement all around as people were preparing the lighting, positioning the instruments on stage, etc. The piano or guitar player to whom I had given a ride earlier made a beeline to come over and say hello. About that time, Elvis came by and the band guy said, "Let me introduce you!" It's been so many years that I don't remember everything; however, my first impression of Elvis was that he had a bad complexion and no hair on his chest.

That was in the days when men were allowed to have hairy chests. This was before they began to shave it all off and then go to the beach or pose for magazines like GQ.

Elvis was going on stage in literally seconds, but he didn't seem a bit rushed. It was as though we were meeting someplace where he had all the time in the world. This was in the days before his beaded and sequined outfits, and I honestly don't recall what he was wearing. He was, however, very respectful—if that's a word still used today. He shook my hand, looked at me intently, and said politely, "Nice meeting you. I heard all about how nice you gals were to my band and helping them get here today." I think he wanted to say more, but suddenly he was distracted by a little commotion just outside the stage area. A group of girls surged for the door shouting, "Just a piece of his shirt! Just get a piece of his shirt!" We heard it and laughed. I thought those teenagers were so silly.

Suddenly, the music started. Elvis and I stood side by side waiting for his entrance cue. Once given, Elvis strode out on the stage. The crowd roared! I had completely forgotten that Harold was somewhere out there, but I didn't particularly care. I was totally into the whole Elvis thing—me, almost on the stage with Elvis!!

At one point in the concert, Elvis was at the end of the stage close to where I was standing just off-stage and was down on one knee getting ready to sing "Hound Dog." I blurted out in my best hillbilly accent, "Ohhhh Elvis, just a piece of your shirt!" This struck him as very funny. He got up and walked over to where I stood, grabbed me by the shoulders, and kissed me! It all happened in seconds and I stood there dumbfounded thinking, "Nobody is going to believe this!"

I stayed there just off the stage for the whole show. When his show ended and he walked off, the crowd went wild. By now I had completely forgotten about my date but did remember that my girlfriends were somewhere in the crowd. As the room emptied I wanted them to see me, so I peeked out around the curtain, first a little, and then a little more. I have always been terribly near-sighted, and before I knew it, I was all the way out on the stage and still hadn't seen my friends! Suddenly I heard my name. "Arlene!! It's you! How did you get back there!?" Four or five of my friends were down front, begging me to get them backstage. I smiled, waved to them, and then walked backstage, loving every second of it.

Again, I saw one of the guys in the band. Was he the piano guy or the guitar player? I can't remember. Anyway, he invited me to go with him to the Royal Peacock Club, for a cast party. I said, "Sure" and we hopped in a car with some other people and drove over. It was a total mob scene. Ten minutes after arriving I lost the guy in the band, but I saw a few people I knew. It was fun! I had a great time, and none of them knew that I was only sixteen years old! Somebody gave me a ride home a few hours later.

By now my mother sure knew that Harold had not forgotten me. See, after the show Harold had driven to my house, awakened my mom, and told her I was "lost." The last he had seen of me was when I was heading to the backstage door. "And you know those terrible show people," he had said. As I arrived home at 2:30 in the morning, my mother, Mollie the Terrible, was waiting by the front door.

Man was she mad! Foolishly, I lied to this woman who could see though steel doors. She grounded me for a month. When I walked through the door, she was on the phone with the police, to have Elvis picked up for abducting a minor.

Of course, if I remember correctly, he did like them young; wasn't Priscilla fourteen when she met him?

And, finally, there's the old expression that when you're in love, the whole world is Jewish. And, as difficult as this might be to believe, Elvis is "technically" Jewish. Under Jewish law, if your mother is Jewish, then you are Jewish. Elvis's maternal great-grandmother, Martha Tacket, who lived from 1852-1887, was Jewish. Her daughter, Octavia "Doll" Mansell, was the mother of Elvis's mother, Gladys Love Smith. Funny how things happen.

Me and my panda, year not to be revealed

James Avery...He Really Was a Prince

You may know James Avery from his role as the father in *The Fresh Prince of Bel-Air,* but he appeared in numerous other television and movie roles. He was the host of the PBS series *Going Places.* I observed to James that he always seemed to play classy roles, like judges. I had first met him at a celebrity ski trip a few years prior to his first appearance on my show. I commented that I knew he was classy back then!

James appeared on my show one time with Mike Farrell and James Cromwell. One of our topics of discussion was—gasp!—unions. There had been a recent vote on merging the Screen Actors Guild (SAG) with the American Federation of Television and Radio Artists (AFTRA). That particular vote went against the merger, although the two organizations did ultimately merge in 2012. (For more on the SAG-AFTRA merger controversy, see my story about Sally Kirkland.)

Mike, perhaps best known for his role in the TV series *M*A*S*H,* was then the Vice President of SAG and had been in favor of the merger. James Cromwell, known for his roles in *The Green Mile, Babe,* and *LA Confidential,* was also in favor of merging the organizations. For purposes of full disclosure, and just being my good old upfront self, I said that I had voted against the merger, partly because I was against consolidation in general.

I asked James Avery about his opinion. He responded, "I'm political in my own quiet way." He had been torn about the merger issue. He said his first instinct was to be opposed, but then as he thought about it he realized that the industry and Hollywood had changed so much since the separate unions were first formed. For example, there were so many things going on with technology and different media types that the separate unions weren't structured to deal with. He also recognized the overlapping areas of responsibility between the two unions. He believed that people in the business needed a strong union that could deal with changing times, so he was now supportive.

We talked about ageism in Hollywood, how people over 40, particularly women, have a tough time getting hired. James Cromwell said that he got the part in *Babe*, for which he received an Academy Award nomination, when he was 54. But he had worked in films and TV for 30 years before landing this landmark role. He added that SAG helped him through those years with insurance benefits, and he was able to make enough on the shows he did do to send his kids through private schools. He said there's no way he could do that now with the escalating costs, even with SAG's help.

James Avery added that by the time you're 50 you know what you're doing. But then, just as you get to your most creative point, you have trouble getting jobs because you're not young enough. And the same problem exists for writers and directors.

I told the guys that this is the first union I'd ever belonged to; I've always been anti-union. I mentioned my Subway and Walgreen's commercials, adding, "All of a sudden I have to be a union person!"

James Avery said that the only color that matters in Hollywood is green. He had recently been in a panel discussion at the Trumpet Awards on the images of blacks in the media. He said to the panel that if you're upset about the new "blacksploitation" films and other black images, then don't go see them. He added that TV is not a realistic reflection of the nature of the country in the first place.

On my set with James Avery, Mike Farrell, and James Cromwell

I learned more about James's background during another appearance on my show. He was raised by a single mother who worked as a teacher's aide. James said that "she never got the memo that a single woman wasn't supposed to raise a male child." He was a latchkey kid. He said he didn't mind it, that he even kind-of liked it. He joked, "My room, my books, you don't have to share."

James had just finished a role on some show about Nancy Drew, where he played a journalism professor. And he was at the time a celebrity spokesperson for Cal-Tech. I asked about the influence of teaching and education in his life, because he seemed so classy and well-spoken and often played well-educated characters. James said that he had been greatly influenced by several teachers in his life, including his mother. He added that he himself had tried teaching for a few weeks, but it didn't work out because "he wanted to whip some kids' butts!"

James grew up in Atlantic City, where I used to visit as a child. James said that he saw the Supremes there for the first time at the Steel Pier. We reminisced about the town and its attractions such as The Diving Horse. We both remembered that your mother could cut you loose with just a dollar and you could spend the whole day having fun.

James talked about differences in Hollywood now versus his early years. He said that in the past there was a lot of work for character actors, and you could make a living doing that without being a star. He mentioned shows such as *Hill Street Blues, Law & Order,* and *Simon & Simon.* But now, he said, the producers have "plugged up the financial holes," and there's not as much character work. Another change he mentioned about acting in a TV series is that now you'll often be designated a "series recurring" instead of a "series regular" so they don't have to pay you "series regular" money. Quality work, according to James, had moved to cable.

He also talked about the roles available for African Americans. He noted that in the early days, *Beulah* and *Amos & Andy* were the only shows out there. But he added that, still today, the black characters are often "buffoons and clowns," and they're mainly young parts. He wished there was more variety. Images should cover the spectrum, he said, adding that "not everybody is a ghetto child."

He talked about how *Fresh Prince* and *The Cosby Show* were groundbreaking in their depictions of black upper-middle-class families. He said these shows are examples of the few programs that the family can watch together. He commented how *Fresh Prince* dealt with family issues; it just happened to be a black family. James noted that the show was timely in that it depicted a blended family; the Will Smith character was his nephew, not his son. So another big issue in the show was how to impose parental restraints on kids that aren't necessarily yours, how to deal with these kids when their parents haven't laid down guidelines. I mentioned how popular *Fresh Prince* was when it aired, and he said that it was still popular in syndication, maybe even more so.

On a related subject, James made a few comments about the show *Friends*. He said that New York is the most ethnically diverse place in the world, but the (white) characters on that show interact only with each other. "No way that would happen," he added.

I asked James about his wife. He said that she used to be the Dean of Students at Loyola Marymount but had just gotten a job as the VP of Students at a college in Oakland. So, they had gotten a house up there and were going back and forth. I said, "See, I knew you'd be involved somehow with education! You wouldn't have married a dummy." And James responded, "No. And I wouldn't have married an actress either. Noooo."

I agreed and said, "There's something dysfunctional about actors and actresses. I've known a lot of them." James responded, "Yes, we're crazy. We are, I admit that. We're insecure, we're needy." On the topic of relationships between actors, he added, gesturing up and down with his hands, "One time one is up, the other's down; this one's depressed, that one can't celebrate. Then the depressed one goes up and the other one goes down. It gets like that you know."

James said that when an audience sees you playing a character, they're supposed to believe that's who you are. And if you're good at your job they believe it. Unfortunately, though, that often means that the casting people believe it too. Some casting directors become "myopic," assuming that you can only do a certain type of role. James said that he used to always say that most of the actors and actresses in L.A. are oceans, or at least lakes, filled with talent and the ability to really develop characters, but most of the time "they only get asked for a cupful [of water]." I responded, "Oh, that's so profound."

On the other hand, James, who had extensive theater training, said that some people think you can just take a class and then you can act. He added that L.A. was the first place he had ever been where he ever met anyone who had *never* done a play.

As our time was drawing to a close, James talked about his volunteer work for books on tape and reading for the blind and dyslexic. He had a wonderful voice; those recordings must be a joy to listen to.

I asked James for some words of wisdom, something to remember him by. He said, "If you're gonna come into this business, make sure you do it out of love. If you wanna drive a Mercedes and live up in The Hills, you can be a mechanic and do that." I commented, "Or a plumber!" and he laughed. He concluded, "The arts are something that require a certain passion, commitment, and love. Something that you would do anyway, regardless. So make sure it's something you would do without anybody's help."

On my set with James Avery...

It's sad now to think that I had innocently asked James for "something to remember him by." James was far too heavy, and I used to nag him about his weight. He suffered from diabetes for years. He eventually lost his foot from this disease, and it was a significant factor contributing to his death in 2013. His passing was a great loss.

...and with James and Ed Asner

Pat Boone...An Oldie But A Goodie

Pat Boone is a doll!! Our paths have crossed over several years and continents, from Israel to the Academy Awards. When I introduced him during one of his appearances on my show, I said he's the only grown-up who can wear a yellow patent-leather suit or black leather pants and get away it. You see, years earlier I had seen Pat at an Academy Awards party, and he was wearing a yellow patent-leather suit! I do not lie.

Pat has been a long-time supporter of Israel. We were once in the country at the same time and happened to be staying at the same hotel, the Hyatt. Pat was there with a group of Christians he had brought over from Los Angeles. In fact, as I learned at a luncheon where Pat was being honored, Pat was there with this group of Christians as part of his role as the "Christian Ambassador to Israel."

I thought it wonderful that this group had come to support Israel and were helping to fight terrorism. However, some of them had the tacky habit of trying to proselytize to the Jews about "finding Christ" and getting to know "The Lord." I felt like they had forgotten that they were visitors in a Jewish country.

So one of the first things I brought up with Pat on the show was the Christian tour groups in Israel and my concern about their proselytizing. I said it was like being invited to dinner but saying that you want to eat on paper plates because you don't trust your host's dishes. Pat said he had brought about a dozen tour groups to the country over the years, with 1,200-1,500 Christian tourists at a time. He believed that they were offering a gift, but he completely agreed with me that he didn't condone trying to convince somebody of something they don't believe in or don't want.

Pat was one of my more fun guests. On the subject of Christianity and Judaism, I just had to tell the "How do you know Jesus is a Jew?" joke: Because he didn't leave home until he was 30, went into his father's business, and thought his mother was a virgin. And she thought he was G-d.

Pat told us that he considers himself an "adopted Jew." In fact, he had recently written an article about why he became a Jew. He believes that he "was adopted into the family of God's chosen people through my Messiah, a carpenter's son." Pat showed us the Magen David that he was wearing around his neck.

Still on the subject of Judaism, I told our viewers that Pat had written the lyrics to the classic song from *Exodus*. But what they didn't perhaps know was that he wrote them on the back of a Christmas card! I showed a clip of Pat on the Masada lip-synching the song, with its opening lyrics, "This land is mine, God gave this land to me."

It wasn't until I received his bio in advance of the show that I realized how smart Pat was. We both attended Columbia University in New York. He entered college thinking that he would be a high school teacher who also preached. He thought that was one way he could make a contribution in the world. He said that at the time he wanted to be a singer but didn't think that was possible. How about that! Pat graduated *magna cum laude* from Columbia. And I must admit, readers, that I did not receive that honor!

On this show Pat was wearing white shoes and white pants. Oy! Throughout his career, particularly in the early years, Pat has had a reputation for the clean-cut look, and I asked him about it. "I elevated squareness to another plateau. And bland," Pat responded. "Bland and square, the two words that defined me the best."

**With Pat
Boone, and
his white
shoes, on
my set**

In particular, Pat was famous for wearing white buck shoes. Pat said he wore them because every high school and college kid in America was wearing them in the mid 1950s; he just happened to be one of the first ones to wear them on TV. Kids would see him and say, "Hey, there's one of us." I'm sure that if he didn't go into singing, he would have been a great politician.

I told our viewers that Pat has sold over 50 million records in his career. I mentioned something about Halls of Fame; Pat said he's not in the Rock and Roll Hall of Fame, and suggested that maybe it had something to do with that clean-cut wholesome reputation we'd been talking about. But he is in the Gospel Music Hall of Fame. Pat said he expects to be singing some of the gospel songs "through eternity."

We also talked about the power of prayer. He told a moving story about his grandson Ryan, who had fallen 40 feet through a skylight from a roof in West L.A. about four years prior to this taping. When the paramedics arrived they thought he was about to die. Ryan sustained multiple injuries, including a fractured skull and a traumatic brain injury. He needed 36 pints of blood at the UCLA Medical Center. The doctors thought he would have to live the rest of his life in a vegetative state and told Pat that he'd better be thinking about how long he wanted to sustain Ryan. Pat said to the doctors, "You're the medical team, we're the faith team." Ryan's story gained national attention, and people across the country were praying for him. And Ryan, after several years of therapy and prayer, was now in a wheelchair and had regained some movement. As to prayer, Pat said, "All of our understandings are so finite, so incomplete; we're imperfect and flawed." I shared my experiences, which I have related elsewhere in this book, about asking for prayer during my brain surgery.

Michael Lerner arrived for the last part of the show, and things heated up a bit. Michael had been listening in the other room and took us back to the subject of Pat's Israel tours. Pat stated again that he doesn't condone proselytizing, which he described as twisting someone's arm trying to get them to agree to something they don't want. But he added that sharing, offering something and being ready to accept being turned down, is something else.

Michael then asked why the intellectual Jews were in bed with the Christian evangelical conservatives. He said that Pat Buchanan thinks they're together because the evangelicals believe that Israel is the Holy Land, and the Jews believe that they're his chosen people; but at Armageddon the Jews have to convert to Christianity, and if they don't convert they go to hell.

Pat responded that Christians believe the Old Testament as well as the New Testament and that, for Christians,

Jesus is the fulfillment of the Messianic prophecies. Michael asked about what happens to the other people—Buddhists, Muslims, atheists, etc. Pat said that only God can decide that.

Michael continued to argue gently for awhile, but then seemed to realize that the last few minutes of my show wasn't the right time to have a religious argument. So, to lighten things up, he said to Pat that he'd been thinking while waiting in the back room that they both had kissed Diane Baker. Pat nodded and said that he'd kissed her in *Journey to the Center of the Earth*. And then they discussed how they've both kissed me. I said "No, you haven't!" and Pat said "How quickly they forget!" As we closed out the show they were singing "When I lost my baby, then I lost my mind!" What a great ending!

When I was introducing Pat another time he was on my show, he kept sticking his face right up close to the camera and making comments. I would say "actor" and he would stick his head in and say "bland"; I'd say "songwriter" and he'd say "dull"; I praised him as a singer and he said "old." I laughed and just gave up on the intro! He doesn't seem to take himself too seriously!

I quoted from a recent article describing him as "wholesome, charming, and intelligent . . . one of America's 10 most-watched men." I asked Pat if it was hard to live up to that image. Pat responded, with characteristic humility, "Well, these things come and go . . . I think I'm on the most-watched list because I'm always popping up; you can't get away from me, whether it's Easter seals, talk shows, or promoting something."

With Pat on my set, in our younger days

My fondness for Pat turned into total adoration when he compared me to Stephanie Powers. During the eighties and nineties, not a week went by when someone didn't tell me how much I looked like Stephanie Powers. Pat was sitting across from me on the set and said, "You know who I think you look like?" I asked, "No, Pat, who?" Totally innocently he continued, "A younger Stephanie Powers." I just smiled and thought…YOUNGER!!! And I captured it on tape!!

Naturally, I was flattered, as I thought of her, and still do, as a pretty woman. But Stephanie didn't see any resemblance, as I found out one morning at the crack of dawn. I was in the Delta Crown Room waiting to catch a plane. I looked up at a woman sitting on the couch opposite from me and saw that she was "the" Stephanie Powers. She was sitting there with some guy who kept telling her how fabulous and flawless she was. She did look great, while I, on the other hand, was having a very bad hair day.

Finally, I couldn't hold it in any longer and leaned over and asked, "You're Stephanie Powers, right?" She smiled, fluffed her "good" hair, and said, "Why yes, I am." I then continued, "Well, you may be surprised, but over the years,

I quite often hear from people that they think we look alike." She responded with a look close to absolute horror on her face, and said, "Really...and who would that be?" I actually named one or two mutual acquaintances of ours and she said, "Oh, yes, I know them." Then I gave her the topper when I added, "And, Pat Boone once told me that he thought that we resembled each other." I could tell she was not pleased as she replied with shock, "Pat said that!?" Shortly after, I walked away, totally embarrassed and mumbling to myself.

At a party with Pat, 1995

Ed Asner...Gruff Pussycat

When we were young(er)...With Ed Asner, 1982

Ed Asner has been a friend of mine for over 40 years, which in itself is amazing. It's really strange that I still think he's wonderful, even though I've rarely agreed politically with anything he's ever said or done.

Ed is possibly best known for his award-winning comedic and dramatic portrayal of journalist Lou Grant. For this role, as well as others he played in *Rich Man, Poor Man* and *Roots*, Ed received seven Emmys and five Golden Globes. He's starred in many TV sitcoms, including *Thunder Alley*, and dramas like *Gone In The Night* and *A Case of Libel.*

Some of Ed's motion picture credits include *Fort Apache, The Bronx*; *They Call Me Mr. Tibbs!*; *The Wrestler*; and *Gunn*. Ed has done numerous voice-overs for animated characters. You'll hear Ed in *Captain Planet and the Planeteers*; *Batman: The Animated Series*; *Spider-man*; and *Gargoyles*, to name just a few. He drew widespread praise for his voice role in the movie *Up.*

Ed served as the President of the Screen Actors Guild (SAG) for two terms (1981-1985). He was *finally* inducted into the television Academy Hall of Fame in 1996.

Ed has appeared on my show seven or eight times. I want to share with you some of the many highlights.

When Ed was my guest on a show in the late nineties, he was wearing a coat and tie, which was unusual for him—for his appearances on my show, at least. During my introduction, when I mistakenly said that he had won seven Emmys and two Golden Globes, he stopped me, saying "five Golden Globes." Oops! But Ed wasn't mad; he was just needling me. For all the accolades he's received, he's a very modest guy.

I told our viewers (and reminded Ed) that I had driven him around Atlanta in the early seventies. I don't think he remembered me from that time, but he furrowed his brow and said, "Wait, it's coming back to me..."

On the subject of Ed's two terms as president of SAG, I told him that I'm SAG-qualified, because I did the movie *Your Mother Wears Combat Boots*. (I later became a member.) I added that "I was a bitch in the airport." Ed asked, "Now where did you go to study how to be a bitch?" I responded, "It was an inbred thing," and Ed retorted, "Did Atlanta teach you that?" I replied, "Didn't have to."

Although Ed and I disagree politically on many things, such as the ACLU, we both support animal rights and abortion rights. Ed has been active in the abortion-rights group NARAL. Ed said that one of the biggest reasons he's pro-choice is that people can find a needy kid to raise in this country and around the world. When Ed stated that he cared very much for animals, and I said that I did too, he commented, "I think you're an animal. Your stir the animal in your viewer." I should have roared!

Getting older...With Ed in 1990

Ed didn't understand why I was down on the ACLU. He said, "You don't truly appreciate democracy if you don't fight for something like that." I told him that I was angry when the ACLU wanted to allow the Nazis to march in Skokie. Ed said, "Yeah, yeah, yeah. But fighting for civil rights is what democracy is all about. Civil rights organizations have to fight for the ugliest so that the less ugly will have a better chance."

I said that I didn't like Vanessa Redgrave marching for the PLO and that she must be anti-Jewish. Ed said, "No she's not; she might be anti-Zionist but she's not anti-Jewish." And I replied, "But they're the same!" Ed said, "No, they're not," and I responded, "To me they are."

It took me a little coaxing, but Ed finally admitted that he had been in Hollywood since—gasp!—1961. He started acting in Chicago. He commented that the theater is the only place where you learn how to act. At least one of my other guests, including Jack Klugman, said the same thing.

Ed added that the theater is also where you go if you need to "refresh your motor."

Ed told us that he likes doing TV better than movies. He said that movies "just take a long time; they're arduously, painstakingly slow." But TV, on the other hand, "keeps you go go go" he added as he moved his arms like he's running.

I asked Ed for some final words of wisdom. First he quoted the Golden Rule, and then the second was "Turn the other cheek." Not surprising—Ed is a long-time pacifist.

In 2005 we taped two shows with Ed on the same day. When I introduced him for the first show, I said, "When they say this man needs no introduction... love him or hate him, you know who Ed Asner is." I told the audience about asking Ed before the show what we should put under his name on the screen, and he had responded, "Stud." Ed laughed now and said, "I like to dream, you know?" But, he added, "They chickened out in the back and didn't do it."

Early on in the show Ed mentioned that Eugene V. Debs had made an impression on him. I told Ed that I once read a book and wrote a paper about him. I think Ed was shocked that I knew who Eugene Debs was! But then I set things straight when I said that Ayn Rand had been my biggest influence. Ed wasn't surprised. Quite a difference in our philosophies of influence!

I kidded Ed that he would appear at a fish fry if it had the word "homeless" in it. In fact, he had just done a play about the homeless, which I thought was horrible. The play, that is, not the fact that Ed was in it. People had left during the show. I stayed for the whole thing but told Ed that I had "tushie fatigue" when it was over. He said, "You should have called on me," and told me he would have given me a massage! Ed had only a few lines in the play, but he did it because he thought it was important.

Ed always showed his great sense of humor on my show, and this one was no exception. When I remarked on how busy he stays, suggesting that he must have to kidnap his assistant Patti to help him with his many commitments, he said that yes, he does restrain her, but he uses "velvet handcuffs, and they don't leave marks." I noted the large ring on his finger, and Ed said that he got it from another actor. I commented how nice that was. "Well," Ed said, "I killed him and took the ring." Another time I kidded Ed that he was a dirty old man, and he responded, "Just dirty."

When I told Ed about how I got barred for being an activist after six years of doing my prison program, Ed said, "What happened to you?" implying that I used to be involved in causes but now had sold out. I said, "I *am* an activist, on good causes." And Ed responded, "Yeah, but you're on the wrong side."

On my set, 2004

At this point I told the audience that we'd known each other since the early seventies but rarely talked politics. And Ed said, with a stern but bemused look on his face, "Yeah, because we knew what would happen." Boy, all that was about to change!

At the time we were in the middle of the Iraq war. Ed noted that there were 500,000 kids killed by the UN sanctions and bombing even before we invaded. We really got into it for several minutes about how to stop Islamic fundamentalism. Finally, I said, "I don't happen to trust George Bush." And Ed responded, "You're becoming enlightened, Arlene."

I turned to the subject of Israel. Ed said he had supported Israel in the past but wasn't doing so now because he found them "too bellicose to gratify my democratic instincts." I raised my eyebrows, waiting for him to continue. Ed said, "You really wanna know my opinion about Israel?" And then he gave us a little lecture. He said that after World War Two anti-Semitism was reduced to the lowest point it had been for centuries because of the six million dead Jews. After the war, he added, it was felt we had sufficiently paid the price for being "Christ killers." Israel was founded with all the good will of the world behind it; a few million Arabs were displaced, but the world didn't care because it wanted the Jews to have their place. And in the beginning everything was fine. The Arab League banded together a few times and invaded to restore the Arabs to their land, but they failed.

Then Ed said, "By the way, prior to Israel's founding, Jews suffered far less from Islam than from Christendom. There were no crusades by the Muslims." When I commented, "There were no Arabs there then!" Ed replied, "Oh cut that crap!"

My director was signaling that we were running out of time, so Ed said, "OK, I'll finish. Since that time, since the failure to establish a Palestinian state, that anti-Semitism has grown." He added that the Arabs have spread the Protocols of Zion to people who don't know any better, creating this hatred of Jewry, and now the poison has spread into Europe and other places.

But when he said that Israel could have done more to establish peace, I couldn't hold back, and we talked over each other about the various peace agreements, land for the Palestinians, etc. Here's a portion of that exchange:

Me: *There is no Palestine.*

Ed: *There was no Israel.*

Me: *Yes there was. Israel goes back to the Bible.*

Ed: *You've got about a 2,000-year gap in there.*

Me: *Our deed goes back to God.*

Ed: *Then we should give the Indians back their land.*

At that point it was time to end the show. I said my blood pressure had gone up. Ed admitted that he was kind-of down when he came in before the show, but that I had fired him up! We chuckled as we realized that we had broken our unspoken promise about not talking politics!

At dinner

Somewhere else

I started out the second show that day with Ed, which we taped that afternoon, by saying, "OK, I'm going to calm down. Maybe if I took tranquilizers." I noted how truly multi-talented Ed is, adding "eclectic, is that the word?" But then I said, half-jokingly, that Ed is very misinformed when it comes to Israel. I added that I wanted to do this second show because Ed got the last word on the first one!

First we got into a little give-and-take about Muslims in France. When I said that France had been taken over by the Muslims, Ed asked, "How can you say that when they won't let women wear head scarves?" I retorted, "In five years everyone there will be wearing a burka." Ed said, "I'll bet you'd still look good in a burka." So here was Ed, deflecting potential confrontation with a compliment! Although I certainly cannot imagine myself ever wearing such an outfit.

Continuing on the subject of my fashion choices, Ed said he liked my pink suit better than the one I had worn earlier in the day, which was black. "Hot pink," he added. Then out of the blue he asked me what "Wow!" stood for in my show's name, and I told him: "Watch out World."

By the way, Ed had a pretty stringent Jewish upbringing. He said that he had a 5,000-word Hebrew vocabulary at one point in his life. At the time of this show he was doing readings at the Westside Jewish Community Center and the Wilshire Boulevard Temple. I asked Ed why Hollywood never speaks out about violence against Israelis by radical fundamentalists. Ed responded, "How come the newspapers don't talk about Israel being the third largest holder of atomic weapons in the world?" At some point Ed used the Yiddish phrase *Der mentsch trakht un Got lakht*, which translates as "Man plans and God laughs."

On the topic of terrorism, Ed said that Bush had declared the war on terrorism, which is obviously a war that will never end. When we got back into our morning's discussion of Israel and Palestine, I said that I consider the West Bank to be a suburb of Israel, and Ed responded, "Oh, you want the West Bank too, do you?" Then he added, "There is nothing more that I can say to you." But once again he smiled to let me know he was kidding—for the most part.

Drifting away from politics, we discussed ageism in Hollywood. Ed said that it's always been there, reflecting our society's emphasis on youth and beauty. Ed added that it applies not only for actors but for writers, producers, directors, cameramen, etc. He said that Hollywood can take people with experience and "exile them to the old folks' home. I think it's criminal."

By the time of this show I had joined SAG and had done a few commercials in addition to my infamous "airport bitch" role in *Combat Boots*. I said to Ed maybe I should also do voice-overs because I can do seven accents. Ed responded, "I only hear one, honey."

We briefly discussed the issue of movies shooting outside the U.S. for tax relief purposes. Ed said he's for globalism as long as the local people are getting good wages and treated well and we retrain people here. But that is not happening, he said.

Ed once appeared on my show with his friend Scott Wilson, who is also a fine actor. Scott's first role was with Rod Steiger in *In the Heat of the Night*. I think Scott was best remembered for *In Cold Blood,* in which he had a starring role, and for playing the priest in *Dead Man Walking*. In recent years, Scott has become well-known to TV audiences through *The Walking Dead*. We showed a clip of some of Scott's earlier roles.

While we were talking about Scott playing a priest, Ed informed us that Pope John Paul II was once an actor, and we somehow got onto the topic of televangelists. I told him my feeling about these men; I watch them stand on stage saying "Send your money to the Lord at Box 724, Tupelo,

MS," and I've always wondered how they know the Lord's P.O. Box number. Rabbis never do that!

On my set with Ed and Scott Wilson, 2008

At one point during this show, while I was very engaged talking to Scott about his various roles, I looked over at Ed and he appeared to be dozing. So I hit him on his knee with my rolled-up notes and said "Wake up!" At another point I noticed him fiddling with his hands and asked what he was doing. He said "callouses," and I asked "From hard work?" He responded, "Walking on my knuckles."

And at another point Ed said, "You look very good today; that face, and that mountain of flesh that's showing." I gathered he was speaking of my low-cut top! I asked how a man like him ended up in Kansas. He smiled and said, "They need butchers there. I've been a butcher all my life." Ed's father, too, was a butcher in Kansas.

Ed also appeared on my show with Alan Rosenberg and Anne-Marie Johnson. Let's just say that, politically, I was outnumbered three to one. But we had a blast!

Alan starred as attorney Eli Levinson in two TV series, *Civil Wars* and *L.A. Law,* and also played Cybill Shepherd's ex-husband in *Cybill*. Anne-Marie is perhaps best known for *In the Heat of the Night*. When I told Alan and Anne-Marie that I've never agreed politically with one thing this man (pointing to Ed) has ever said or done, Ed exclaimed, "God Bless America!" I added, "Personally I love him! He's a pussycat. But politically I don't see how he exists. I mean, the ACLU—he actually thinks it's a *good* thing."

On my set with Ed, Anne-Marie Johnson, and Alan Rosenberg, 2007

Whoa, that got us started! They talked about how important the ACLU is and how they all love it. Anne-Marie raised the issue of women's equality. And, OK, they got me to agree with the concept of equal pay for equal work. But then I commented that I've always been against equality because women are so superior that they'd have to lower themselves to the level of men. At one point during the discussion, Ed said, "When I'm with you, women's equality gets set back 100 years." And we all laughed.

Alan was the president of SAG at the time. He said that Ed is one of his heroes: as an actor, as a previous president of SAG, and as a political activist.

When someone pointed out that Anne-Marie was married to a Jewish man, she said, "Yes, I joined the tribe."

So we started joking around about Jewish men. Ed said, "You know what Jewish lovemaking consists of. It begins with nine minutes of pleading."

When Ed appeared with Shirley Jones in 2007, we somehow got on the topic of the Michael Richards "incident," the one in which he shouted some racial slurs at a few hecklers in the audience at his comedy show and then went into a racist rant that was well-publicized in the media. As I told Ed and Shirley, I was there!

At one point I was talking about my years at the University of Alabama, before I went to Columbia. I said, "Well, you know, in those days, nice Jewish girls didn't leave their nice Jewish houses until they met nice Jewish boys and then they had nice Jewish children." And Ed responded, "Well, you know, you missed out on the first part: Nice Jewish girl."

And we also somehow got on the topic of Billy Barty, the famous "dwarf" actor. Ed said, "He may have been short in stature, but boy was he hung!" When we speculated that "it" may have hung to the ground, I commented, "Well, it didn't have far to go!"

We often talked about other actors on my show. Ed has worked with some of the best; after knowing Ed all these years, I believe that he still *is* one of the best. Two of Ed's stage roles come to mind. First, I find it ironic that he, with his leftist viewpoints, was able to carry off, so terrifically, a role in a play about Jonathan Pollard. Interestingly enough, Ed played the part of Israeli Rafi Eitan, a man who betrayed Pollard, which ultimately led to Pollard's capture and destruction.

And a few years ago Ed invited me to a reading where he played the part of FDR. For three hours I watched Ed, well into his 80's, do a one-man-show, and he didn't miss a word. Even more impressive, it was hard to figure how this stocky Jewish man could play so convincingly the part of Roosevelt, the elegant New England Episcopalian.

Ed still seems to pop up everywhere. One week I saw him in three shows: as the voice of the old man in the film *Up*; then a few days later in *Elf*, where he was Santa; and finally, playing a grumpy old man as usual, in an episode of *Criminal Minds*.

Although I usually disagree with most of Ed Asner's political viewpoints, he was always an exciting guest on my show! However, when we're not talking politics, I find him a lovable man and consider him a good friend. Despite our differences, I still think Ed Asner is a pussycat.

Maybe not so gruff after all

Elie Wiesel...The Sexy Peace Prize Winner

From time to time, people ask, "You've interviewed so many people, who was the sexiest?" Frankly, I am a very basic woman and, to me, a sexy man is one who can make me feel sexy. So, immediately my mind conjures an image of the sexy humanitarian, Elie Wiesel.

I remember that in 1998 Mr. Wiesel and I were both staying at the Tel Aviv Hilton in Israel. As luck would have it, we also both had privileges to the Executive Suite on the 16th floor, where selected guests would gather for happy hour and late-night coffee. I noticed people staring in his direction wherever he walked, and, you know me, this sparked my interest! I wanted to know, who was this man? He looked over seventy, slim and not very tall. He carried himself with an air of authority, and he had the most amazing, hypnotic eyes. Without any verbal exchange, just looking into his eyes, I found myself wanting to talk to him. Were we connected? I was surprised to learn, during one of our later conversations, that he had once worked as a stringer for my newspaper.

Anyway, at some point we ended up in the same elevator together. I remember, at the time, I still didn't know exactly who he was but thought he had to be someone I knew or should know. He was certainly someone I wanted to know! So, I smiled at him and said, "I know who you are." He smiled back and said, "You do?" Nodding my head, I replied, "Uh huh, you're Simon Wiesenthal." He laughed and said, "Not exactly. I'm Elie Wiesel." Undaunted, I shrugged and said, "Well, I knew it was a 'W' name anyway." Shyness has never been a trait of mine. So, without hesitation I told him that I wouldn't let him off the elevator unless he consented to meeting me for coffee, conversation, and an interview.

He was the busiest of men. However, during this stay in Israel, he found time to meet me several times in the lounge before or after his talks with world leaders. As a reporter, I had so many questions I wanted to ask him. I remember that I took a notepad to capture his words for posterity. I even went to the Hilton's business office to research this elusive man. There were hundreds of pages written about him. He had written and done so much!

I learned he was born in Romania on September 30, 1928, and led a life representative of so many of the Jewish children growing up in a small Romanian village. His life revolved around his family, his religious studies, and his relationship with G-d. However, his life, as he knew it, changed when he was deported with the rest of the Jews in his community in 1944 and sent to Auschwitz. He then endured the horrors of a Nazi concentration camp. After the war, Wiesel became a journalist in Paris, and eventually ended his silence about his experiences during the Holocaust with the publication of *Night* in 1958. This book, his harrowing account of his experiences at Auschwitz and Buchenwald, contains arguably the most powerful and renowned passages in Holocaust literature. *Night*, which was by the way his first book, has been translated into thirty languages, with millions of copies in print around the world.

Wiesel devoted his life to ensuring that the world does not forget the atrocities of the Nazis and that those events are not repeated. He advocated on behalf of many repressed peoples and races, and spoke out about our shared responsibility in fighting hatred, genocide, and racism. The world has been changed by his tortured memories and forgiving attitude.

Wiesel wrote over forty books and won numerous awards. He served as the Chairman of the President's Commission on the Holocaust and was the founding Chairman of the U.S. Holocaust Memorial Council. In 1986, he won the Nobel Peace Prize. At the end of his life, Wiesel was still teaching at Boston University and travelling the globe advocating for human rights and ethical issues.

With Elie Wiesel in Tel Aviv, 1998

So, armed with all this new-found knowledge after researching Elie Wiesel, I looked forward to returning to the 16th floor at the Hilton to share an intelligent conversation with him. In my mind, I remembered his famous quote, "To remain silent and indifferent is the greatest sin of all." I knew I had better be a good talker when we conversed.

But, to tell the truth, when I looked into his soulful eyes, I forgot everything. I do remember, though, he was very reluctant to talk about himself. So, there I was, with probably one of the most interesting men in the world, and I was talking about myself; which, actually, is one of the topics I don't mind discussing. Amazingly, he wanted to find out what made *me* tick. And that is why I found him to be a very sexy man. It has been said that the eyes are the windows of the soul. Well, on that alone, I'd give Mr. Wiesel a Nobel Peace Prize—his eyes were awesome!

He probably thought that this was one of the more outrageous interviews he'd ever done. Perhaps for this reason, from time to time over the years he continued to meet with me and answer my questions over coffee.

On one of these occasions, in about 2002-2003, we had agreed to meet at the Ritz Hotel in L.A. Only for Elie Wiesel would I drive fifty miles. I am admittedly not the best driver. But I somehow made it to the hotel, and on the dot at 4:30 P.M. he met me in the lobby, and we had a chance to speak about the world over an overpriced cappuccino. What else could you speak to Elie Wiesel about except "The World"? Plus, even the L.A. *Times* wrote about him once as being the most important Jew in America.

I think Elie appreciated my way of communicating. I didn't talk with him the way you're supposed to talk with a Nobel Peace Prize winner. On this occasion I had so many things on which I wanted to get his opinion that I almost didn't know where to start. Since Jonathan Pollard was a topic uppermost on my mind at the time, I decided to start there. Mr. Wiesel had visited Pollard in prison several times, including at the hellhole maximum security prison in Marion, Ill., where Pollard was kept under deplorable conditions. Wiesel also visited Pollard at a prison in North Carolina.

At the time we both thought that the prospects for Pollard's early release were very dim. As we sat over coffee, I told Elie about my recent dinner with Jonathan's father, Dr. Morris Pollard, and how heartbroken he had been since Jonathan had married his second wife, Esther. Elie nodded his head, and followed my thoughts with, "His wife has alienated everyone who could or would help him." When I asked, "Do you mean Annie?" Elie answered, "No, she was faithful to him." I commented that Bill Clinton hadn't released Jonathan when he had the chance but instead pardoned millionaire Marc Rich, a major donor to the Clinton Foundation. Elie didn't dispute that, but stated his belief that the FBI and CIA were primarily responsible for preventing Pollard's release. And he felt that Caspar Weinberger's voice was still influential in the case.

Coffee with Elie

At the time, the Iraq war was close on the horizon. As we discussed the blowing "winds of war" he looked at me with those eyes and said that he wasn't marching in peace movements this time around. He supported intervention in Iraq as part of the effort to eradicate international terrorism. He said that Saddam had gassed thousands of his own people in the 1980s when he had the weapons and had of course invaded Kuwait. Elie felt, and I agreed, that Saddam was a madman who had to be stopped. And he didn't seem to like the French and Germans (who had united in opposition to the Iraq war) anymore than I did.

All too soon, he had to leave to speak at the Civic Center in Thousand Oaks, which could have been Honduras as far as I was concerned. The reason I mention this is because, as I indicated earlier, driving is not my forte. Nevertheless, Elie said, "Why don't you follow my driver, and you can hear me speak?" This sounded great to me, so I got in my car and prepared to follow Mr. Wiesel and the chauffeur. However, within minutes, it began to pour (I don't do rain) and the man in front of me was driving like a madman at 80, 90 miles an hour, while I was following, nearly hysterical, for 65 miles! I had thought we'd be going just a little way down the road. Every few miles, an arm would reach out of the car in front of me, and I assumed it was Elie cheering me on.

By the time we arrived at the Civic Center, I was not a happy camper. Ah, but that was before this great man spoke. There wasn't an empty seat in the house. There is an old expression, "He walks softly but carries a big stick." I think of Elie Wiesel when I hear that. His demeanor was soft, but his impact was powerful. He captured the audience immediately and spoke for an hour and a half, with no notes. In a quiet voice, he spoke of the seducer and the victim of seduction. As he wondered aloud about what had happened to civilization, and how history was sick today, his audience sat in rapture.

There was so much for him to remember, but not enough time to tell it all. He spoke of his painful years and said, "My goal is to be sensitive, to become sensitive to the other's pain, or joy. G-d is alone. Human beings shouldn't be alone." Wow! He continued: "Commitment is memory. Forgetting in ancient times was said to be a blessing. But, once you start forgetting, where do you stop?"

I felt as though if I kept really good notes of his lecture, they should be printed in a book somewhere. Almost hypnotizing his audience, he spoke of how 1939-45 was preceded by the "winds of madness." He said that if in

1934, or '36 or '38, the world had reacted to Hitler, the madness could have been stopped. He then added, "Why not? That's the question I want an answer to. Why did so many people listen to him?"

With a direct, penetrating look at his audience, he softly said, "How did we remain sane after the war?" He said he never believed he'd see the end of communism or apartheid. Yet, it did happen.

Earlier over coffee Elie had told me that he felt that the transfer of Arabs into Arab nations was never going to happen and was utterly impossible. I also was sorry that I didn't have the chance to discuss the comments on Palestinian statehood he made during his talk. I was saddened to hear him say, "They will have a state and it will be a peaceful state of two peoples living side by side." Yet he then continued, "It's a miracle that the Israeli people don't go into psychosis. How can they live with the terror that they do? Even terrorism must know limits. They are destroying their own chance for a state." And he later predicted that the Palestinians would have their own state in three years, adding they there should be a "three months' moratorium on violence." Hearing these comments I admittedly thought him naïve, and I disagreed with his synopsis.

When I had asked Mr. Wiesel earlier about the rise of Anti-Semitism, he answered, "They can't forgive us for being here. We could have disappeared so many centuries ago. We are the only people who have survived antiquity, and they cannot forgive us for that." So it was almost comical when during the question-and-answer session after his talk, one questioner asked, "Would the United Nations today vote to create a State of Israel?" Mr. Wiesel laughed and responded, "You're joking. Abba Eban said if Moses brought them the 10 commandments, they would vote him out."

Beverly Hills, 2002

A number of years ago I sent Elie a column that I wrote about him, and he wrote me back and said he was amused by my description of him. When I was beginning to write this book, I knew I would include a story about Elie, so I asked if he could write a comment to include in the book. He responded that he would be glad to and to let him know when the book was finished. I have a tendency to procrastinate, and thought I had all the time in the world to contact Elie as I was continuing work on the book.

But then, in July 2016, as I was putting the finishing touches on this book, Elie Wiesel died. Many wonderful things were written and said about him following his death. I thought about our experiences together as I read through the obituaries and watched the television news reports. After vowing to not speak or write about what he had seen while imprisoned at Auschwitz and Buchenwald for 10 years, he broke his silence when he exposed the horror of the Nazi death camps in *Night*, and his words resounded throughout the world. In a famous passage from that book he used the phrase "Never shall I forget" several times while describing some searing memories from the camps. He spent the rest of his life speaking out against forgetfulness, violence, and hatred. I remember when President Reagan was going to Bitburg, Germany, to place a wreath in a cemetery where SS officers were buried. Wiesel told Reagan, "This place, Mr. President, is not your place. Your place is with victims of the SS." And I remember the ad he took out in the *New York Times* in 2013 urging President Obama to insist on fully eliminating Iran's nuclear program and to condemn Iran's continued harmful intent against the Jewish people. Finally, in one of its obituaries the *Times* even talked about his eyes, as I do in this story. I will never forget those soulful, mournful eyes.

Dr. Carole Lieberman...The Shrink to the Stars

Unlike most of the doctors in Los Angeles, who seem to have earned their diplomas after a six-week internet course, Dr. Carole Lieberman has earned the right to put the "MD" after her name. She was a member of the clinical faculty at UCLA's Neuropsychiatric Institute and has a Master's Degree in Public Health. Known as the "Shrink to the Stars," her other accomplishments include: host of her internet radio show, "Dr. Carole's Couch"; author; a three-time Emmy nominee; and a voice to Congress for the ratings system on television. To me, she is blonde, has a "little girl quality," gets things done, and is an expert on everything. Before I knew Carole, I religiously read her article in *The National Enquirer*. We were friends many years before I learned that hers is the calming voice heard on earphones while on a plane. She has been a guest numerous times on major media channels. I feel that Carole is everywhere, just like a fungus. When I think she is gone, she pops up, and I am delighted!

Carole has "popped up" on my show several times. After I introduced her, letting my viewers know that she is a "real" doctor and not one of those mail-order types, she acknowledged that there are some people who put "Doctor" in front of their name who do have a legitimate PhD but not in psychiatry or psychology.

During this show Carole told us about her experience with the TV ratings system. In 1992, after testifying in Congress about violence in the media, she recommended a 10-point plan to get violence off TV and the streets. One of her recommendations was to have a TV ratings system. And, eventually, such a program came about. But, unfortunately, under the new system the individuals doing the ratings were producers and others from the business. Carole had recommended that the ratings group should consist of child psychiatrists and other mental health professionals who have expertise in deciding what's appropriate for children of certain ages. She had also recommended making a simpler classification system than the one used for the movies. Carole speculated that the system is intentionally confusing to just show they're "doing something." But she was pleased that at least some progress had been made.

Carole added that *Teenage Mutant Ninja Turtles* was one of the first shows that brought violence down to the level of little children of preschool age. Kids were copying the martial arts moves of the turtles; teachers were talking about it, and studies in which experts observed kids through one-way mirrors watching and reacting to the shows had confirmed the anecdotal evidence.

One of Dr. Carole Lieberman's appearances on my show

My title for this show was "Bad Boys Revisited," because one of our subjects was Carole's book, *Bad Boys: Why We*

Love Them, How to Live with Them, and When to Leave Them. In this book she describes 12 different types of Bad Boys. We talked about this subject on this show and returned to it in a later one, and I found our discussions to be fascinating.

According to Carole, most women have had at least one Bad Boy in their lives. Women are attracted to a particular type of Bad Boy because of some issue in their relationship with their fathers. The nature of that relationship sets you on the path towards a particular Bad Boy type. The situation gets more complex when a stepfather is added to the mix.

For each Bad Boy described in the book, she uses an example from a fairy tale. For example, the "Frazzled Frog" or "Fixer-upper Lover" type of Bad Boy never wants to grow up. He's like a tadpole. He doesn't have his act together, particularly his career and finances, no matter how old he is. Women who are attracted to a guy like this were often abandoned by their father in one way or another— perhaps they lost their father through death or divorce, or the father was a workaholic or not emotionally available. Women unconsciously look for a guy who is *least* likely to abandon them, and the Frazzled Frog seems like that type of guy. Bad Boys usually have dysfunctional relationships with their mothers, and the Frazzled Frog is looking for a woman to mother him.

The problem is that if the woman takes care of him too well, that "mothering need" gets satisfied, and then he "hops away" to find another woman who can take care of him even better.

Carole asked me if I ever went after a Frazzled Frog, and I responded that they turn me off, but that they went after me! I added that these days I'm "just happy to find a man who's heterosexual and pays his own bills!"

Another Bad Boy type Carole talked about was "Mr. Power Mad," like the prince in Cinderella. This guy is very controlling and, according to Carole, is looking for a woman to fit into *his* shoes. He seemingly has his life together and seems like a "catch." Women whose fathers were weak compared to their mothers tend to go for a Mr. Power Mad type. Because their mothers "wore the pants" while they were growing up, they perhaps felt ashamed of their fathers. These women conclude that they're not going to marry a man like their father and are therefore attracted to powerful-seeming men. What often happens, though, is that the women enjoy the relationship at the beginning, but the guy turns out to be too controlling.

I told Carole that I yearned for the days when men were men. In Israel they still are. Also, older women are considered to be a national treasure there; I speak from experience!

Carole stressed that women are drawn to Bad Boys unconsciously to somehow make up for not feeling loved by their fathers. The common denominator with the Bad Boys is that they break your heart in some way or otherwise hurt you.

I asked Carole how she came to write the book. She said that her co-author contacted her and suggested the idea. At first Carole wasn't sure, but after thinking about it realized that if anybody were going to do this it should be her, because she's been with each of the Bad Boy types at least once. And I commented, "I knew their brothers!"

When I shared my observation that women seem to go for the same type again and again, Carole said that Freud called this the "repetition compulsion." Women are trying to fix something from childhood and feel more love from a male figure than they received from their father, so they're drawn to these similar situations. They're trying to live the same story but make it have a happier ending. But, Carole noted, if you haven't learned about you, why you are the way you are, you'll keep making the same mistake. She said that you have to feel you deserve not a Bad Boy but a prince.

Finally, we briefly discussed whether to talk about old relationships when we get involved in a new one. Carole thinks it's important to do so, that you can learn a lot about your new relationship through talking about old ones. For example, how previous relationships ended, or a history of short-term relationships, can be warning signs in a new partner. I said that some people might want to make the next one pay for what the last one did, and added, "The only thing I want to hear about an ex-wife or girlfriend is how she died."

I asked Carole for a closing remark for this show. She responded that she wants to get people to recognize the power of the media and how it is affecting us unconsciously every day.

After writing and publishing her book, *Coping with Terrorism: Dreams Interrupted*, Carole and I went to a conference on terrorism in Dallas. I remember sharing a room with Carole, and the phone in our hotel room rang. I answered, and someone from *People Magazine* was on the line. I was eager to hear Carole tell the listener her viewpoint on terrorism; instead, the caller wanted her opinion on Britney Spears, who had been rushed to the hospital with a drug overdose. I mean, really, this Britney Spears incident was considered headline material! Meanwhile, here we were, at this intense, newsworthy conference, hearing from experts that terrorists were trying to take over our country from outside and within and that the Muslims had learned how to use our own laws to destroy us.

And, in my heart, I felt this was true. I remembered that I had noticed an area in the airport where Muslims washed their feet for prayer. Does that mean there will be a private section for nursing mothers or a private section for Orthodox Jews to say their prayers at airports? Carole commented, "Mentally, we think the war is 'over there' but it is really 'here,' and this is a rude awakening."

Carole appeared on my show a few times after this book was released. I noted that it was quite the change from *Bad Boys*. She said she would have never considered writing a book on terrorism prior to 9/11, and if she had, people would have said she was crazy. After 9/11, as a native New Yorker, she felt compelled to act. First, she developed "Shrink on Board" for the airlines, providing relaxing music and narration (with her voice) to ease the stress of airline passengers who may not only have a fear of flying but now have to worry about terrorists.

**With Carole on my set showing her latest book…
Oh wait, that's me on the cover!**

Carole said that the threat of terrorism is having negative impacts on our daily lives, leading to problems such as eating or drinking too much, losing sleep, issues with our jobs and relationships, etc. She feels it is important that we recognize where these problems are coming from. We must bolster ourselves psychologically and get more active politically to keep ourselves safe.

I expressed my frustration that people in our country still seem to have no conception of what it's like to live where terrorist actions are common occurrences. People don't understand terrorism. I added that I've been to Gaza and Beirut and found out that terrorists live for death.

Carole said that yes, that's the important part; many terrorists seek out situations for their martyrdom. After 9/11 people couldn't believe it was real. People don't want to hear it and put their heads in their sand. But one day they're going to wake up and discover something else has happened, she added.

She continued on about what we could do. She said that we must prepare ourselves, but we can turn it around and make something good out of it. Perhaps the dangers of these times can make us appreciate what we have in our lives, to make the most of each moment, live a more fulfilling life, and put more into each day. We're focused on the wrong thing—getting more sneakers, status symbols, iPods, etc. While it's nice to have luxuries, you not only miss out on so much of life but also may not see what's coming.

As to her book title, she said that "Dreams Interrupted" is a double entendre. One, terrorism can interrupt your life's dreams, as 9/11 did. And two, our night dreams are interrupted by terrorism; people are having nightmares and not sleeping well due in part to this new fear in the backs of their minds.

One of Carole's appearances on my show occurred soon after the Virginia Tech shootings. She had been following the story closely and had commented extensively in the media about it, specifically about the shooter Seung-Hui Cho. Carole remarked how much his Internet video reminded her of the videos that the terrorists made, and how he spoke of himself as a martyr. She said that often abuse and neglect in the family fills children with rage, and the violence in the television shows and movies they watch and the video games they play seeps into their unconscious minds. Kids with access to guns then bring them to school. According to Carole, people would rather say they don't understand this than to do something about it. Carole believes that our exporting of violence through movies, television, and the media has been fueling violence not only at home but all over the world.

Out to dinner with Carole, 2001

I was very pleased to receive a compliment from Carole on my articles. She said that she finds them well-written, funny in a sardonic way, and well-researched, and added that I know what I'm talking about. I also thanked Carole for giving me the title for my book, *Prison Cheerleader: How A Nice Jewish Girl Went Wrong Doing Right.*

Carole feels deep compassion for the pain she sees people going through in our troubled and violent times. She said that her current branding line is, "I'm the doctor who helps you stay sane in an insane world."

At the end of one of the several shows on which Carole appeared, I said, "Well, today we talked more about men and less about terrorists." And she responded, "We need to learn how to protect ourselves from both: Bad Boys and terrorists!"

Joan Rivers...My (Said) Twin

This title, "My (Said) Twin," reminds me of my mother's famous words. She used to tell me that had I been a twin, she would've drowned the other one because I was such a hard child to raise, and she could handle only me.

Joan Rivers and I were not very close friends, but our paths crossed on several occasions. Although we were nothing alike, people always told me I reminded them of her. It must have been our energy or karma. However, when we finally met I noticed she was tiny—and I am anything but tiny! But we had daughters the same age, and in the early days, I often wrote articles about my daughter, Dana. Dana gave me good reason to be a qualified writer on the subject of the "Southern Jewish American Princess." (I wrote a chapter on this topic for a book called *The Ethnic American Woman: Problems, Protests, Lifestyles* in the late seventies and for the book's second edition in the late eighties.) Joan's daughter, Melissa, seemed to leading a similar kind of life.

One day, on a whim, I sent Joan a couple of my newspaper columns about Dana, who was leaving for college at the same time as Melissa. She apparently liked my style of writing, and her office contacted me about being a guest on her new show. This was during the time she was serving as guest host of *The Tonight Show*, which she did many times. I was beyond thrilled and almost had my suitcase packed before hanging up the phone. Unfortunately, the invitation came the week her new show was cancelled, and my chance to appear with Joan ended before it had even started.

Years passed, and around 2009, I bumped into Joan at the Cannes Film Festival and mentioned our "almost past history." I found her to be darling and real. Joan said she remembered me, and I thought that was very gracious of her.

Our paths crossed again a few years later. I was at a play with my BFF, Jackie Zeman. During intermission, I found myself standing next to Joan Rivers. G-d, she looked fabulous!! I started the conversation by saying, "I don't know who was the King of your 'nip and tuck,' but I would love to set up camp in his office." Joan replied, "Dr. Leafe, with an e." I am telling you, she was about 80 years old and didn't look a day over 50. I told her that if I could, I would let Dr. Leafe start at my knees and go up, to make me a clone of her. I said, "It isn't easy being a sex goddess when you are getting Social Security and Medicare." Somehow, I mentioned Betty White in the conversation. Joan laughed and kiddingly said, "That bitch is taking all my work." A week later, I turned on the television and saw Joan in *Hot in Cleveland* playing Betty White's evil twin sister. Of course I thought of our conversation!

I think if Joan could have seen the tremendous support and love that was shown when she died she might have been surprised, but I wasn't. It is true, she was one of a kind, and she will surely be missed.

With Joan Rivers at a play opening in L.A., around 2009

Art Linkletter...Not Older, Just Better

I have an attraction to young men; however, if they are too young, I say, "I don't know whether to date you or adopt you." Readers, I was a "Cougar" before it was in style. However, I developed older man syndrome when I met Art Linkletter.

Art appeared on my show twice; after his first appearance I had been dying to get him back because he was so damn interesting. When he appeared again in 2007, just a few years before his death, I introduced him as an icon, legend, entertainer, author, lecturer, and "one of my younger men." As I was in the process of stating that "he's ninety-..." Art said, "Oh no, I'm just celebrating the 45th anniversary of my 50th birthday." But at age 95, Art had the energy of a 30-year-old.

When I said, "Look at this man, he looks fabulous!" Art responded, "I take good care of myself. The secret is that if your body and mind are working together, that is a successful life." Art swam every day, calling himself a "professional swimmer." He was a lifeguard for years in Del Mar and La Jolla. He said that he "saved many beautiful girls who had no idea they were in trouble. They were when I got to them." Art never smoked or drank and, as he said, "never chased girls, other than in high school and college." And I guess as a lifeguard when saving girls from "drowning"! Art also used the stationary bike and weights. He said that he was the same weight that he was when he graduated from college. Incredible!

Art was born in Moose Jaw, Saskatchewan. I said that you've got to be Canadian to pronounce that. He was—literally—left on the doorsteps of a church and was raised by a preacher. Art said that the worst thing about being a preacher's kid was that you always say Grace at the table. He added, "I was 14 before a bite of hot food passed my lips. They would pray about things I'd never heard about, and there was the lamb getting cold and the toast going stiff." He said his father didn't have a church of his own but churches would sponsor him.

As an adopted child of a poor preacher Art lived in many different places as a child. He lived in an old folks' home for a year when he was five or six. Art told us that they didn't have retirement homes in those days. Houses were donated by the pastorate for old people to live in. There were no nurses or anything like you have in today's retirement homes. Art lectured at about twenty retirement centers a year. He also spoke in hospices where most of the people have six months to live.

Art went to college to become a schoolteacher. However, he got a job as a radio announcer and never took up teaching. Can you believe that he never had an agent? When he started at the local station, no agents wanted to get 10% of $15.00, so Art learned that he could sell himself. Readers, who knew that Art and I would have so much in common? In the first segment of his long career in entertainment, Art spent 20 years just playing county and state fairs, out in the hot sun in South Dakota.

But Art believed that of all the things he'd done, he was probably best known for being "the guy who talks to kids." Art joked that he "invented children." He told us how he came up with the idea of interviewing children. In 1941 he was in his home office in San Francisco, testing a new kind of recording machine that used a tape. His son Jack came in the office and asked Art what he was doing. Art showed the boy the tape recorder and then interviewed him. Art asked, "What did you do today?" Jack (who had just started school) responded, "I went to school." When Art asked Jack if he liked it, his son replied, "I'm not going back." When Art asked why, Jack responded, "Well, I can't read, I can't write, and they won't let me talk! Why should I go back?"

Art played that tape on a local radio station and the mail came flooding in. Art said that at that point, he knew this was it. He had come up with something nobody else was doing. He knew there were lots of "professional kids" in the entertainment business, but none who were just kids. "So then I started interviewing children. And I interviewed 27,000 of them." Amazing! Art said that he doesn't go anywhere in the U.S. where "some old man with a beard doesn't come up to me and say, 'Do you remember me? I was on your show when I was 5.'"

Art said that after his son gave him that idea he learned how to talk to children, and "now I know better than anybody." He told us about just a few of the hilarious "interviews." One time he asked a kid what church he went to, and the boy responded that he couldn't remember if he was a Catholic or a prostitute. Another time he asked a child what kind of animal he would be, and the kid said he'd be an octopus. When Art asked why, the boy responded that there were a lot of bad kids in his class, so when they were mean to him he could hit them with his testicles. As the audience howled, Art said "Tentacles!" and the boy responded, "No, testicles!" They didn't cut it out, because it was innocent. Art said, "Children have said things to me that have never been cut be a censor."

Art asked a girl one time what's fun to do around her house, and she responded, "I get to wake up my baby brother." When he asked her how she did that, she said that her brother is two years old and has his own room.

She gets the cat and goes down the hall and throws the cat in the room. He asked, "What's fun about that?" And she responded, "My brother sleeps with the dog." Art said that people at home could relate to his segments with children. "When you hit the family right in the heart you've got an audience that will be with you forever."

Art said that Bill Cosby was on his show for three years and that he was great, but, as he told Bill, he had one problem. Bill was a wonderful comic and stand-up star, but when you're talking to kids *they* have to be the star. Art could tell that Bill was always waiting to get a joke in. "You have to be the straight man," Art said. "Bill was very good but he could never be as good as me at it because I'm a natural straight man. And I know all the questions."

On my set with Art Linkletter, 2006

Art found many of the kids for his show by going to schools. He said, "Before arriving at a school, I would ask the teachers to give me the names of four children they wanted out of their class for a few hours." These were the children Art selected for his questions, because he knew they were vocal and wanted to talk. Personally, readers, I feel I would have been one of those kids selected!

At one point I said to Art, "You're a lot of things, but boring and forgettable aren't two of them." Art replied, "No, because I have a sense of humor." He said that Steve Allen used to sit in his audience when he was a DJ at KBX. Steve told Art that he wanted to watch him because they had the same sense of humor. Steve and Art became great friends. Art even "did Steve's funeral" in Glendale. Art added for my viewers, "I do funerals, by the way. Free."

He earned 17 honorary degrees and 1 BA degree. When Art told me that as a teenager he lived in Africa and Argentina all by himself, I said, "People today in the U.S. are scared to cross the street at the age of 30!"

Art enjoyed entertaining on cruises. I remember being on the *Queen Mary* and each time I entered my room, there was Art on the in-house television telling me how to stay young. Actually, my biggest fear on that cruise was that my aging shipmates might run me over with their walkers.

Art said that his sense of humor had been instrumental in the success of his long marriage. When he appeared on my show the second time Art had been married for 73 years. I expressed absolute amazement. Art said that he and his wife had never had a serious argument. He explained that everybody has arguments, but that when he and his wife were having one and it started to "get disagreeable," Art would mention to her that the argument was getting too heated and that if it got too much worse "I may have to kill you." And she would laugh, because she knew he didn't mean it.

Having been married to Lois for 73 years, Art stated that he and Larry King have a relationship around the number "7" regarding marriages—he being married for 7̲3 years to the same woman and Larry King having had 7̲ wives. Art met Lois at the gym while going there for free dances.

Together they had five children and 18 great-grandchildren, who practice religions from Buddhist, to Jewish, to Catholic. Now, that must have made for interesting prayers when they were all together!

I mentioned that Art had never changed his name. Art said that he was about to change it one time, because it was a "funny name." People would call him things like Stinkletter. But Jack Benny said to him, "Don't change your name. It's a different name, don't change it." And now people come up to Art all the time on the street and say, "Didn't you used to be Art Linkletter?" He said that a lady had recently approached him on the street smiling and asked, "Did anybody ever tell you that you look like Art Linkletter?" Art replied, "They tell me that all the time," and she responded "I'll be it makes you mad, doesn't it?" And Art said that the lady meant that as a compliment!

Art was so good at what he did and had so much experience that he usually preferred to improvise on the fly. He said, "What I say depends on the audience. A guy will be introducing me, I'll have something in my mind about an opening joke and a general idea of what I'm going to say, but he'll say something in the introduction and I can take off on that and never come back to my original plan. That's what makes it fun." Art said when he was doing a show he would usually get a big stool to sit on, with no podium and no notes. And then he would "just talk, like I'm talking to you."

I then asked, "But you were a very good dramatic actor as well, weren't you?" Art agreed, but said that he didn't like it as much because he didn't like the way it worked. He didn't like saying the same thing over and over again each night. Art told us a story about a time he was doing a "serious play." After about two weeks Art said to the producer, "Can I go out after curtain and entertain the audience?"

With Art on my set, 2007

Art became involved with the anti-drug campaign after enduring a personal tragedy involving drugs. His daughter had been given LSD at a party and she leaped to her death from her apartment on Sunset Strip. She was only 20 years old. Art described her as a "beautiful, lovely young woman" who was an actress and ready to be in show business. Then, looking wistful and sad, he said, "I still can't get over it." I replied, "You never can." That experience changed his life, Art said. He began to speak on the dangers of drugs and other problems with children, and ultimately he became a lecturer. He also wrote a book on the subject, called *Drugs on My Doorstep*.

On the subject of lecturing, Art said, "I'd rather lecture than be on any show that you could mention. I love to have thousands of people sitting out there; when I talk on a subject I never say it the same way. Sometimes I'll be walking into an auditorium and some lady will say, 'Oh Mr. Linkletter I can hardly wait to hear what you're gonna say!' And I say

'Me too!' And she'll say, 'You don't know what you're gonna say?' And I say, 'Well I know the subject but I don't know how it's gonna come out.'" Like I said, the man loved to improvise and he was great at it!

Art was telling me a story about President Bush. He said the President asked him, "Tell me how to be successfully old." I had to stop Art right there to say, "I was hoping you were going to say that he asked you how to be successful!" And, with that comment, we continued to another topic!

Art Linkletter wrote 27 books. Art ended his first appearance on my show by talking about his recent book, *How to Make the Rest of Your Life the Best of Your Life*. He said, "Life is what happens to you while you are making other plans. Do what you love to do—your passion—take chances so you don't get stuck in a rut. Then, you will never work again." Do you see why I am in love with an older man?

Art won three Emmy Awards, including a Lifetime Achievement Emmy. He said, "That was the big one, I'm very proud of that one."

Art traveled around the world. He journeyed all over South America and skied in Austria and Switzerland. When I asked him if there were any place he'd like to go he hadn't been, he said "probably the South Pole." Art also spent some time in Israel. He said that one time when he was there he was going to have a Christmas party. He tried to get a Christmas tree but couldn't find one. At one place he went the guy said, "Well, uh . . . it's not a big day around there." Art also did a Christmas service at the tomb of Christ.

As we were wrapping up Art returned to the importance of having a sense of humor. He said that he tells people that they need to laugh; they need the endorphins up in the brain to make them feel good. He said that your sense of humor is something you can cultivate, that your attitude is something you can do something about.

Art added that when you change the inner attitude of your mind, it changes the outer aspects of your life. He said that he had even learned how to do that when shopping. He told us a story about a recent visit to the jewelry store with his wife. She was looking at some valuable and expensive jewelry, and he sat down "right before he collapsed" from shopping exhaustion! He said the store manager was standing there with her arms folded, looking like some plumbing had burst somewhere, and he got up and walked over to her and asked, "Are you happy?" She replied, "Yes I'm happy!" And Art responded, "Why don't you notify your face?" Art concluded about this story, "She had to smile. I got her to laugh. You gotta laugh."

I said that would be a good ending for the show, but Art said he could come up with a better one. Then he recited the following:

> I never want to be what I want to be because there's always something out there yet for me. I get a kick out of living in the here and now, but I never want to feel like I know the best way how. Because there's always one hill higher with a better view, something waiting to be learned I never knew. So 'til my days are over, never fully fill my cup, let me go on growing, growing up.

I said, "Oh my God, it can't get any better than that!" And we rolled the credits. Art Linkletter, like a good wine, got better with age.

Shimon Peres...The Serial Loser

It was June of 1982 when I first met Shimon Peres. I was visiting Israel and staying as a guest at the Dan Hotel in Tel Aviv. It happened to be the very day that Israel went to war in Lebanon. At the time, I had no idea that a war was starting. I do remember a lot of planes overhead but felt no danger. Instead, I was running through the hotel lobby, wearing my bathing suit, going for a morning swim in the beautiful Mediterranean. While rushing into the sunshine, I noticed Shimon Peres at a corner table. He was sitting with a few other men, deep in conversation. I wasn't sure at that moment who exactly Mr. Peres was; however, I knew he was important. I knew he worked in the government but wasn't sure of his position. Israel plays musical chairs with its politicians. Someone may be Prime Minister one term, and then the next term he may be moved to Minister of Tourism, or Minister of Trade. I believe that Shimon Peres was the Foreign Minister or Defense Minister at the time. I can't ever keep up with the changes. Whatever his position, I knew the man sitting there was important.

An hour or two later, I finished my swim. On impulse, I took a detour to where these men were still sitting. I introduced myself, still in my bathing suit, and told them that I was a journalist. I smiled and said that it would be remiss of me as a reporter if I didn't request an interview with Mr. Peres while I had the chance. Surprisingly, he said, "Give me your card, come see me at the labor office tomorrow, and I'll see you're cleared to enter."

Fortunately, the labor office was almost across the street from the hotel. So, bright and early the next morning, wearing a summer dress that was perhaps a little too low cut, I walked into the building. Within a very short time, I was ushered into Mr. Peres' private office...simple as that.

1987   **1988**

With Shimon Peres in Jerusalem

The first thing I noticed was the wall of books behind his desk, most of which appeared to be either written by him or about him. I thought that was most impressive. Secondly, I was awed by his attire. It was a warm day in Tel Aviv, and most everybody was walking around in shirtsleeves. Not Peres, however. Israeli men are not known for their sense of style, but Shimon Peres was impeccably dressed. I think he was impressed with what I was wearing, as I remember being a little self-conscious about my top being low cut and kept pulling on the strap to make it higher. Actually, I don't think it was *that* low. It's just that Mr. Peres' eyes seemed to be gazing at my ample breasts, which didn't surprise me. Israeli men, thank G-d, are sooo heterosexual that a woman living there gets used to it. But, I was a little surprised at the vibes this man was sending out, especially considering that there was a war going on.

It's been so long, so I don't remember too much about our conversation. Probably, it was about the impending war. I do remember that as busy as he must have been, he made no effort to rush me out.

I did get the sense that he was flirting with me. But since flirtatiousness is a common trait among the men of Israel and Italy, I didn't give my instincts too much credence. However, when I rose to leave and thanked him for the interview, I went to shake his hand. Instead, he put his arms around me and gave me a "farewell hug." Then he said something about "being available anytime for me" and "how far did I want our interview to go?" I firmly pushed him away and graciously said, "I think our interview has ended."

With Shimon Peres in Tel Aviv, 1993

After that, our paths crossed several times, and we spoke each time we saw each other. However, those brief moments in 1982 were never mentioned, again. In the mid-1980s I was having lunch with the Ambassador of Turkey in Israel. We joined Peres' table at the restaurant. Then, another time, as a fluke, I sat next to him during lunch at some international conference. Each time, he was totally charming to me, although I never thought he remembered who I was.

By the time we had lunch together at the Hilton Hotel in 1997 or 1998, I had become so disgusted with his policies during the 90s that I had to struggle to keep my opinions to myself. I remember I did say to him, "Shimon, you are a mah-vel-ous dresser. Other men are suave. You, darling, are a good dresser *and* you are suave." I was afraid I'd be kicked out of Israel if I told him what I really thought concerning his destructive policies and his leadership, or lack thereof.

In the old vaudeville days, when a bad comedian or act came on the stage, they got the hook. Well, that's what I grew to feel about Mr. Peres. He deserved a Nobel Peace Prize about as much as that terrorist Yasser Arafat or Jimmy Carter. Truly, I think that the reason Peres always managed to come out kissing when it came to photo-ops with Arafat was the shame he must have felt. Why else would he have continued to defend the PLO chairman knowing he was a proponent of terrorism? Because, if the world accepted Arafat as a terrorist, and Peres was there jointly, then what does that make him? In my book he's not an elder statesman. He, I believe, caused so much of the violence that Israel has experienced. And, in addition, he armed more than 40,000 of those damned terrorists under the guise of being Palestinian Authority policemen. Israel should have given Peres the hook long before he left office.

And, speaking of Arafat, our paths crossed in Italy sometime around 1998 in Rome. It was accidental how I happened to end up in his company. I had been staying in Rome at the Excelsior Hotel. One particular morning, I came into the lobby and noticed security men and a few press with the ever-present cameras slung around their necks. But

Tel Aviv, 2000   **Some other time in Israel**

Show me a camera and I'll smile with anybody

unlike their American press counterparts, these Italian press men were nicely attired. Italian men are born to dress well; you could throw them in a garbage can and they come out looking like GQ. The concierge, Mario, had been there a hundred years and knew everything that was happening within a fifty-mile radius. Not wanting to miss anything, I wandered over to his desk and said, "What's going on?"

Mario looked a little over his shoulder and said in a very quiet voice, "Arafat is staying here and is about to come out for a press conference in a few minutes."

Since I had my press cards in my purse and I wanted to hear what Arafat had to say, I answered, "I think I'll go in and get my own clearance." The stairs to the mezzanine were right alongside the lobby desk, so I just walked up and found myself in an enclosed area by the elevator. It was surprisingly easy. All I saw milling about were a few young Arab body guards and five or six Italian press. Nobody actually asked to see my press cards, but I presented them to a nice young guy who was standing by the entrance and he motioned me to pass.

Within a few minutes, there was a little commotion, and then Arafat entered the mezzanine from the side door.

G-d was that man ugly! He just looked nasty. What really amazed me was the lack of security that surrounded this man. Honestly, while I was standing there, the elevator stopped, and an American couple got off and the wife yelled in a Yankee accent, "Oh my Gawd! Harry, get out the camera! It's Yasser Arafat!" I remember thinking at the time, "I could just see something like that happening in Israel. What a total lack of protection!"

It was amazing to me that a man like him was standing by the mezzanine elevator holding a press conference, which was hardly covered by security of any consequence. I also didn't understand a thing that he was saying as he was speaking in Arabic, which was being translated to an Italian journalist.

I probably could have taken a picture with him, but chose not to even stand next to this man. In person he looked like a giant lizard wearing a dirty tablecloth on his head. His aura was one of deception and danger.

Within a short period of time, the few people who were there dispersed and I was left standing alone by the entrance talking to their secret service guy. He seemed like a nice young Arab kid, and I wanted to find out more. So, casually I commented, "You know, I've covered many Israeli politicians and never would I see such a lack of body guards".

He looked at me like I was crazy and said, "What do you mean? He has fourteen of the best security men in all of the Middle East." I replied, "Really? Fourteen you say?" The fact that I was being told such a confidential thing was astounding to me in itself. After a few minutes, he also relayed to me that his father was the third in command to Arafat and somehow connected with the Holy See in Rome... whatever that meant. I became even more interested and wondered where "daddy" might be. He wasn't too far, the young man told me; at that moment in the dining room in the hotel he was having lunch. He then asked, "Would you like to meet him and do an interview?"

Would I ever! However, when we walked over to his table, the gentleman was having lunch and deep in conversation. Nevertheless, I did get to have that introduction. He half-raised himself from the table and said, "Very nice to meet you. May I have your card and maybe I can call you later." He also gave me his card. I said, "Sure, I'd like that" and headed out for the afternoon.

However, I made a call to the Israeli Consulate in case they might also be interested in my yet-to-be-set-up interview. The Consulate seemed incredulous when I told them that this guy with connections to the Holy See had given me his cell phone number in case I would want to reach him. They replied, "HE GAVE YOU HIS CELL NUMBER?!"

Anyway, it was never to happen. By the time he called, I had left the hotel and the city. However, obviously he didn't forget me. For years at Christmas time, I received a packet of propaganda at my home describing the plight of the poor Palestinians. Perhaps he wanted me to write about their oppressors from the Israeli occupation. That wasn't going to happen.

Finally, folks, in case you were wondering, Shimon Peres is not the only Israeli Prime Minister I ran across over the years, as you can see . . .

With Ariel Sharon, Tel Aviv, 1993

With Bibi Netanyahu, L.A., 2001

Rabin   **Shamir**

With the two Yitzhaks, Jerusalem, 1989

Shirley Jones and Marty Ingels...A Marriage of Opposites

Shirley Jones, Academy Award winner for Best Supporting Actress, star of numerous movies and Broadway shows, and mother of the Partridge Family, appeared on my show several times. Ms. Jones and I had known each other for several years. Los Angeles is a very big place to most people, but to those in the entertainment circles, it could seem a very small town. As a result, we must have had many mutual acquaintances, and our names apparently were on the same invitation lists, because we kept bumping into each other. Our casual visits were always very cordial, and eventually I asked Shirley if she'd like to be a guest on my television show. She said "Sure" and referred me to her well-known Hollywood publicist, Edward Lozzi.

With Shirley Jones and Marty Ingels at Academy Awards Party, 1995

Now, on several of these occasions Shirley had been with her husband, Marty Ingels. I didn't know much about Marty but had heard that he was a comedian. I soon found out that Marty wanted to be on my show, too. I wasn't so sure about this, but as it turned out he ended up being my guest before Shirley was. And looking back, thank G-d it was only a half-hour spot, because that was the closest thing I've ever done to a televised therapy session.

I titled this show "The World According to Marty Ingels," and boy was it ever. The show had a crazy beginning and stayed that way for the duration. I somehow managed to introduce Marty, although he was talking a good bit during my intro, making comments about himself and what I had said about him and tossing in a few cracks about my studio, at one point saying, "Anne Frank lived here." One of his self-assessments during the show's beginning was that he was "crazed but talented."

I knew already that he and Shirley were in a trial separation period. Marty said that he was very proud of Shirley and himself, having been married for 25 years (they were eventually married for almost 40 years), with no booze problems in the relationship or other such serious types of marital difficulties. He said that her kids—Sean, Patrick, and Ryan, her sons with Jack Cassidy—"never really bought him or gave him a break." He claimed that the kids "went out and got successful, then said 'Mom you're welcome in our home, he isn't.'" He noted that they tried smoothing things out with different holidays, etc. but that didn't work. So without any lawyer involvement, they went to a psychiatrist, who suggested a six-month separation, with three months of no communication, which was intended as a chance for him to focus on himself.

I interjected, "Did you discover anything bad about yourself?"

Marty responded that an absence of self-esteem could sometimes make people "big-mouthed." Then he went on to say that the "loneliest, saddest people are the loudest, most obnoxious boobs." But, he said, "the most talented people are the most troubled...creativity comes from suffering." He added that Shirley didn't necessarily agree with all of this.

When I asked him what he was insecure about, Marty responded that he was born on his brother's fifth birthday and that he grew up in the shadow of his "perfect brother Arthur." He remembered his mother telling him to be more like his brother. So his identity was the "brother of Arthur." Arthur eventually became a dentist. "That's the baggage," Marty said, and added that if he had wanted to be happy and content he would have been Arthur the dentist. But, he noted, it was also ironic, because "at this point Arthur is jealous of me."

Marty acknowledged how different he and Shirley were, commenting, "Talk about marrying your opposite." He contrasted the two of them further by saying, "Shirley is someone who gets up in the morning and likes who she is."

I managed to get Marty to talk a little bit about his career. He said that he had his own series and almost had a second one, but that "my own emotional craziness hurt my career." He pointed out that Hollywood is an unforgiving place and that he didn't have mainstream acceptability. When people would say "Ingels is crazy," he bought it. I speculated whether this was sort-of a self-fulfilling prophecy, and he seemed to think that maybe it was.

Then Marty shifted the focus to me for a minute, asking, "You speak so fast, do people understand what you say?" And I replied, "No." Hah! We talked for a bit about why I did my show. Marty asked, "Do you enjoy it or do you need it?" And I responded that I enjoyed it but didn't think I *needed* it.

Then Marty said, "I think it's a need." He went on to say that he liked being on my show, but that if he were really happy with himself, why would he want to come on television and open his guts like this, spilling things that most people would not spill, being a "total boob," just hoping that somebody out there liked him and would laugh? "Believe me, that's not the objective of a well-adjusted person," he added. Then he joked, "Am I gonna have a breakdown right now?" This was getting weird, but it was still kind-of funny!

Marty asked me where I got the most peace, and I told him that I live on the beach, which I find to be very peaceful. He pushed me a little bit on whether I thought I was well-adjusted.

I then tried to change the subject by asking why comics were such miserable people, noting that I knew many comics because my daughter Dana was manager of the Laugh Factory. Marty responded, "When you take off the layer, why do you find angry, bitter people? Because comedy comes from pain." He said that when he gives lectures to kids at school he tells them to take the pain and make it work for them. This would help them work out a language that nobody else has. I couldn't help but wonder what school would have Marty in to lecture to students.

As this bizarre show was winding down I asked Marty if he had any final words, and he responded, "Life is a never-ending work-in-progress." This was a great closing line, but my relationship with Marty Ingels was far from closed, as you will soon see.

With Marty Ingels on my set

When Shirley finally appeared on my show, she talked about how she got her start in show business. Although Shirley had been singing since she was six years old, she never thought of it as a career while growing up. She had wanted to be a veterinarian. The summer before she went to college, Shirley and her family took their annual vacation to New York City. When the rest of her family was about to head home to Smithton, PA, her father gave her $120 to stay in New York for awhile longer, which he knew she desperately wanted to do. Shirley had a pianist friend in the city and took him to an open audition for Rodgers & Hammerstein's casting director, who was selecting roles for the film adaptation of *Oklahoma!*. It was her first professional audition ever. The casting director was impressed, and he got in touch with Rodgers, who in turn called Hammerstein, and Shirley ended up singing, for both of these theater greats, "Oh What a Beautiful Morning," "People Will Say We're in Love," and "Oklahoma!".

Shirley got a reading for the film, but they didn't choose her at first, partly because she was too young. So they put her in *South Pacific* and then in a traveling show called *Me and Juliet*. Meanwhile Rodgers and Hammerstein were screening people all over the east and west coasts. Finally, after about a year they came back to Shirley and asked her to come to Hollywood for a screen test. And she got the part in *Oklahoma!*. Shirley said that the New York audition was "serendipitous," that she was in the right place at the right time.

Shirley never ended up going to college. She said that she still wanted to go, even after being offered the role in *South Pacific*, but her parents told her that she should give the show business thing a try. Good thing she listened to their advice!

Of course we had to talk about *The Partridge Family*, so I showed a clip from the show. Shirley said that one reason she took the role was so that she could be home and raise her three young sons. She had been on location doing movies her whole career up to that point. Shirley knew that at the time it was considered a "step down" for a movie actress to do television. People warned her against it, saying that it would ruin her career, but she thought the show was going to be a hit so she did it. And she was right! But she acknowledged that in a way the role did "ruin" her movie career. She added that the younger producers and directors knew her as "Mrs. Partridge" and not from the movies she had done previously.

Shirley said that when David Cassidy was young he wouldn't have anything to do with her, probably because she was his stepmother. They didn't get close until "Partridge."

Shirley also observed how it is not easy to raise kids in L.A. Sometimes she wished she was back in Smithton. She commented that the value system in Hollywood is "in the toilet."

By the time she appeared on my show, Shirley had been a spokesperson for the Leukemia Foundation for years. She started working with this organization when she was doing *The Partridge Family* and caring for her children. Leukemia was a big killer of children at the time, so the cause was very important to her. She did a film role about Alzheimer's and worked for the Alzheimer's Foundation, and has also been involved in animal rights causes, having retained her love of animals even though she never became a vet.

I played a great clip from *Elmer Gantry*, which I mispronounced as "Gentry" a few times and Shirley politely corrected me (As you may have realized from reading the other stories in this book, I'm always screwing up names!). When I commented that Shirley looked so "pure and virginal," Shirley responded that they wanted somebody pure and innocent-looking, who "didn't look like a hooker," because the character Lulu was a minister's daughter. She added that she had always been a fan of Burt Lancaster— when she was 16 she had pictures of him all over her wall— so working with him on *Elmer Gantry* was a dream come true for her.

At the time of this show Shirley and Marty were back together, so I said, not altogether sarcastically, "Marty is a sweet dear man." Shirley responded that people don't see the other side of Marty. She described him as very sweet and kind, as a marvelous husband who made her laugh all the time. She said that he drove her crazy but was a very good person. She echoed Marty's comment from my show when she said, "We're very opposite; he's my stimulation and I'm his reserve."

Shirley worked with so many famous leading men in addition to Burt Lancaster. On this show I asked her about Marlon Brando. She said she had a great experience working with him on a comedy called *Bedtime Story* (*Dirty Rotten Scoundrels* was the remake of this film). She said that Brando loved doing comedy, even though he wasn't in that many funny movies. Shirley felt that Brando liked her. He had just finished doing *Mutiny on the Bounty*, which Shirley thought had been "a disaster" for him, and that doing this comedy was fun for Brando. She said that Brando liked to do more than one take, and clarified that when she said "more," she meant that 50-60 takes was nothing for him. Shirley joked, "I always say he was the greatest American actor because he wore down all the other actors!" David Niven, an actor she "adored and respected," was also in this film.

I was very impressed with Shirley and found her to be pleasant, well-spoken, and charming. Near the end of this show I told her she "gives out good vibes, good energy." As I would again learn soon, she must have needed all of these qualities to handle her husband Marty.

Here's what happened...Shirley was on my show with John Savage, who starred in *The Deer Hunter*. Marty was supposed to be on the show too, but he had yet to show up when we were ready to start taping, so we just went ahead.

John told us that he had his professional stage debut at age 14 in *The Drunkard*. This was great for me to hear, because I was in that play one time, too, and of course I had to mention it! Shirley said that she was delighted to be on the show with John because she was such a fan. John returned the compliment, saying how it was a dream to be sitting there with Shirley.

Then, as John was talking about first being in the theater and then coming out to "film town," Shirley looked offstage and started laughing. I looked up to see Marty, seemingly on a mission, walking past the camera men towards us. He walked on set and sat down on the floor in front of us, but with his back to me. On my show! He was wearing this elf-like hat and baggy shorts. Under his hat his grey hair was sticking out in total disarray—what a disturbing image!

Shirley joked to Marty that she was only there because she had heard John was going to be on the show. They all bantered back and forth as I was vainly trying to regain control of my show. At one point Marty said to Shirley and John, "Listen, do you two want to get a room somewhere?"

Honest to G-d, Marty was talking a mile a minute. I had a choice. I could have either stopped the show or given him a mike and asked the studio engineer to bring an extra chair so he could join us. I chose neither. I told Marty to "just lie down, lie down," and thankfully he obeyed.

So, Marty was stretched out on the floor like a misbehaving puppy while I continued my show. I tried to turn attention to *The Deer Hunter,* noting how disturbing the film was to watch, and John agreed. But Marty must have been too distracting for him, because John commented, "There's a leprechaun in the room. A Jewish leprechaun." Oy!

John also had played the priest to the Corleone family in *The Godfather Part Three,* so we started discussing this movie. John said it was about a family trying to assimilate into "regular life," or as regular as it could be for that particular Mafia family. Marty chimed in, wondering "why Three failed when One and Two were so great." His theory was that "nobody wanted to see Al Pacino as an old grey-headed impotent man after what he was in One and Two." Nobody really commented on that, although I think I patted Marty on the head.

John told us that he got the role in the movie when he was in South Africa working for the anti-apartheid movement.

Then he began talking about the current situation in that country and all the problems associated with instituting a democracy there. It was clear that John knew a lot about Africa; he talked about several other countries such as Zimbabwe and Lagos. I chimed in on the democracy issue, saying that Israel is perceived as the Great Satan because "they hate democracy," just like the Middle East hates the U.S. for the same reason. John diplomatically responded that I was generalizing. Then he made some statements about cooperation between the Arabs and the Jews, and of course we argued for a bit about that.

About 10 minutes into the show, Marty left. So we finished without him. John was still gushing about Shirley. At one point he said, "God, I can't believe this. You inspired me. We could sing together and have a Jewish leprechaun follow us around." Funny!

Actually, despite the fact that Marty was disruptive and, I thought, made a total fool of himself, it was one of my funnier shows. Not one that I would want to repeat, but it was one of my more interesting experiences doing the show.

Before I move on to the rest of my story about Shirley and Marty, I've got to relate a few exchanges that occurred when Shirley appeared with Ed Asner on my show in 2007. I told Shirley she was "Jewish by injection" by virtue of being married to Marty. When I asked Ed, "Your kids didn't marry anybody Jewish?" he responded, "They met Marty and said 'No more!'"

At another point in the show I commented that men my age don't like me, maybe because I have too much energy. I said, "They look at me and think, Oh my God, that woman would kill me." And Shirley joked, "Marty would love it. You're the female Marty." Aaaahhh!!

**With
Shirley and
Ed Asner in
my studio**

So, after Marty the leprechaun appeared on my show, I may have thought I was through with him, but he wasn't through with me. At some point he called me, wanting to talk about some big production deal he had in the works. Marty told me how he was about to produce a movie about Haym Solomon. FYI, Haym Solomon was a wealthy Jewish man who saved America by funding the Revolutionary War as the "money man." Solomon supported the American army through fundraising and personal lending, made it possible for our country to win, and never asked for anything in return. Legend has it that when George Washington asked this wealthy, Jewish Philadelphian what he would like as a personal reward for his services to the Continental Army, Solomon said he wanted nothing for himself but that he would like something for his people. The 13 stars in the Great Seal of the United States are arranged as a Star of David in honor of Solomon's contributions. Although Solomon saved the Army through his financial contributions, he died a pauper. I found this story interesting as Marty was talking, but wondered why he was calling me about it.

Marty continued by telling me that he, Marty Ingels, was going to produce a movie about this great American hero and have Sean Penn star as the lead. All he needed was a "little funding" to make this possible. I still couldn't imagine what I had to do with this, but it seemed that Shirley's husband was under the misconception that I could put my many "contacts" in touch with his own "money man" who could make this movie happen. And, for my help with introducing him to people who could fund this great American project, I would get a very nice commission for my efforts. I held the phone thinking, "Why me?"

One thing I've learned is to always go with my instincts. I believe those little hairs that rise on the back of my neck when someone is asking for money, or has a "deal for me," is G-d's way of telling me not to get involved. This conversation with Marty Ingels was one of those times that my instincts said, "This is not a person you want to become mixed up with in any way!" So, as nicely as I could, I told him that I was sorry, but I really didn't know anybody who would want to finance his movie. However, if and when I thought of someone, he'd be the first person I'd call. And, that, I thought, was that.

Evidently not! Some time later, I had booked Shirley for another appearance on my show. The day before her scheduled appearance, I got another call from Marty. "Hey Peck," he said, "the last time we spoke, you neglected to mention how much you plan on donating to our charity." Since I didn't have a clue as to what this man was talking about, all I could answer was, "Huh, charity; what charity?" Marty continued, "Anybody who thinks they're going to do business with Shirley Jones has to go through me, and we have a special charity we've established. She's not going anywhere until you pay your fair share."

I had been booking celebrities on my show for 20 years and had never had to pay anyone to be a guest. I knew it would be best to get off the phone before I lost my temper; I said, "I think I should talk to Shirley about this." At which point Marty shouted back something like, "If you want my wife to go on your show then you pay! Nobody gets her to go anywhere unless they go through me! Period!"

I had Shirley's cell number and immediately dialed it. When she answered, I calmly asked what was up with her not appearing on my show unless I paid. I thought I was calm at least, which, considering my mood of the moment, was an amazing feat in itself. Shirley soothingly put me at ease when she responded, "Arlene, what time do you want me at the studio in the morning?" I let her know the time, adding that I hoped she'd be arriving alone. This time I specifically asked for Marty not to come on the show with her. I told her that I found him "a little disruptive" and I hoped she would not mind if she appeared by herself.

And this show was great. We began by talking a bit more about her childhood in Smithton, PA. She said that her family owned the Jones Brewing Company in Smithton, which had a population of 800. Her grandfather had come from Wales and worked as a coal miner, but he eventually built a hotel and a brewery. Shirley was crowned Miss Pittsburgh at age 17.

I knew that a few years earlier Shirley had appeared with her son Patrick in *42nd Street*, so I asked her about this. She said that she hadn't done a Broadway show in 38 years; her last one had been *Maggie Flynn*, with Jack Cassidy. She did *42nd Street* for five months, and said it was an incredible experience, bonding with her own son while working with him. I played a clip of Shirley and Patrick from that musical.

I also played a few other clips of Shirley that I had not shown previously. In one of them, she is receiving her Academy

Award for Best Supporting Actress in 1961, wearing a big ball-gown. Then I showed a few great "kissing scenes" with Shirley and various leading men. We saw her with Robert Preston in *The Music Man* and with Richard Widmark in *Two Rode Together*, which Shirley noted was one of the last John Ford films. And in various other films she kissed David Niven, Marlon Brando, James Garner, Lloyd Bridges, Burt Lancaster, Charlton Heston, and Bob Hope. Wow!

While we were on the subject of leading men she had worked with, I knew there was a story about Shirley and Frank Sinatra, so I asked her about it. She said they were both cast in the movie version of *Carousel*. They had done all of the rehearsals and pre-production, and traveled to Booth Bay Harbor, Maine to begin shooting. She said they were doing two separate filming processes, Cinemascope and Cinemascope 55, so they had two cameras there. Shirley said that everyone knew about this ahead of time, so she assumed Sinatra did, too. But when Frank arrived on the set and saw the two cameras, he asked the director Henry King about it, who explained how they would be shooting. Frank asked, "Does that mean I might have to do more than one take?" And King responded, "Well, maybe sometimes." Frank said, "I signed on to do one movie, not two" and then left and never came back.

Shirley said that she tried to talk to Sinatra about this situation a few times afterwards but he didn't want to discuss it. Shirley couldn't understand why he left the movie, because he had been so excited to play Billy Bigelow, which she described as a "great part for a leading man, the best." I suggested that he might have been bipolar and that maybe they just caught him on a bad day.

Shirley ended up calling Gordon MacRae in Vegas and asked him if he would like to play Billy Bigelow in *Carousel*.

He responded, "Give me three days, I've got to lose ten pounds." And MacRae got the part.

I told my own Sinatra story. When I was five I was in Atlantic City at the same time as Sinatra. I was waiting for an autograph, and finally Sinatra's manager took my name and address. I waited for weeks, and finally received a signed picture. Years later I was looking at this picture and realized it was my father's handwriting in the autograph. Such a sweet thing for him to do so his little girl wouldn't be disappointed!

Shirley said that she did 30 movies before *The Partridge Family*. And though doing that show may have negatively impacted her movie career, as I mentioned earlier, it didn't end it. We talked about some of her more recent films. She had done one with Adam Sandler called *Grandma's Boy*, in which she plays an old-lady character who has a tendency to go to bed with guys in their twenties. Shirley described it as "lewd but funny." And she had recently been in a Hallmark movie called *Hidden Places* that had been nominated for an Emmy.

**With Shirley
on my set**

And Shirley was still doing theater work. When she had received the Richard Rodgers award years earlier in Pittsburgh, she stayed on and played Aunt Eller in *Oklahoma!* She had also been in Waltham, MA, doing *Carousel.* Like so many of my guests who worked in theater and films, Shirley loved the theater the best. She said that there's nothing like the camaraderie, becoming a family with the cast and crew.

We also talked about another charity endeavor that Shirley and Marty were engaged in. They had bought some land up near Big Bear Lake, in a town of about 300 people called Fawnskin where she had a house, with the purpose of doing a memorial for 9/11. They created a beautiful park with tables and chairs, and a stage for summer musicals. Rudy Giuliani sent them a girder from one of the towers, and they were raising money to get a memorial built around the girder. OK, I thought, this must be the charity Marty was talking about on the phone. By the way, they were ultimately successful in building the memorial.

Soon after this taping I saw Shirley and Marty at an event in front of the Israeli consulate. Thousands of people had come to watch the Israeli flag being raised along with the California and United States flags. About a hundred dignitaries and guests were seated on a special platform that had been set up to watch the mayor give his speech. Somehow I ended up as one of these guests and found myself sitting a few chairs from Shirley and Marty.

I smiled and waved (at Shirley at least) and she responded with a warm greeting. I remembered that she had brought to the recent show's taping a VHS tape with the movie clips. It dawned on me that I wasn't sure I had returned it. When I mentioned this to her she said, "No, I never got it. Do you still have it?" I replied I would check when I got back to my house.

When I returned home, I found the tape still sitting on my desk. I sent it back to her along with a note. A couple of days later, I received an envelope with the return address "Suite One Productions." Upon opening it, my mouth dropped. In it was the note that I had written—which, by the way, said,

> *Shirley, it was so nice seeing you yesterday— and I was wrong. I had meant to mail this to you but it was still sitting on my desk. Hope our paths cross again—Arlene P.S. Oh and here is this week's show!*

Marty and Shirley's names were on the letterhead next to Suite One Productions. My note card had been torn in half and stapled onto a letter, which was just a single page but a piece of work. At the top, written in black marker, was, "Say, Peck, how do I get through to you with the way things <u>ARE</u>?" Then, typewritten under this bold statement, it said, "Last Time, Kid. We now start returning your mail and restricting your phone calls."

I assumed the letter was from Marty. "We?" I never called the man. What in the world was he talking about?

In large letters he had typed three paragraphs, each labeled with a big number in a huge font. He underlined several words in each paragraph with his black marker. The text of the letter was:

1. *My wife and I have a <u>FAVORITE CHARITY</u>! These days, after a lifetime of showing up for everybody and every<u>THING</u> every time we were asked, we embarked on a new policy of "<u>MONEY FOR OUR 501(c)(3) CAUSE BEFORE SHIRLEY DOES ANYTHING</u>. <u>Period</u>! (Laugh, call us names, write your Congressman, get*

mad, take a nap—I could care less—That's our reality . . . Perfectly sane and reasonable);

2. *Since that policy-implementing, our standard precondition of our 9/11 memorial donation has been "discussed" about 66,000 times in the 66,000 requests for our free time, with ne'er a cross-word — Just a "YAY" or a "NAY";*

3. *Only Arlene Peck took the very QUESTION ... the REQUEST ... as some sort of "attack", and went dadblame BERZERK ... ranting, raving on about "extorting money" etc. etc.*

Then, in black marker again, Marty had written, "'Medication' problem? Bad hair day?" Finally, the letter concluded as follows:

> *I could care less. You were off the wall, over the top, rude and offensive AND AS "WRONG" AS YOU COULD BE! And, without a genuine apology (that phrase underlined in red marker), for that hair-brain tantrum aimed at 2 good people who deserved better, your mail, your calls, your social advances will be rebuffed. Give it up, Arlene...or your contacts will drive us to more "discomforting" measures.*

Readers, it was about this time that I became absolutely certain that I was dealing with a disturbed person. Although I had never attacked or gone berserk on the phone with Marty, I had perhaps commented negatively when I had said something like, "In all my twenty years of having a cable show in Los Angeles, I have never had anyone demand money from me at the last minute as a condition of appearing on my show."

Looking back, the only other guest who even came close to asking me for money, not to mention leaving me with dead air space at the last minute, was Buzz Aldrin, the astronaut. He, however, didn't even remember that he committed himself to the show until I called to remind him of the time. All he could say was, "Who arranged this and how much am I going to be paid?" I reminded Mr. Aldrin that he said he'd be a guest when we had met at a party a month or so before and had spoken on the phone two more times. But, by this time, I found him so disagreeable that I just cancelled him and went with the other guest that I had booked as Plan B.

After I had finished reading the letter I stood there aghast...shaking my head and thinking, "What is wrong with that man?" The only mail that I had ever sent to Ms. Jones was the tape that she had left at the studio. Calls? We had spoken a couple of times but that was only to re-affirm the studio time. As I said earlier, after he disrupted my show with John Savage, I told her to keep Marty home, which she seemed perfectly okay with. Never had I made any "social advances" to them, although we had bumped into each other at events over several years.

Shortly afterwards, I left for a trip to Atlanta and tried to forget about the whole ridiculous issue. However, while in Atlanta, I received a frantic call from my daughter, Dana, who was getting my mail in my absence. "Mom, what did you do to Shirley Jones and Marty Ingels?" I was taken aback but answered, "I didn't do anything to them. What are you talking about?" Dana told me that when she went to my condo to get the mail, there was a letter from a lawyer threatening to make my life miserable if I continued to harass Ms. Jones and Mr. Ingels. I'm not kidding.

My daughter read me the letter over the phone, and I couldn't believe what I was hearing. The letter stated that I had repeatedly ignored requests from Shirley and Marty to have no further contact with them. My kid was saying, "Wow, what are they talking about?" To which I didn't have any answer. The letter said that they would seek a protective court order if I continued to harass them. What the...?

I speculated what they might be angry about. Was it because I had told Marty that I wouldn't help him finance his movie? Was I being threatened because I wouldn't donate to their 9/11 charity as a condition of Shirley's appearing on my television show?

I could understand why my daughter's voice was a little shaky on the phone. The letter made me sound like I had been stalking Shirley and Marty, and I found myself incredulously looking at the phone.

Wow. Should I call *The Enquirer*? Or should I call their attorney to clarify that these accusations were for real? Letters from lawyers always make me nervous, which probably, in this case, was the desired effect. In the end, I decided just to drop it.

Well, that's my story about Shirley Jones and Marty Ingels. She and Marty stayed married until he died in 2015. When Marty wasn't there with her, she was a terrific guest on my show. If I were still doing the show I'd probably invite her to be on again. Although it's doubtful that she would accept. Marty's appearances were bizarre but entertaining. I don't know, maybe I did something wrong, but I truly don't think so.

Ted Turner...and His Polyester Jacket

I first came in contact with Ted Turner while growing up in Atlanta. He was dating a friend of mine who was a hostess in a restaurant. One night I was at this restaurant having dinner with a date. I remember, it was a cold winter night and I was standing by the door wearing a full length mink coat. While my date was paying the bill, Ted Turner walked towards me. Of course, I knew who Ted was, but I didn't want to give him the satisfaction of recognition; something about him was just so damn arrogant. So, I just nodded in his direction while my friend introduced us. Without saying a word, Mr. Turner leaned over and opened my coat so he could get a better look at my body, which back then, considering I was all of twenty years old, was pretty fabulous. Remember Readers, in those days Southern gentlemen just didn't do such tacky things. I closed my coat and said something about his "crass manners." Mr. Turner seemed to enjoy the comment. I have to tell you, all these years later, I still think of him as white trash with money.

Several years later, Ted Turner was buying CNN and looking for a location. They ended up buying a country club. Here is the story of that country club...

The Southern WASPs didn't allow Jewish membership into their clubs. As my father said, "The hell with them," and the Atlanta Jewish community started their own clubs; three to be exact. The clubs survived because my father, like many others who built those country clubs, had returned from the Second World War. For lack of a place to go, they decided to build their own bigger and better country clubs. My dad became one of the "charter members" of one of the clubs.

This club was antebellum gorgeous and glorious with big chandeliers, ballrooms, swimming pools, and tennis courts. They even had gambling and card rooms downstairs where women were not allowed to go. The custodian, who answered the phone and brought the drinks and food to the men, made a fortune. The husbands would tip him 50 bucks each time the wives called to ask if their spouses were there. He would loudly exclaim, "Lawd no, m'amm. Your husband doesn't come down here." The rumor was that this custodian invested all of those tips into real estate, and ended up owning more land than many of the members. This country club was called the Progressive Club, and it eventually became the first location for CNN at the suggestion of Ted Turner. I even received a bit of cash from the deal, as I held original stock that was sold to Turner.

I remember going over there once after he had taken control and I felt very sad. The palatial ceilings and crystal chandeliers became his offices. The large gorgeous ballrooms had desks and didn't look elegant anymore. And the three large, swimming pools were used to house satellite dishes.

I had another encounter with Ted Turner after he had bought the rights for the classic film, *Gone with the Wind*. I was invited to the festivities during the fiftieth anniversary for the movie. I went to dinner and the movie with Danny and Susan Selznick. Danny Selznick's father was David Selznick, the producer of *Gone with the Wind*, and his wife, Susan, was from the New York Times family. At the movie, I was sitting directly behind Ted Turner and his date and Larry King and his then-current girlfriend. Frankly, watching the Ted and Larry show was the best entertainment of the evening. Truly, they spent the better part of the movie gnawing on the arms and shoulders of their dates, and Lord knows what else. I was so busy watching them that I missed half of the movie.

I have to mention that twenty years after that *Gone With the Wind* celebration, I saw Ann Rutherford. I had previously seen her speak at a luncheon given for the Young Musicians Foundation at the opulent Beverly Wilshire Hotel. I remembered Ann was a benefactor of that foundation. She spoke about her part as Scarlett's Sister, Careen. I was shocked that was she still around and that, at the age of 90, she looked wonderful—gorgeous hair and make-up, darling in her outfit. I reminded this lovely woman how she had been my first interview when I had moved to Los Angeles twenty years previously. We recalled that night of the Turner event, when she had mentioned that I should call her when I moved to Los Angeles to come for tea. Which is exactly what I did, and Ms. Rutherford had me over to her mansion for tea.

Now, back to Ted Turner...

I would see him from time to time. Considering that here's a man with billions of dollars, I found it ironic that I have two pictures of him, taken fifteen years apart; in both pictures, there he is wearing the same tacky polyester jacket. Do I need to tell you anything more?

With Ted Turner in Atlanta, 1994

Mary Wilson...the Supremest Supreme

With Mary Wilson during
ski trip to Canada
in the late '80s

And here we
are years later
at my condo in
Marina Del Rey

Of all the nicest celebrities I've known, Mary Wilson is at the top of my list of favorites. We go back a long way; I've seen her in good times and in bad times, and she's always shown her kindness.

We first met in the eighties. We had both been invited to a celebrity ski tour in Quebec, Canada, she as a celebrity and me as a journalist. Others on this trip included Carrie Fisher, Carol Alt, Brooke Shields, Alan Thicke, Margot Hemingway, Woody Harrelson, Gregory Harrison, and Margot Kidder. I must comment on Carrie Fisher. She of course played the princess in *Star Wars*, and I think she believed she should play her "princess" role in her real life. I remember that she was standing next to me on the plane. Before I reached in the overhead compartment to put my luggage inside, I asked her nicely to hold my coat. From the look she gave me, you would have thought I had offered her poison.

Soon after we arrived in Quebec we attended a very elegant, formal party at the top of the slopes. We were all wearing ski outfits—it was so damn cold. I laughed and wondered whether the coffee from the silver pitchers would come out as icicles. Actually, I was thinking about Mary and wondering how she was going to ride in the next day's celebrity parade half-naked waving to the crowd. Mary had the answer, though; I later learned she had a heater under her dress!

Mary was a different breed than the other celebrities there. Although she was a star before most of the others, she displayed a humility that was both friendly and refreshing. Most of Mary's family was from Atlanta, where I lived, and we kept in touch after the ski trip. From time to time, she came to visit family and sometimes stayed at my house.

Mary's visits were a "big deal" in Atlanta, and I wanted to show her off and party. Once, while she was at my home, I fixed her up with Atlanta's Police Chief, Eldrin Bell. Eldrin was one handsome man who I thought could be a clone of Smokey Robinson. So, being the matchmaker, I arranged for them to meet at Atlanta's Steeplechase, the "yuppie event" of the year. Let me tell you about the Steeplechase. The local women worship at the shrine of Laura Ashley! The "Laura Ashleys," wearing outrageous hats, and their boyfriends spend a day walking around the track, attending tailgate parties, and drinking fancy drinks. Okay, so I arranged for us to go to the Steeplechase on a chartered bus that left from one of the clubs. Let me tell you, mimosas were served from the minute we pulled out until we arrived at the site of the Steeplechase, an hour or so away in Forsyth County.

For those of you who aren't aware, in January 1987 Forsyth County had been the site of two civil rights demonstrations during which racial tensions exploded. In the first, a march to the Forsyth County Courthouse was disrupted by militant segregationists who broke through police lines, and violence quickly ensued. The march eventually was halted and multiple people were arrested. In the second and larger march, thousands of demonstrators determined to complete the journey to the courthouse were again confronted with hundreds of counter-protesters carrying racist signs and shouting racial slurs such as "Nigger, go home!" Several thousand National Guardsmen and police officers were present. Oprah Winfrey broadcast her new show from there in the following month in an effort to address racial tensions.

So, here we were driving into Forsyth County. Of course, nobody ever told Mary that she wasn't white, so I didn't give it much thought at first. But it was clear Mary had been following the news when she noticed the county signs as we drove by. She gave me a look and said, "Girlfriend, where are you taking me?" All ended well; in fact, Mary and Eldrin Bell connected so well, that later she sent me postcards from somewhere in Jamaica where they were on a trip together.

I remember when the Martin Luther King parade was in its formative stage; Mary and I somehow were on the original committee for the parade. Mary, I believe, was the Master. As a committee member, I agreed to bring celebrities. Also, someone promised me an all-day limo ride with Kris Kristofferson! Kris wasn't in my limo in the end, but I did ride to the parade with Miss Universe, Miss America, and the fighter Evander Holyfield! When I drove Mary in the parade in the convertible, I remember being scared

**Heading out to dinner with Jermaine Jackson,
Mary, and Atlanta Police Chief Eldrin Bell**

because the crowd adored Mary; thousands of spectators were trying to rush to the car shouting, "Hey Mary!" We were the last ones to leave the parade because Mary didn't want to leave until everyone who wanted it had her autograph.

Years later, I visited Mary when she was living in Las Vegas. At the time, Kris Kristofferson's ex-wife, Rita Coolidge, was also there visiting Mary. When I was introduced to Rita, Mary told me that Rita was also a singer and would be appearing that night in a lounge on the strip. At that time, I didn't know that she had been married to Kris Kristofferson, and I also didn't know diddly-squat about music (and I still don't). I have to interrupt this story to mention that one reason I hate Vegas is because Vegas gambling men are so oblivious to women. A gorgeous, naked woman could ride in the casino on a white horse, with her hair on fire, and the gambling men wouldn't notice because they are so absorbed in their games.

**I didn't get a limo ride,
but did get a picture, with
Kris Kristofferson (1991)**

**But this time I got to
ride in the Rolls. Check
out the license plate!**

Although I had no idea who Rita Coolidge was, she was already very famous. That evening Mary and I went to hear her perform. Naturally the crowd cheered. After the show, I made one of my more astute comments of the week; I told her that I really, really thought that she was going to make it. Rita Coolidge graciously thanked me for my encouragement. Readers, take note, she was nice enough not to tell me how much of an idiot I was.

When I moved to Los Angeles, Mary was living there also. One day, while Mary was driving back from Las Vegas, her SUV flipped, and her fourteen-year-old son, Rafael, was killed. I attended the funeral and the guests were like Motown's "who's who" list. Everyone came to express their condolences to this good lady. Soon after that, Mary moved to New York. I believe she moved because of too many sad memories.

Readers, I can't forget the time Mary invited me to meet her at the Hyatt Hotel, in Century City, where she would be appearing. I was told that the dress code was formal. I arrived looking fabulous...and when I walked in, I noticed that the male to female ratio was certainly in my favor! There were great-looking men wherever I turned, and all were wearing tuxedos. I found a table where I was the only woman, and I was in heaven! The ambiance was great until the music started; then about 500 men got up to dance... with each other! Nobody asked me for even one dance. I learned that I was sitting at the "Gay and Lesbian Annual" something or other. Let me tell you, with this group, I would never have gotten a date for the prom.

I have to tell you another story about Mary...

When the Supremes had planned to get together in 2000 for a last reunion tour, Diana Ross, in my opinion, once again lived up to her "bitch" legacy. It was widely reported in the news that rather than being a lady and working together on this tour, Diana Ross planned and arranged everything, including the monetary arrangements, without consulting Mary on anything. Although the fame had been shared among the three of the Supremes, Diana wanted to keep all the money. As a result, Mary decided not to do the tour; and, the tour was a total failure. People connected with the tour relayed this information to me. Mary, true to her nature, never said one bad word against Diana. Diana Ross, however, badly underestimated the audience draw of Mary Wilson. People stayed away in droves.

I don't know if this was the reason or not, but after I said that I wanted to publicize what Diana had done, my friendship with Mary slowly dissolved. We were good friends for years; but, I know, people do drift apart. Mary asked me to be her friend on Facebook. I tried to answer "yes" but I am a computer moron so I must not have responded correctly. However, I will always wish Mary the very best in life.

Out and about

Having dinner, 1992

Vidal Sassoon...More than a Hairdresser

Vidal Sassoon may be a common brand, but Vidal himself was anything but common, which was evident to my audience when he appeared on my show. I told my audience how I met him on the Queen Mary, which was such an appropriate place because he's such a classy man. Vidal was born in 1928, but he was still so hot and such a babe. I added, "I've never liked older men, but I think I'm switching over."

Vidal was such a wonderful role model, and I sat in awe as we discussed his background. He was born to Jewish parents in London, and his father left when Vidal was three years old. After a few years his mother could no longer afford to take care of him or his brother, so they were both sent to a Jewish orphanage in London. Soon after the war broke out in 1939, the British government took the kids out of London to the country because of the bombing. He was there until 1942 when he returned to London. Vidal said, "I had seen enough cows."

Back in London, Vidal started shampooing at age 14. He said that his mother had this dream, which she described as a premonition, that he was going to be "in hair." She took him to Adolf Cohen, the renowned hairdresser in London's East End. Vidal described him as a great disciplinarian. Even though the war was still going on and they were living in shelters, he had to come in with his shirt and trousers pressed and clean nails, "looking like he'd stepped out of a shop window." He added that it was pretty wild but taught them all discipline. This was probably the reason Vidal was always so clean and dressed so beautifully. No wonder the Vidal Sassoon slogan was "If you don't look good, we don't." Every time I saw him he was elegant.

I asked about school. Vidal said that he received his education through the "auto-didactic" method. He said he had Wednesday afternoons off and would take the bus to the theaters in the West End. There he and others did the "elbow thing," standing in the back with their elbows on the railing, watching the show. He said it was relatively cheap, and he used his tip money for his theater fare.

Vidal's mother got remarried, to a boxer. I asked him what this guy thought about Vidal being a hairdresser. Vidal said that his stepfather was a great guy who "never made more than $75 in his life." The boxer ultimately "gave in" to him being a hairdresser, mainly because of his wife's premonition about her son. He said they lived in a Jewish ghetto in Aldgate/Whitechapel, which had a "marvelous atmosphere." He remembers hearing a lot of funny Cockney Yiddish jokes.

Vidal also became politically active during and after the war. He said that Sir Oswald Mosley, a famous British fascist who had been jailed by Churchill, recreated the fascist movement, complete with anti-Semitic speeches and uniforms, when he was released from prison in 1943. A group of ex-service men formed the 43 group to oppose the fascist movement, and he and some other kids joined the group. And he added that in 1948, "when Israel came alive, we all volunteered." So Vidal joined the Israeli army at the age of 20. He was stationed in the Negev.

Vidal's mother was a powerful Zionist who held secret meetings in their house, which, he noted, was a very dangerous thing to do during a time when the Irgun and the Stern were fighting British soldiers in Israel.

With Vidal Sassoon and Kate Linder on my set

Vidal spoke with conviction and enthusiasm, and with that wonderful English accent! We transitioned to present circumstances. Vidal said that he had always been involved with being Jewish in a very positive way. He noted that we were sitting there on television today, as Jews. But we have to look back from '48 onwards, when we found our dignity, and it was Israel. That's why we must always keep it powerful, keep it strong, especially since it's surrounded by millions of enemies. At that point I expressed my frustration at the desire of some to bring displaced Arabs to Gaza, an area of just a few square miles.

Vidal said that he had been involved with the Hebrew University Center for the Study of Anti-Semitism for 25 years. He said he's been fascinated most of his life with the question, "Why do people love us or hate us?" He believed that it goes back to the time of Constantine and particularly Saint Chrysostom, who used terms such as "perfidious Jews." He added that Martin Luther in the 13th century spoke of the "Jews and their Lies." And then of course there was Hitler and his belief that he was doing the Lord's work. Vidal called all of this "outrageous stuff." What's happened, he said, is that fundamentalist Islam has taken over the worst of the Christian excesses and has bought into myths and lies such as the Protocols of the Elders of Zion and the "blood libel."

Vidal stated his conviction that we should work for more assimilation, adding that the national anthem should be for all Israelis, Arab and Jewish. "I do believe we should cultivate our own Arabs," he added. That didn't sit too well with me, so we had a bit of an impassioned discussion.

Vidal said, "Look, we've got 1.2 million Israeli Arabs; they can either be a fifth column or they can be Arabs. Many of them could be good allies, just like the Druze." I responded, "No, I disagree."

Vidal then said, "Maybe not this generation, but the next. Especially if they went to the same schools; now they go to different ones." I responded, "No, I don't think so." I mentioned that I had just written an article arguing that now would be the perfect time to annex and transfer.

I realized that this topic wasn't one we could cover in the time we had left, not even in the full 30 minutes. Plus, how could I argue anymore with this handsome, suave, debonair man? So I asked him about Jewish food, and he said, "Talking about Jewish soul food is like talking about Chinese food." This got me thinking, have you ever noticed that every Sunday night you see Jewish people in Chinese restaurants? I wonder if you went to a deli on Sunday, would it be filled with Chinese people?

As we neared the end of the show, I pointed out that when you say "Vidal Sassoon" people go "Oh, yes!" Vidal responded, "But then some say, 'He's a butler, isn't he?'" He was so funny and self-deprecating!

I said that I had to have him back on the show so we could continue our discussion. Plus, I added, "You're an icon, and a hottie." Vidal responded smoothly, "Plus, we can disagree, which is wonderful." I wish I could have had another chance to have a disagreement with this wonderful man.

With Vidal on the Queen Mary Two, 2006

Julio Iglesias...Hmmmm

I remember the first time that I heard the music of Julio Iglesias. It was in the early eighties, and I thought of him as a Spanish, very heterosexual Johnny Mathis. I had traveled to Italy and several Latin countries in South America, and I was used to the "sexy sound." However, Julio's voice and music were something new. And, oh was that man someone to see!

Our meeting was one of those post-divorce encounters that I later thought was directed by G-d to give me back my confidence. I was living in Atlanta at the time. Somehow, I had caught the attention of one of the casinos in Atlantic City and was invited to go on one of their gambling junkets. To this day, I don't remember the casino, but I've never forgotten my time spent with Julio Iglesias.

I don't gamble. For me, gambling and the use of drugs were G-d's way of saying, "You have too much money, just throw it in the garbage can." I did, though, always enjoy the shows that were offered in that sinful city. When I arrived on this particular trip, I left a note for the managers of Mr. Iglesias stating that I'd like to interview him for my newspaper column. I honestly never really thought I'd hear back. However, I did graciously accept the comp ticket his manager handed me. I went to the show that evening, along with several thousand other females. About fifteen minutes into this gorgeous man's act, one of the security people came to my table and said, "Mr. Iglesias will see you for five minutes after the show." He said that I should stay in my seat and someone would come and escort me to the dressing room.

Gawd! After the show, I felt like a fabulous celebrity as I followed the security guy though the mass of women who had somehow managed to get backstage passes. Yet, even they were not cleared to go where I was going, to see "the man," alive and in person! I swear, when I traveled to the Middle East, I had to pass through fewer "check points" than I did in the tunnels of this New Jersey casino! But, when we arrived, it was worth the long path of twists and turns. Julio opened the door with that perpetual George Hamilton tan, wearing white loafers, tight jeans, a white tee shirt, and a white sweater tied casually around his neck...and he gave me a big, lazy smile. Gorgeous!

He is looking at me and I am posing for the camera. Does that make me a bad person?

It was obvious that my time with Julio would be limited, because other people were waiting. So, when he said, "What can I do for you?" I blurted out that I wanted a lot more than five minutes...without the escort present! While we sat in our respective chairs, it was difficult to concentrate on what, if anything, I wanted to ask this man. Oh yes, did I want to "interview" him!

Years later, I remember little of the conversation. I do remember feeling sad for him, which was odd considering who he was. But, he had a wistful look in his eyes when he told me about one of his favorite things he used to do, which was to shop along the boulevards in Spain and go in and out of the stores. Once he became famous, everything changed. I imagined that with all the fans pushing to get a glimpse of him, it was impossible to go anywhere without being recognized. So, shopping and browsing, as he had so enjoyed in the past, was something that he couldn't do anymore. Now, if he needed to buy clothes, stores would send a dozen suits to his hotel suite, and from there he "went shopping."

What do I recall about our time together? Time flew!

When I was back in my room that evening, the red message light on my phone was blinking. The message was from Julio's manager, telling me to go, at four o'clock the next afternoon, to the ballroom where Julio would be rehearsing for his evening show. The manager said that Mr. Iglesias had set aside time for another "interview." Lucky me—very lucky me! When I arrived this time, I didn't see hordes of females or security guards. I merely walked into the dimly lit ballroom and sat in a front-row chair directly in front of the stage. Other than the waiters and bartenders, who were preparing the room for the evening, I was all by myself. Soon, the band and backup group walked in and started to set up. I was still sitting right up front, wondering what I was supposed to do. A few minutes later, the lights dimmed, and about five feet from where I was sitting, Julio Iglesias casually walked out. He looked directly into my eyes, smiled "that smile" with his incredible white teeth, and began to sing his song, "To All the Girls I've Loved Before." Truly, I thought I had died and gone to heaven. For over an hour, this man rehearsed by singing his songs directly to me.

Truly, it was one of those moments that come once in a lifetime, and I didn't want it to end. I have to tell you, when Julio walked onto a stage, women didn't scream; they enjoyed the music and his gorgeous smile because he was a total class act. He was every woman's fantasy, unlike Wayne Newton, who was also appearing that evening at the same time. And the girls in Julio Iglesias's audience were throwing roses on the stage rather than underpants and room keys like they threw at a Tom Jones show!

After the show, Julio and I met once again in his dressing room. Yay, this time when we spoke, I actually remembered to ask him some questions. I told him that I wrote a column in Jewish syndicated newspapers. He gave me that lazy, sexy smile and commented that Jewish women were always his favorite. I could have been from Honduras, and he might have said the same thing about Honduran women, but who cared??

He asked me how long I would be in town, and I told him I was leaving late that evening. Then the moment of truth came! Very casually, he said, "If you would consider missing your plane, I would love to see you after the show." I don't remember ever turning down something I wanted so badly...a night with Julio Iglesias; what could be better? But, I knew where the night would lead, and knowing my mentality, I knew he would have ruined me for all future men. So, with great regret, and I do mean *great* regret, I said, "Good-bye." But, to this day, I still have that Florida phone number he gave me stuck in my phone book.

Our paths didn't cross again until November of 2002. I had been invited to a formal dinner given by the Los Angeles Police Department. It was an absolutely incredible night! Sylvester Stallone and Astronaut Buzz Aldrin were there, and Lionel Ritchie sat at my table. And lo and behold, the entertainment for the evening was...sigh...Julio Iglesias! I was sitting so close, yet, so far away. I was positive that somehow Julio would notice me and remember our "ships that passed" and he would sing to me as he did that night fifteen years before. Ah, but that wasn't meant to be. Really, though, he still looked wonderful, and the audience of 1,500 came under his spell as he displayed the same charm I remembered.

Probably just as well I passed on his invitation years ago; I wouldn't have wanted to break his heart.

Jack Klugman...Not So Odd

"This guy just keeps going," I said when introducing Jack Klugman. I told my viewers that I had started to print out his credits from movies and the theater so I could read some of them but my printer had run out of ink. I said that most people know him as Oscar from *The Odd Couple* and from his role as Quincy in the show of that name. But, I added, you've also got *Days of Wine and Roses* and all the others!

As a good segue from my mentioning Oscar Madison, Jack said he thought this was going to be a radio show and apologized for the way he was dressed. I said I thought he looked precious, which he did! He said he thought I looked terrific...which I did!

We talked about Jack's throat cancer. Jack had part of his larynx removed in 1989, and his voice is hoarse. Jack told a story about working with Humphrey Bogart in the 1950's. Bogart, Jack said, "could have been the poster boy for cigarettes." Jack said that each cigarette you saw on the screen represented about 10 that he had actually smoked; he would light one with another. Jack said that Bogart's weight went down to about 77 pounds, and he died at 57. "From cigarettes," Jack added.

Jack said he himself used to smoke two to five packs a day when he was gambling in Vegas. He said after the larynx operation he felt worthless, like the horse John Henry, who won $6 million, but when he was done racing was worthless because he was a gelding. Jack sympathized with the great horse. He couldn't talk, and therefore couldn't act. One day he was functioning and the next day, nothing, "worthless." So he worked with a voice specialist, and got some of his voice back. Now he can talk for two hours in a one-man show, like the one I had recently seen him in at Garry Marshall's Falcon Theater.

I told Jack about my breast cancer and brain operations. We talked about the importance of getting multiple opinions. He said one doctor had told him he had to have a complete laryngectomy or he'd be dead. But another doctor said he didn't see any reason to completely remove the larynx.

Jack talked about Ethel Merman, with whom he had a "great platonic love affair for years and years." I raised my eyebrows, wondering about how "platonic" it was, and he joked that she always had "real" affairs with the leading men! He said he and Ethel realized that they had such a good thing going, why ruin it? I told Jack that my mother took me to see him and Ethel in *Gypsy* on Broadway when I was very young. Ethel died at 75 of brain cancer, and Jack went to see her right before she passed away. He talked about how sad it was to hear her barely able to form words.

I named just a few of the other great actors Jack had worked with, including John Garfield, Henry Fonda, Lee J. Cobb, and Jack Lemmon. Jack loved his time with all these greats, adding that he had worked with very few actors and actresses with whom he couldn't get along. Jack was such a nice guy!

When I asked Jack about how he developed his acting talent, he said one reason he loved doing the theater was because "you've got rehearsals," and "that's where you learn you to act." You've got "selectivity"; that is, you have to figure out what works during rehearsal and use, or select, that. With TV and movies, he said, the shooting is so fast.

He also called the movie industry an "impersonal business." Jack was with Lee Remick in *Detective* in addition to *Days of Wine and Roses*. About *Detective*, he said of Remick, "I never met the woman!" Their scenes and therefore shooting schedules were all different. That's another reason he loves the theater; you go to lunch and dinner with each other, you become a family. He said that the only picture he did that was like that was *12 Angry Men*. He talked about the great cast in that movie, including Fonda, Cobb, and Jack Warden.

**On my set with
Jack Klugman,
2003**

In the early days, television was live, and Jack loved doing that because it was similar to the theater, and all the people were from the theater. He said in those early days of live TV they were doing adaptations of Faulkner and Hemingway on shows like *Playhouse 90*. Jack's first show was *The Front Page*. If he was a photographer he got $10 a show, but if he had a talking part he got $25. When the actors' union came in, the pay went up—some. Jack said that you got $60 if you had under five lines and $125 for at least five lines.

But the powers that be decided to start taping shows so they could make more money. Their justification was that they were giving the people what they wanted, but nobody in the viewing audience, as far as Jack knew, had ever said to get rid of live television. The producers did what they wanted, and the people eventually accepted that.

He talked about some of the other changes in television. It surprised me when he said that "we never had a dead body on *Quincy*." Everything the characters did was intended to help the living. Now the camera has to focus on the gory dead body. "I'm glad I was around in the good old days," he said. Jack felt that television could have been a magnificent influence on the world, but it hasn't been. It's all about sensationalism and, of course, the money.

We talked a little bit more during the show about money and actors. Jack said that he made $900 a week shooting *12 Angry Men*. As to the current money available in acting compared to the earlier days, he said that the "kids doing *Friends* make more in two days than I made in five years on *The Odd Couple*." But he's not resentful: "God bless them. Better them than the producers."

Jack had just done the play *On Golden Pond* in a traveling show, covering 35,000 miles in nine weeks. He loved it. I told Jack I could never see him getting bored, and he said no. I was also struck by how very grateful he was for his blessings and his life. He stressed the importance of appreciating what you have.

I asked him about his role in *Quincy*, wondering whether fans who saw him ever thought he was really a doctor. He said he wasn't sure about that, but added that he had spoken at a lot of doctor's and forensics/coroner conventions but had never been asked to speak to an acting group! He said the same was true with E.G. Marshall, who was in *The*

Defenders. He spoke to a number of lawyers' conventions but no gatherings of actors.

When my director was giving me the "wrap it up" sign, Jack said, "Wow, it's almost over?" I said what an easy interview he was, and he responded, "Well, I talk a lot." But then he added that I talk too much, too! Somewhat mortified, I said, "You think I talk too much?" and he responded, "Yeah, for an interviewer you talk too much, but you're wonderful. I enjoyed listening to you. Plus I got plenty of my stuff in." I was so relieved, and thrilled, to hear that!

With Jack at Garry Marshall's Falcon Theater, 2006

I ran into Jack at the Falcon Theater and at various other social events over the years. I was deeply saddened when he died in 2012.

Lou Ferrigno...The Incredible Hulk, and Hunk

The opening credits for my 2007 show with Lou Ferrigno said that today's topic was "The Incredible Hulk." During my introduction I observed that I wasn't sure whether it should be "hulk" or "hunk." I showed the audience one of Lou's bodybuilding books where he's posing on the cover in one of those Speedos that those guys wear. Lou commented that he was only 44 when that picture was taken 11 years ago. He told us that at the time he had weighed 325 pounds with 2% body fat. As he sat across from me at age 55, he still looked pretty good!

Not long after his birth Lou lost close to 80% of his hearing due to several ear infections. As a child he had to study and master phonetics and learn to match body language with words so he could both understand people and be understood. Lou stressed to my viewers that this was a "lot harder than bodybuilding." He said he can hear very well with his hearing aids, which I noticed you can't even see.

Lou has acted in 37 movies; prior to the show I had received pages and pages of credits from Lou's publicist, Edward Lozzi. Lou noted that he likes doing comedies. He particularly enjoyed his work on *The King of Queens*, which he was on for seven years.

And of course we talked about Lou's most famous role. The darling man, Stan Lee, created The Incredible Hulk for Marvel Comics. I showed a clip from the TV show. Lou said it was from a 1989 episode called "The Return of the Hulk." Lou told us that the makeup took three to four hours to apply. He had to stay "refrigerated" when he wasn't shooting to keep from sweating too much and ruining the makeup. Lou said that he had just finished working on the new Hulk movie with Edward Norton, Tim Roth, and William Hurt.

I had to ask Lou about "Arnold," since each of them is both an actor and a bodybuilder. Lou talked about doing the documentary *Pumping Iron* with Arnold. He said that he unfortunately finished second to Arnold in the competition on which the documentary was based.

Lou played football for awhile in Canada. He said he did it because people kept telling him he had to play because he's so big. But he didn't like the game because he didn't like hitting people. I commented, "You're a pussycat. Guys your size don't have to be intimidating." Lou is a gentle giant.

Lou is committed to helping people with hearing loss. He said that his wife Carla once told him that the deafness issue was his "thing" and has been very encouraging and helpful to him. Lou is the spokesperson for the Starkey Hearing Foundation. He told us that 30 million people in the U.S. are hard of hearing or deaf, but also noted the amazing advances that have been made in helping people with hearing loss. He said that if he had been born today he would have gone into theater to learn a different accent, with all the technology available for deaf people. Because, he said, his accent is "very Brooklyn!" As to actors with hearing loss and other disabilities in Hollywood, Lou would like to see Hollywood hire more actors with disabilities instead of hiring healthy actors to play characters with disabilities.

Lou is also in the personal training business because, as he says, "people need motivation." He talked about the home gym equipment company that he was just starting. He said he still trains five or six days a week. I told Lou that he looked so young and great; I said if I didn't know his age I'd put him at about 44-45. He credits his continued good health to "good living, good diet, and working out," but added, "and no skeletons in my closet." I didn't pursue that one!

I told him that I have a love/hate relationship with working out. If I go to the gym, afterwards I feel great and love myself; if I don't go, I feel fat and hate myself. But I don't see the results; I go to the gym to stay my basic chubby. Maybe I need some help from a professional like Lou!

With Lou Ferrigno on my set, 2007

We talked about what makes a man sexy. I said that a sexy man is "one who makes *me* feel sexy." Lou said that he respects Sean Connery—he'd never met him but had always idolized him—and Harrison Ford. Since he had mentioned Mr. Connery, and Daniel Craig's first Bond movie had been released recently, I asked him about his favorite Bond actors. He said that, next to Connery, Pierce Brosnan was his favorite.

I complimented Lou on his aura of calm and assurance. I added, "Even though you're so big I wouldn't think you were a bad guy." Lou suggested that this might be because he's a Scorpio. When I told Lou that I'm a Leo, he said that Leos have an incredible energy about them, a great "gift of gab," and good leadership traits. Scorpios are very focused and intense. I liked what he had to say about Leos, but added that "we're so egotistical, Leo people. I just found out there are other signs!"

As our interview was ending, I asked Lou if he had any closing words to tell our viewers. He responded, "You only have one life to live. Live it to fulfillment, because no one has ever come back to tell us where we go from here...We don't know what happens afterwards, so we must live every day." My reply was, "I always tell my children if Mommy can't come back, I'm not going!" Lou laughed and added one more parting phrase: "Your health is your greatest wealth." And that inspiring comment ended my show for the night.

Dianne Feinstein...Guess Who Is Coming to Dinner

Back in 1985, when I was a journalist, the Fairmont Hotel in San Francisco asked me to write an article about the hotel and invited me as a guest to do my "research." The Fairmont was gorgeous; but soon after I arrived the dinging of the trolley bell through my window made me crazy and I had to leave my room. Although it was early in the morning, the elevator was already crowded, mostly with people wearing press badges and carrying video cameras, which, of course, stirred my interest. When I got to the lobby and inquired about the crowd from one of those men whose main job seemed to be walking around looking busy, he told me there was a major conference of the United Nations taking place in the hotel. Now my interest was really sparked!

The same guy, who was carrying about a dozen cameras around his neck, looked at me and added, "It's a secured event and only for the working press." Well, I *was* "working press." Just because I was dressed nicely, and technically hadn't been sent to the Fairmont to cover this conference, didn't preclude me from going to the press office and requesting my credentials! Let me just say at this point that media people always seemed to come to events looking so tacky. Frankly, I was usually appalled when I saw how the media people dressed! I've always felt that the ability to distinguish "us" from the animals is our ability to accessorize. For instance, I've always told my kids, "Gold is good, but diamonds are better."

Okay, back to my story...

So, after showing my press cards to the lady at the desk and answering a few questions, I was in. I wasn't quite sure what being "in" meant, but the adventure had begun. Looking fabulous and, of course, totally accessorized, I walked around the opulent lobby of the Fairmont. Secret Service agents and delegates from countries represented in the United Nations surrounded me. I learned that this conference was being held as part of the 40th anniversary celebration of the United Nations. The original charter was signed in San Francisco in 1945.

Somehow I began spending time with two men who looked like they were one year younger than G-d but who were, actually, kind-of cute. They turned out to be one of the original signers of the United Nations Charter, Carlos Rómulo of the Philippines, and Herbert Armstrong from the United States, founder of the magazine *The Plain Truth*, who had attended the 1945 conference.

**With Herbert Armstrong, United States,
and Carlos Rómulo, Philippines**

I wondered what they had been thinking when they first had the conception of how the United Nations was supposed to function. I also wondered if the U.N. founders, even in their wildest dreams, had imagined countries like Syria or

Iran being allowed on the Security Council. I thought of asking them, but I didn't want to draw too much attention to myself; remember, I had just gotten, i.e. sneaked in, there. Actually, I have to tell you, I didn't see those two doing much politicking; they just sat in their wheelchairs. And sadly, both of these gentlemen passed away within the following year.

I was having a wonderful time, because the ratio of men to women was about as good it was back when I was covering the war in Beirut in June of 1982. I think I told you elsewhere that back then in Beirut, there were 67,000 gorgeous, sex-starved Israeli soldiers and four female correspondents, with bombs dropping in the background. But, I don't think I mentioned this part: often, one of those wonderful men from the Israeli Defense Forces (IDF) would jump out of his tank, run over and say, "I give you rose for a kiss." God bless those Israeli soldiers; they're never too busy for fun. This group at the Fairmont, however, didn't look so "gorgeous," and they all looked busy.

Suddenly, there were chimes announcing that lunch was being served. The walls opened and the reception hall became a beautiful dining room with sparkling chandeliers everywhere. The Press was told to stay outside; a lunch invitation was not in the packet. I was thinking this might be a little problematic; however, lack of an invitation didn't worry me. No one ever stops me from going anywhere I really want to go, and this lunch was no exception! Besides, I had dressed the part! All my fellow journalists, walking around with notepads and cameras slung around their necks, still looked so tacky—more like tourists who should have been taking their pictures at the zoo or other places tourists go!

The tables filled quickly and I didn't want to be left standing in the middle of the ballroom. However, I held back for a few moments while my eyes gazed across the room. I searched for an empty seat, hoping there would be an absent delegate. As luck would have it, I was standing in front of a table occupied by several men from the Arab nations. Knowing how much of a pushover they were for blondes and redheads, I winked at the chubby Arab who was wearing what looked like a dirty checkered tablecloth on his head. He almost broke his neck as he jumped up and asked, "Would you like to join our table?" In my best Southern accent, I smiled brightly and said, "Oh my, yeeess."

So, here I was, at a table with the delegates from Saudi Arabia, Yemen, Sudan, Jordan, and a couple of those other countries that I just loved so well... NOT. I found it interesting that when an Arab delegate spoke during the luncheon, these men clapped forcefully. However, the minute the delegate from Israel began to speak, those at my table all stood up, as if prearranged, and walked out together, leaving me sitting all by myself. Considering the relative charm of this group, I wasn't bothered in the least. Then I noticed, sitting in the chair next to me, a large, white envelope that had obviously been left by a member of the Arab contingent. Looking to my left and then my right, just to make sure nobody around me was watching, I picked it up.

Boy! What a bonanza! Enclosed in this packet were the invitations to all the parties and all the entrance badges for the next four days. Now, normally, if someone loses something, I'm the first person to rush to return it; but, that mindset changed in this situation. Right then and there, I decided to spend the rest of my trip going to every event. And, let me just tell you this—these people knew how to party with our tax dollars! I went to lunches, dinners, and a whole list of other events. I have long forgotten who the Israeli representatives were to the United Nations at that time; however, I do remember meetings and lunches with them.

My four-night charade culminated with a dinner invitation to the home of Mayor Dianne Feinstein. Yes, and this, Readers, is how "guess who" had dinner at Dianne Feinstein's.

I had managed to introduce myself and make acquaintances while mingling and holding drinks at previous parties. At one of these events, one of the delegates from an African nation, Dr. Davidson Nicol, who was President of the World Federation of United Nations Associations, took a liking to me. So, as I was standing there pretending that I knew what the hell was going on, he mentioned the Feinstein dinner event. At that moment, I reached into my purse and pulled out the embossed invitation and showed it to Dr. Nicol. He gave me a wide-toothed grin and said in a very British accent, "Oh! Then you must attend with me in my limo." Bingo! I was in!

With Dr. Davidson Nicol of Sierra Leone

Promptly at seven, I met him in the lobby and we walked outside. Within seconds, our limo arrived. This was fun; I noticed others getting into their stretch limos at the same time. Frankly, I was loving life, although I had no idea what I was doing. I was getting a kick out of how nobody questioned me about anything. When we arrived at Ms. Feinstein's house, the Mayor herself was there to greet us. Dr. Nicol she obviously knew, but she looked at me with a bit of puzzlement. I smiled and said, "Don't worry; you'll be thrilled I'm here." (I later wrote nice things about her in an article.) She might have questioned me, but other cars arrived and she began greeting other guests. I stood there for a moment while they pondered why there was a mix-up and my name wasn't on the guest list. Surprise, surprise! The two women who were the gatekeepers for the event scrambled and quickly designed a nameplate for me. I think they gave me the seat of the Ambassador from China, who never made it to the dinner.

The dinner was not as big as I had expected it would be. Out of the estimated four hundred who were attending the United Nations conference, maybe only sixty had been invited to this shindig. All I know is that I was seated at a table with a lot of important people. Everybody at my table was a "Head" of some place. I think I was seated with the President of Boeing Airlines, and maybe the CEO of Lockheed...maybe even Lee Iacocca.

Finally, the evening ended and we all prepared to head back to the Fairmont to pack for our departure following the farewell brunch the next day. As I was doing my "Jewish good-byes"* I edged toward the door. But, before I left, I noticed a couple of the paparazzi taking pictures of me, in the hopes that I was somebody whose photos would bring the big bucks. A few of the wives of the delegates approached me asking, "Who are you? We've all been wondering." I laughed and said, "I'm a star!" and walked out the door to my waiting limo.

*Have you ever noticed that when Jewish people leave a party it takes a half hour from the first good-bye until they actually depart? It's true. People of other religions say "Bye" and just walk out the door. But Jewish guests have to work the room for another thirty minutes before they actually leave.

Hector Elizondo...Garry Marshall's Lucky Charm

I begin the interview by saying, "This man is always working. I can't remember when he has not been working." Then I said that my guest today is "Hector...Oh God, I've asked him 14 times already how to pronounce his name... Elon...Elizondo!" He wondered what's so hard about his name, and remarked, "Say 'Schwarzenegger.'" We were off to a fun start!

I used to bump into Hector Elizondo often at Garry Marshall's theater, the Falcon. For years I had been trying to get Hector on my show. But his agent or manager would always say that he couldn't appear. Finally, we scheduled a date and time. But just before Hector's appearance date, his agent called to say that Hector was cancelling because "he does not do cable shows," and hung up. Frantic that I would have dead space, I called Hector. He calmed me down and asked me to confirm when and where to show up...and show up he did! As he says, "I am a man of my word."

As he talked about his youth, Hector said he was "a New York City born and bred lad." He said that he was very sick and "neurasthenic" while growing up in Harlem. But one day, after he had been "running behind his mother's skirt for the 400th time," his father stated very clearly to him that they were not going to move, so Hector was going to have to figure out how to survive. His father said they were going to the gym, where Hector was going to learn how to box. Hector said that he wasn't a very aggressive kid and didn't want to learn, but he finally gave in and did. He said he figured, "Maybe at least I could fake it." Hector feels that this moment was a rite of passage for him and was ultimately a way of surviving in a tough neighborhood.

Hector said that becoming an actor was never on his radar screen. He was always a singer, though, specifically a jazz singer. Hector started singing at a very young age; he joked that when he was little he thought his last name was "Sing," because whenever his father saw him he would say, "Hector, Sing." He said that by the age of eight or nine many kids know that they want to be a pilot or an "Indian Chief" or whatever. Hector wasn't that way at all; he was just a kid having a good time, playing ball, etc. But he was always the "class singer." It was an "accident" when he was discovered for the first time, at age 10. Hector was in a school play, singing a song, and the song's composer just happened to be in the audience!

While on the subject of jazz, I told him that it was my favorite kind of music, at least good jazz. Hector responded, "Jazz is how I float, how I think, how I feel." He added, "When they dig us up 5,000 years from now, there will be only three things that are remembered as purely American constructs: the First Amendment, baseball, and jazz."

Hector was also a jazz dancer, another career move that he said happened accidentally, when he was in his 20s. He began playing conga, first for a jazz class, and then with a jazz dancing troupe. One day, during rehearsal for a particular piece, the choreographer asked him if he would walk through the piece while the choreographer was figuring out the "blocking." As it turned out, the choreographer needed another dancer for the show and was planning to conduct auditions, but, after watching Hector, asked him if he would be interested in dancing. Hector responded, "So I have to stop playing conga? I get 10 bucks to play conga. What do I get for dancing?" "Nothing," the choreographer responded. Hector said to forget it. But the choreographer finally convinced him to be a dancer in this show, and he ended up joining the dance company for a few years. But Hector left dancing "because dancers don't make a living. And I'm a family man; I have to make a living."

With Hector Elizondo on my set, 2004

I told Hector that he has such a "nice" aura about him, which is hard to explain since he grew up in Harlem. I went to Columbia and knew of Hector's "stomping grounds." I told him that I knew the area was scary—I recalled that my biggest expense was the cab fares! He said, "Oh yeah? I drove those!"

When I told the viewers that Hector had received an Opie award when he was a kid, Hector responded, "That's the first time I played God. Since then I've played God four times. There must be something wrong with the universe.

That's why things are so fakakta." One translation of this word, readers, is "crappy." He is a funny man!

I told Hector that he always seemed to play the nice guy when he acts. He said that before *Pretty Woman* he enjoyed doing a lot of roles playing "what they call in the business 'Bad guys.'" He mentioned *The Taking of Pelham 123* from the seventies in which he played Mr. Gray, who was, as Hector described, "The Bad Guy."

Garry Marshall had told me that Hector was his lucky charm. Hector appeared in every movie that Garry directed! As I mentioned earlier, the word "nepotism" sometimes comes up in association with Garry. Hector feels that Garry didn't believe in nepotism just for the sake of nepotism. He said that he believed in using his friends and family as long as they could "cut it, do the job," adding that Garry didn't "float or featherbed anybody."

But, for Hector, Garry's first love was the theater, and he feels that one reason Garry did movies was to fund the Falcon Theater. Hector had just finished a performance in Garry's play *Wrong Turn at Lungfish* at the Falcon. I had seen it, and Hector was wonderful! I said that this was his first play in 12 years and wondered if he had been away from the theater so long because he had been so busy. Hector said that he doesn't want to be in the theater "just to be in it." He always wanted to choose particular works, and *Lungfish* was one in particular that he wanted to do.

The play had premiered 18 years earlier; Hector said that he was too young for it then, but not now. We talked about Ana Ortiz, Hector's co-star in the play. When I said that she reminded me of a young Judy Holliday, Hector agreed, saying "She's a Latin from Manhattan, a Latina Judy Holliday." Hector said that she has a "heart of gold" and is "very, very bright."

Hector remarked that Garry created another generation of theater lovers with the Falcon, which is so important. "Theater is the oldest way to express yourself," Hector said. "The first theater was around a campfire. Telling the story is an essential part of being alive. We're still around a campfire." He added that the Falcon has become an essential part of the fabric of the Toluca Lake neighborhood.

I told Hector that the first time I met him was when we both played roles in the made-for-television movie *Your Mother Wears Combat Boots*. I had never done a movie before, and I haven't done much movie acting since. I recalled that I played a bitch at the airport, adding that this was a role I felt very comfortable playing! Hector just smiled.

Hector supports many great causes. Through his work with the Creative Coalition, he goes to D.C. to talk with the House Ways & Means Committee about getting more funding for arts in education. I remarked that they're closing up libraries for budget reasons. Hector just shook his head and said, "In Salinas they're closing, are you ready, The Steinbeck Library...One of our literary icons, they're closing the library that's named after him. We're turning into a country that I don't quite understand."

Hector continued with a story about Churchill meeting with his other ministers while bombs were falling on London in World War Two. Some of the ministers said that they would need to cut arts funding from the budget. Churchill responded, "No, we don't cut a penny from art. Why do you think we're fighting?" Hector added, "You survive through the arts, through expression, whether it's singing, dancing, writing..."

Hector is also involved with Alzheimer's, the Heart Association, and the Red Cross. I let him know that I have a beef with the Red Cross. I told him that Israel was one of the few countries not allowed into the Red Cross because the Jewish star can't be displayed; however, they have no problem allowing the Arabs and the Muslims to display symbols with the lions and the crest. I continued, "I once wrote an article, 'Red Cross, Double Cross,' stating that Israel is the first to come in a time of crisis with help and medicine." I told him my daughter now goes to Cedar Sinai to give blood rather than going to the Red Cross. Hector gave me his wonderful smile and said that he would look into this.

We turned to the topic of ageism in Hollywood. I commented that Hector may not be worried about that because he's always working. He said that he likes being at this point in his life, but also noted that he doesn't like to think of myself as having a "career." He explained this attitude, saying, "I'd rather think of myself as having jobs, and some jobs are better than others. If you have a career it's something you can lose. It's another moving part, like losing your hair; you've got to worry about it. At this point in my life I'm trying to figure out what I'm supposed to do for the third act." Hector added that he's trying to find out what it is that he wants to contribute, which is one reason that he's involved with so many organizations.

Since Hector had been in a movie with Sophia Loren, I had to ask about her. Hector described Sophia as "a wonderful, a good person, a person interested in living." He said that they spent a lot of time discussing food, which "always seemed to be a metaphor in everything we talked about." They loved to discuss the choosing of food, preparing it, who's sitting at the table, etc.

Hector has been married to the same woman for over 45 years. She is a publisher and book designer. He remarked,

"She is a much better person than me." I don't know her well, but she is lucky to be with someone so adorable.

When it was time to wrap up the show and I asked Hector for some closing comments, he told a story the Irish poet-writer Brendan Behan, author of *Borstal Boy*. Behan, Hector said, was a "heavyweight drinker." But one time, during a "minute-and-a-half when he wasn't drinking," Behan was asked, "What kind of government would you support?" Behan wasn't really into politics. But his response, which Hector relayed in his best Irish brogue, was, "I'll support any government that makes the beer colder in the summer and old people warmer in the winter." Sounds like a great government! And then Hector added, "That's what I'm looking for." What a great ending for this show!

Meir Kahane...the Jewish Activist

Where do I begin? Sometimes events or people come into your lives that are meant, perhaps, to provide a lesson or meaning to a time that would otherwise have been "run of the mill." But the period in which Rabbi Meir Kahane entered my life was way beyond one of those times.

In the 1970s I was chairing a Jewish Discussion Group at the Atlanta Federal Penitentiary. I rarely had more than eight Jewish inmates in attendance; very few of the 2,800 incarcerated in the prison were Jewish. But let me tell you, my program grew to be a popular one; in fact, I eventually had about 75 men coming into my Wednesday night group. I had the elite of the mafia, NAACP, and Muslim Brotherhood present. I used to tell them it wasn't very Jewish to be put in jail, and they were probably children of a mixed marriage.

For a while during that period, Rabbi Kahane was an inmate in Allenwood Prison. The guys in my discussion group used to tell me about him. They said Rabbi Kahane had broken the barrier and was getting kosher food sent to him in prison. Since all other inmates at the Atlanta Penitentiary were given special dinner on holidays such as Easter, Thanksgiving, and Christmas, I thought the guys in my group should have a Passover Seder, especially after hearing about Rabbi Kahane.

The warden and I were usually at odds because of what he considered my "unreasonable demands." When I inquired about this Seder idea, the warden told me, "Lady, we ain't got no money for special Jew food." I answered him, "Really? There is a Rabbi Kahane, who is in jail, and kosher food has been brought in for him, so the precedent has been set. So, see that the guys in my group get kosher food and Passover Seder, or I'm going to file an injunction against you." Eventually the warden backed down. That was the start of my relationship with Rabbi Kahane. Through his distant inspiring influence I was able to break a barrier.

As I've mentioned, for many years I had a nationally syndicated column that ran in *The Jewish Post and Opinion*. Rabbi Kahane was a featured columnist in another paper, *The Jewish Press*. Somehow I ended up on their mailing list, and I soon noticed that Rabbi Kahane and I would write similar columns on the same topics.

One of the Rabbi's articles from 1978 concerned the circumstances surrounding the planned march of the National Socialist Party of America (NSPA), a Nazi group, in Skokie, IL. The march was initially planned for 1977, and the ensuing controversy lasted into the next year, drawing national attention. Skokie was a very Jewish community; thousands of Holocaust survivors lived there. Kahane himself organized a protest in Skokie against the march. In this particular article Kahane expressed his frustration with the Jewish "establishment," which had initially argued that responding to the march would give the Nazis undue publicity. But eventually a Holocaust survivor, Sol Goldstein, who also happened to be a wealthy contributor to the local Jewish federation, complained about the lack of response, and the establishment agreed to hold a counter-demonstration.

And secondly, Kahane expressed in this article his outrage that the ACLU had defended the Nazis in court. They did this even though the ACLU's National Director and the Illinois Chief Counsel were Jewish! And, equally ironic, the head of the NSPA itself was the son of a Jewish father who had survived the Dachau concentration camp! The case went all the way to the Supreme Court, which upheld the Nazis' right to march. Yet the march never happened in

Skokie. It was moved to Chicago. Kahane said that without the ACLU there would have been no march and no publicity.

In my story on Ed Asner I described my ongoing disagreement with Ed about the ACLU. I had been telling Ed for years how disgusting the ACLU is. I agreed with Kahane's outrage at the ACLU's defending the right of these neo-Nazis to march in Skokie. My frustration with the group was engendered then, and my affinity with Rabbi Kahane continued to grow. I liked his attitude and writing; it was apparent that we were pretty much on the same wavelength.

In 1978 I happened to be in Israel for my son's Bar Mitzvah when I saw a flyer advertising that Rabbi Kahane would be speaking that evening. I called him up and asked, "Are you the real Rabbi Kahane?" He answered, "I don't know. Are you the real Arlene Peck?" Apparently, he had heard about me and read my columns, as I had his. And, before hanging up, he invited me to come to his talk that evening. Since we were in Israel, and his audience was Israeli, I knew he would be speaking Hebrew. Since I didn't understand Hebrew, I suggested we meet after his speech. He liked the idea, and we set up a meeting later that evening at the Dan Hotel, where I was staying with my family.

Around ten that night he walked into the lobby. He was a slight man, walking with two young guys, who I assumed were bodyguards. He introduced one as "security." The guy looked large enough to be a refrigerator with a head. I ran back to the room and asked my then-husband Howard if he'd like to join us, and he answered, "No thanks, I'm not interested in meeting that criminal." And with that, he closed the door.

I walked back to the lobby, where the Rabbi and I sat and talked until almost four in the morning. Wow! What an interesting man! Reluctantly I went back to my room and got dressed for another day of touring. At the time I had no idea that spending this one evening with this icon of a man would become a pivotal point in my life. He called again before we left to catch our plane back to the states, and promised to "keep in touch."

However, I was still surprised when, a few days after my return, the Rabbi called and said he would be coming to the states and asked if I would be interested in going with him to speak with prisoners in upstate New York. I quickly agreed. Over the succeeding years I traveled to various prisons around the country with Rabbi Kahane, advocating for better treatment for incarcerated Jews.

**With Rabbi Meir Kahane and prison rabbi,
Greenhaven State Prison, 1980**

When I was still wrapped up in the whole prison "thing" I received a call from a friend of mine, David Ulrich, who was a producer in Atlanta. He was developing a television show called "Scared Straight" and wanted to know if I would be interested in becoming involved in this project. Was I ever! He also remembered I had told him about this amazing

Rabbi from Israel who was heavily involved with the inmates in the prisons. David wanted to know if I could interest Rabbi Kahane into coming to Atlanta and taping something for this new show. Long story short, next time we spoke, the Rabbi told me that he would love to fly to Georgia and meet with the people at CBS and, of course, with me.

A few days later, without telling my husband (at that point our marriage was almost out the door), I left for the airport and picked up Rabbi Kahane. We spent about fifteen hours together while he gave me an introduction to an approach to activism that I hadn't previously known. That man was so smooth; he could have sold a refrigerator to an Eskimo. He may have walked softly, but he really did carry a big stick. Also, this was the year where he didn't wear a grey beard, and I thought he looked like a "hottie." Now, remember, I was so innocent in those days, having been married for so many years, that I really didn't know the details about being a "hottie." However, the Rabbi obviously knew this role well!

The following day when I went over to his hotel to meet him for a press conference I had set up with the local papers, the desk clerk told me that he had already checked out and had left behind a note for me. In it, the Rabbi wrote that he was leaving without seeing me because he was too attracted to me and didn't want to do anything to compromise me or my marriage. I was furious, as I had used up my favors with my press contacts to get them out on a cold rainy day to attend this press conference. The local Jewish newspaper wouldn't even talk to me, as they considered Rabbi Kahane a troublemaker and didn't appreciate me bringing him into town.

At some point in the 1980s the Rabbi called me asking if I knew that the new Consul General to Israel was an Arab and whether I would like to join him and several others to protest at the Israeli Consulate in Atlanta, where the Consul General was stationed. I said "Yes" and again found myself at the airport meeting his plane. This time, however, the Rabbi was really angry, and I had a chance to see his temper in action. We drove directly over to the consulate, and he kept talking about the absolute stupidity of the Israeli government giving an Arab a position of such power. While we were driving, I commented that there were two cars following us and he replied, "Don't worry, I'm used to it." When we stopped for lunch, I noticed the two cars also stopped and parked, and some men from the cars came in sat down at the table next to us, trying to be unobtrusive.

For me, this was a learning experience. This was the time this man taught me what a Trojan Horse was and predicted what the Oslo Accords would become. Among other things, he expressed his belief that chopping the Jewish state into pieces like salami could not bring peace.

When we got to the Israeli Consulate, obviously the word had gotten out because the local press was there without any notification from me. Readers, I wouldn't have been surprised if we had been asked to check our guns at the door. This was not a friendly crowd. This time Rabbi Kahane didn't rush out of town and agreed to be my "date" that evening at the Israel Bond dinner.

After I brought Rabbi Kahane to the dinner as my escort, the local Jewish paper *The Southern Israelite* refused to continue publishing my writings. Rabbi Kahane laughed when I told him what he had put me through. He said, "You would be surprised at the number of closet Kahane followers there were in the 'establishment.' When things would get a little too tough they would go into the closet and shout, 'Never Again … Kahane, Kahane, Kahane!'"

You see, "Never again" was a slogan of the Jewish Defense League (JDL), which Rabbi Kahane founded. More on that in a moment.

I remember so many times when the Rabbi would tell me things like, "What don't they see about the Nazi mentality of these terrorists?" He believed that the terrorists were just that, not freedom fighters or militants. He felt that you couldn't have a normal dialogue with people who target old people, women, and babies. He believed that the terrorists must be defeated, destroyed, not negotiated with by sitting down across a table to discuss the attributes of democracy versus terrorism. The Rabbi said that he preferred death to debate.

He strongly felt that you cannot negotiate with someone you have not beaten, because in their minds they have no reason to negotiate. He would point out that their polls show that most were delighted with the way things were going, and that negotiation just gives them a sense of security and suggests that terror is rewarding them. "Israel must go and remove that security," he said. "The only thing these terrorists understand is military force."

The Rabbi and I helped each other. He called me one time for assistance in breaking into the Atlanta Jewish community. Our local federation, that is, the "establishment," had banned him from speaking in the city. I was somehow able to break the ban by arranging for him to speak at Emory University. From that talk he was able to establish some needed Jewish contacts in the Atlanta Orthodox community.

And, as I describe in my story on Billy Carter, the Rabbi helped me by sending three of his disciples to Atlanta to attend the closed cocktail party that Libya was giving for local politicians as part of its effort to buy land in Georgia.

Needless to say, the presence of Kahane's delegates was disruptive.

In the mid- to late-1980s I wrote several columns about Rabbi Kahane's ideas, including his proposal to transfer the Arabs out of Israel, which for him was a completion of the population exchange that had been going on since 1948 when Jews began migrating from Arab countries to Israel. Kahane proposed financial compensation for Arabs who agreed to leave voluntarily. Yet he did support forcible removal of those who would not emigrate.

The idea of Arab transfer has always had some appeal for me. Transfers have happened successfully in many other countries before, so why not in the cities that rightfully belong to the Jewish State?

I was considered a radical even before then, but I received numerous negative responses to my columns supporting Rabbi Kahane's ideas. I once wrote, "Sometimes, I think that I could write that I had a tête-à-tête with Gaddafi and it would enlist less response. But, Kahane? The letters to the editor are filled for weeks, and usually adversely." The politically correct people of that time shunned my theories and wrote stories of the coming peace between the Arabs and Jews.

Some of Kahane's ideas were pretty extreme. I remember when he was campaigning for the Knesset in 1981 on a pledge to outlaw sex between gentiles and Jewish women. He made no mention about sex between Jewish men and non-Jewish women. Only someone like Rabbi Kahane—or Donald Trump—could have run for office on such a platform. He did eventually serve on the Knesset from 1984-1988, but by that time he had dropped that campaign pledge!

It is hard to believe that it's been over forty-five years since Rabbi Kahane used to tell me about an organization called The Jewish Defense League (JDL) and its plans for the future. JDL National Chairman Irv Rubin recalled for me Rabbi Kahane's motivation for founding the JDL. Rubin remembered how Kahane wanted to change the image of the Jewish community in the United States.

How many of you remember the necklaces that we wore during the plight of the Soviet Jews? Not that many are around anymore to remember, but I am, and do. There were many "Save Soviet Jewry" campaigns, but one of the biggest was when Rabbi Kahane led thousands of people to Washington D.C. in 1971 to protest the treatment of Jews in the Soviet Union with a rally outside the White House, a march, and a sit-in near the Soviet embassy. Kahane was the first one arrested, and hundreds more followed, many of them shouting the JDL slogan "Never again" as they were marched off to jail.

Our paths crossed often over the years, even, sadly, when he died. I was shocked, as most everyone else was, when in 1990, after giving a speech in New York at the Midtown Marriott East Side Hotel, he was shot and killed by an Arab gunman. The terrorist, El Sayyid Nosair, was an Egyptian-born American citizen who was charged but later acquitted of the murder. He was convicted and sentenced to prison for several other crimes. Later Nosair was convicted of the murder when it was discovered that he was a member of the terrorist cell responsible for the 1993 World Trade Center bombing. This time he was sentenced to life imprisonment, and he also later confessed to federal agents that he had killed Kahane.

When Rabbi Kahane was assassinated I was getting ready for a month-long trip to Israel. He was buried the day before I arrived. Soon after arriving in Jerusalem I went with some friends to his town for the shiva, which is the condolence call to the family of the deceased. After a lengthy drive we arrived at the unpretentious home of the Kahane family. Wow! What a crush of people. It seemed as though the entire orthodox community in Israel had come to pay their respects. Maybe the house wasn't as small as it appeared, but the immense crowd made it seem that way.

This was not a group that cared about fashionable dress. Yet, there I was, dressed for the era, wearing a short black leather skirt and jacket accompanied by my favorite gold hoop earrings and lots of clunky bracelets. The contrast between me and the other women in attendance was a bit much. Among the very orthodox women who probably hadn't seen their own uncovered hair in years, my red "big hair" stood out. For a full two minutes it seemed like everyone stopped what they were doing and just stared at the interloper who had just arrived.

Oh, and I was probably wearing my fishnet hose, which were all the rage then. And that reminds me of a story about Rabbi Kahane. The Rabbi that I knew was not the revered, restrictive "rebbe." Once when he was visiting me in Atlanta, it was a hot summer day, and I was walking around in shorts. One of my neighbors, a former Israeli who had suddenly "found religion," invited us over for Shabbat dinner. I thought this would be an informal occasion, so I drove the Rabbi over, not giving my attire a second thought. My neighbor, however, just about freaked out when he saw me. He was carrying on, "The rebbe! You dress like that in front of the rebbe?!" Before I knew it, I was back in my car driving home to change into something more respectful, since I was being watched by the Rabbi's "holy eyes." Of course, on the way over Kahane had been telling me how great my legs looked with the tan I had on them!

Anyway, when I went inside the Rabbi's home at the shiva, I noticed that the men were seated in a room to the right and the women were seated on hard wooden benches across from the female members of the family. The room was overflowing but no one spoke. Finally, one of the ultra-orthodox girls who had noticed my confusion explained that it wasn't proper to speak unless first spoken to by the family. No one wanted to impose on the silence of the mourners. I found all of them, their dress, and customs quite curious, but I'm sure no more unusual than my red hair, cosmetics, and flashy clothes and jewelry appeared to them.

In the other room, the men were telling stories of the Rabbi. I didn't feel like sharing my own recollections to an audience. They were too private at that moment. I recall thinking that the surroundings said a lot about the man I knew. The home was devoid of frills, just like the Rabbi's manner of dress, with his off-the-rack sports jackets and open-collared shirts.

There is no doubt that Rabbi Meir Kahane was a controversial figure. He was vilified by many, including those in the Jewish establishment. He was a militant activist who was arrested numerous times and served time in prison. He was accused of being a terrorist and a racist. Yet Rabbi Kahane was a lifelong defender of Jewish heritage and the rights of the Jewish people. As I said in the column I wrote following his death, "While our methods were different, our hearts were the same."

José Canseco...Ready to Play Ball

I am at a stage of my life where I'm having a hard time remembering what I had for lunch or where I was yesterday, but, when looking back, there are certain people about whom I have total recall. I remember thinking at one time I would give up all my future adventures just to play ball with the ballplayer José Canseco.

As I may have mentioned in another chapter, I used to go as a celebrity to the L.A. Police Department Golf Tournament at the Riviera Country Club every year. This particular year, I managed to get four of my girlfriends invited as my guests. They accepted, because I had told them it was total fun and the price was right! We were escorted to a private tent where we saw Joe Pesci, Mark Wahlberg, Alan Rosenberg, BB King, Tim Conway, and lots and lots of food. It was early afternoon, and we had just gone through the buffet table. All of a sudden, my friend Barbara looked at a guy who had just gotten in the food line and asked, "Who is that??!! He is absolutely gorgeous!!" With that comment, of course we all turned around, stared with open mouths, and said in unison, "She's right, who *is* he?"

Golf is not my favorite sport, but I was ready to learn if I could play with this guy!! I have a lot of good qualities, which do not include patience and shyness—I am working on humility, as I think I mentioned earlier—but in this case, I walked over to this attractive stranger and said, "I don't know who you are, but I've got four adorable blonde California girls who would like you to join us for lunch." And you know what, he did!

At police celebrity golf tournament with José Canseco, 2006

This man's looks were distracting, but somehow during the afternoon I managed to mention that I had a celebrity television show. I commented that since he had been in the celebrity line at the buffet, he had to be someone I knew. I asked if he would like to be a guest on my show. He flashed his beautiful white teeth and said, "Sure."

I knew he had to be somebody I should know, so I went home and Googled José Canseco and found out he was a baseball player. And this gorgeous ball player appeared on my show not once but twice!

During one of his appearances José was a guest with Joe Bologna, about whom I have also written in this book. When I introduced them I said that today I may be hyperventilating because I happen to have two very sexy men here. After I introduced Joe, I said that my other guest is kind-of a new friend, and told my viewers the story about how we had met at the golf tournament. I of course also had to mention that, even though I didn't know anything about baseball, I would watch baseball players because they had the cutest tushies and were the best-looking athletes.

José was born in Cuba and raised in Miami. His family came to the United States in 1965. I learned on my show that he has a twin. He told us that they used to switch classes in school. His brother was good at math, and José was better in vocabulary, so they would switch classes on test days. And they did very well in school, until high school, when they got a car and "freedom." I had to ask if they ever switched girlfriends, and he said they didn't.

José was of course famous as a professional baseball player and had recently gathered a lot of attention for his book, *Juiced: Wild Times, Rampant 'Roids, Smash Hits & How Baseball Got Big.* When I said that this book "blew the whistle on steroid use in baseball," José acknowledged that the steroid issue had given the book a lot of publicity, but that there were really only two chapters on steroids in the book and that it was really the story of his life. In the book, he tells the story of his childhood, growing up in sports, his life as a major league player on and off the field, and why he "disappeared off the map." He also discusses his belief as to why baseball took a stand and tried to get rid of him. José said he wrote the book because he thought his fans needed to know what really happened. He added that he feels that the sport of baseball had sold the public a manipulated lie, and so he wrote the truth.

I asked José about the reaction from specific athletes mentioned in the book, like Mark McGwire. He said that in writing about specific athletes he wasn't trying to throw them under the bus, but felt that he had to bring well-known players to the forefront so that one of them would come out and say that what he was saying in the book was the absolute truth, and they could then take a stand against Major League Baseball. But not one of the players did. José pointed out that now some of these athletes were testing positive and other athletes were coming to the forefront of the steroids issue.

José said that when the book first came out, "everybody thought I was crazy and it was a lie." But now the book had been "dubbed a historical document." He thinks people realize it was written with the truth behind it. And he stressed again that everything he said in the book was the "absolute truth."

Some of his fellow baseball players were not happy with his book. José said that his intention wasn't to "report" particular athletes; he just wanted to bring the steroid situation in baseball out in the open.

Benefits of the job...On my set with José

At one point Joe commented that José looked like he could still knock one out of the park. And José said, "I probably could." He may not be playing baseball anymore, but José is not finished with writing; he said that he's working on two other books.

As to other future goals, José told my audience that he had always wanted to go into acting. He talked a bit about his experience with the reality show *The Surreal Life*. He said with this type of show you've got to be ready to have a camera on you all the time. "You wake up, there's a camera sitting over you. You go to sleep, there's the camera." He said they shot the show for 12 days. But as a professional athlete he was already used to the camera following him everywhere. He'd like to broaden his horizons into "real" acting.

Finally, I have to tell you one more thing about José, which I learned during his other appearance on my show. He told us that he has been in martial arts for 17 years and is a registered black belt in three different categories. José even brought me a video of him doing black belt that I played during the show. I sat there in a trance, trying not to hyperventilate, watching him doing black belt, barefoot and wearing loose sweat pants and no shirt. I announced to the audience, "Folks, see why I love this show!" I then told the engineer guys to run the tape again...I wanted to say run it over and over!

Gloria Allred...Attorney Extraordinaire!

On my set with Gloria Allred, 1998

Gloria Allred first came to my attention at least twenty-five years ago. I was visiting New York, and when I turned on the television in my hotel room, a small woman with a big aura appeared on the screen. She was taking on Saks Fifth Avenue for giving free alterations to men while charging women through the nose. Her list of lawsuits and grievances also included the dry cleaners, for charging a small fee to men for dry cleaning their shirts but charging much more to women for the same service. I thought, "I like this lady." And my opinion hasn't changed since.

After I had moved from Atlanta to Southern California, somehow, at some Beverly Hills party, our paths crossed. I asked her to be a guest on my television show, and she graciously accepted. We bonded and were friends for many years. Considering how different we are in style, I'm always a little amazed that we stayed connected for as long as we did.

For this first of several appearances on my show, I introduced Gloria as a world-famous attorney, particularly in the area of women's rights, who represents her clients in sexual harassment and discrimination suits as well as other cases. I mentioned her radio show, which *USA Today* had described as one of the most important radio talk shows in America.

I asked Gloria about the Saks Fifth Avenue case, in which she represented several women who had been charged exorbitant amounts for dress alterations, while alterations of men's suits were typically done for free. Although Saks settled the case out of court, the company changed its alterations policy nationwide, creating a more equalized price structure.

As to the other case, in which Gloria had sued a dry cleaning company for charging more for women's shirts, I asked, "Why do men pay 99 cents for a shirt and women 5 dollars?" Gloria said that as part of proving her case she sent a few women to the cleaners with men's shirts, and they would be charged from the women's price list. Gloria concluded, "Women should be able to go to the cleaners and not lose their shirts."

I commented that Gloria is just like a fungus; when you think she is gone, she pops up again. Gloria responded, "That's not a very pleasant analogy unless one likes the fungi!" I told the audience that I saw Gloria all the time on TV when I was in Israel. Gloria commented that "the women's movement is everywhere."

Of course we talked about women's rights. I told Gloria what I usually told my guests when this issue came up; that I had my concerns about women's equality because I felt women would have to go down a few levels to be equal with men. Gloria said that the issue is really about equality of rights under the law and in relationships, the workplace, family, business, sports, and education.

In the area of equal pay for women, she was at the time focusing on the concept of "comparable worth." She explained that this idea refers not to equal pay for equal work, but rather that jobs that are mostly done by women should be valued for the worth they provide to society, not just for the fact that the jobs are usually done by women. Gloria asked, "Why should a woman who is a nurse for the county get paid less than a parking lot attendant for the county?" The education, experience, and responsibility are greater for the nurse, but most nurses are women and most parking attendants are male. Gloria said that we need to have all wages rise in jobs that are dominated mainly by women.

I asked her about a case I had heard about involving the Boy Scouts. Gloria had sued on behalf of an 11-year-old girl who wanted to be in the Boy Scouts. The girl had noticed that the Boy Scouts offered much more than her local Girl Scout troop, including leadership opportunities and extensive outdoor activities. Also, she would have the opportunity to become an Eagle Scout, which would enhance her college and career opportunities. The Girl Scouts offered no equivalent version of the Eagle Scout program. Gloria pointed out that the U.S. is the only English-speaking country that doesn't allow girls to participate in Boy Scouts. She didn't think that the courts should assist the Boy Scouts in "gender apartheid." Gloria and her client ultimately lost this case, but not until it went all the way to the California Supreme Court. Also, I remember reading that as recently as 2015 girls in California were still trying to get into the Boy Scouts.

I shared my perception that even though Gloria is so admired and respected, most of her supporters still seemed to be women. Gloria seemed to agree but added, "A man of quality is not threatened by a woman of equality."

Gloria said that she had spoken at the third anniversary of the killings of Nicole Brown Simpson and Ronald Goldman. We talked about how the system had seemed to fail in this case. She felt the system worked better in the civil trial, with different lawyers, a lower burden of proof, O.J. testifying, etc. Gloria added that she had recently recommended a bill in the California legislature that would deny child custody to a parent convicted in criminal court, or ordered to pay damages in civil court, for murdering the spouse.

I had to bring up the "Melrose Place Case," because my daughter had disagreed with Gloria's taking the case. Hunter Tylo had left *The Bold and the Beautiful* when she was offered a role on *Melrose Place*. Then she got pregnant. Melrose Place informed Ms. Tylo that her agreement was terminated because pregnancy constituted a material change in her appearance.

Gloria made several arguments in defense of Ms. Tylo. First, she said that at the early stages of the pregnancy people wouldn't even notice, so she should have been able to work then. Secondly, the show should have been able to accommodate her role to allow for pregnancy. Finally, Gloria said that "you can look sexy when you're pregnant," adding that she herself didn't even need maternity clothes for five or six months.

I said, "Well, I mean, look at you!" I added that I had looked terrible when I was pregnant.

Gloria replied, "Well you may have but some women…" but I interrupted her, blurting out, "I gained 80 with my first and 92 with my second." Perhaps that was a bit too much information, not to mention weight! Gloria responded, "That's a lot of weight gain. I gained 15 pounds." Gloria went on to explain that she and Ms. Tylo were alleging pregnancy discrimination.

I said that this was one case where I disagreed with Gloria. Ms. Tylo was hired as a woman who looked a certain way; she was beautiful, thin, etc. In other words, she was a "Melrose Place type of girl." Gloria chimed in that she still was beautiful. I agreed, but added that in that show the story lines are not conducive to pregnancy; it's just not that kind of show. I asked Gloria, "Why should they have to rewrite the story?"

Gloria responded that Ms. Tylo was not hired to be a certain character. Her character was to be developed as the show progressed. Therefore the pregnancy could have been accommodated. That's our allegation, she said. The case was still awaiting trial at the time of our show.

I was getting the "wrap it up" cue from my director. I asked Gloria about her daughter practicing with her. Gloria replied proudly that her daughter is a pioneer in child sexual abuse cases; she represents child and adult survivors of sexual abuse suing the perpetrators for damages.

I asked Gloria which case she would like to see resolved permanently. She responded, as a good attorney would, "Whichever one is the most important to my client." But she added that there are so many women's issues arising all the time and they are all important to her.

As we closed, I told Gloria, "You look so great." And she responded with a great finish for this show: "Fighting injustice is good for your health."

This woman stays busier than a one-armed paperhanger. She is not the type of friend whom you call and say, "Hey, meet me outside! I'll pick you up and we'll go for Chinese!" Plus, it took seven years of friendship before I saw her dressed in anything like casual. Our styles are quite different. Flamboyant

Two more shots with Gloria on my set

is normal to me. I was raised under the banner, "If you got it, flaunt it!" On the other hand, I could live in jeans. Gloria however, is always, I mean always, attired in something smart. It's usually "St. John."

You may have gathered that Gloria is a petite lady. Also—maybe it's a gene thing, I don't know—this woman wears a size three and can eat like a horse. I mean it! We would go out and she would order an appetizer, entrée, AND a dessert. She would eat the whole damn thing and walk away looking fabulous. I, on the other hand, would order the salad and put on five pounds.

Speaking of eating, I remember one night, a very good friend of mine, Jason Barzilay, who started Packard Bell Electronics in 1986, invited us to Argo, a restaurant he owned with Robert De Niro. After dinner, Jason walked us to the parking valet. The paparazzi were there. When they caught a glimpse of Ms. Allred, several called, "Gloria, Gloria! Look here! Look this away! Smile!" Jason smiled. He caught my eye and said, "She can't be a bad girl." "Huh," I said. He explained, "I can go anyplace and do anything I want and nobody knows who I am. I can be a bad boy." He was right. She can't be a bad girl. Too many people would love to find something, take a picture, and sell it to the *Enquirer*.

With Gloria and Jason Barzilay

There is, I believe, a softer side to this lady who seems to have invented the words "Women's lib." That's another difference we've shared. I grew up in the south in a different era. I love it when men do things for me. Like I said earlier, to be "equal," I would have to step down a few levels.

In the mid-nineties I was in the hospital recovering from a serious operation. Still groggy from the anesthetic, I was half-heartedly watching television. I believe that I was watching "Good Morning America," and lo and behold, there on the screen was my friend Gloria. That in itself was nothing new. Like I said, she is constantly on television someplace. What I shall never forget is that, a few minutes later, my phone rang in that Cedars-Sinai Hospital room. It was Gloria calling from the studio in New York, asking me how I felt and wishing me a speedy recovery. And that folks, for me, is a bonding moment.

When Gloria appeared on my show in 2004, I said, "Folks, I've got a woman here today, I've got to really stay on my toes." I went on to describe her as "probably America's most famous woman attorney, probably one of America's most famous women. I think if you stood her next to the Pope, people would come up and say 'Who's that guy standing next to Gloria Allred?'"

On this show we dove right into the issues. I noted that we're both strongly pro-choice. Gloria had recently joined the March on Washington for Women's Lives. She talked about the amazing experience of marching for a woman's rights to choose with over one million women, and men too. Gloria was concerned about the presidential election coming up that November, noting that at least one Supreme Court nominee would likely occur during the next presidential term. She said that if an anti-choice justice joined the Supreme Court, it could change the course of women's rights in the country. Abortion could become restricted or even a crime, and we could return to the days where abortion was illegal and unsafe.

Doesn't everybody take pictures before radiation?

Out to dinner with Gloria

And then, well, I introduced some controversy when I said, "You're a hero of women's and feminist rights. But some of your causes I've questioned." As an example, I said, "I like Arnold Schwarzenegger." Whoa, big mistake! Gloria said she assumed I was referring to the lawsuit that she had brought against Governor Schwarzenegger on behalf of Rhonda Miller.

Then Gloria explained this lawsuit. She said that it was really a libel lawsuit. When Ms. Miller had come forward with allegations of sexual misconduct against the Governor, the suit alleged, the governor's office had reacted by releasing some damaging information about *another* Rhonda Miller, seeking to hurt her client's reputation. Gloria said that she was defending the right of women to testify about sexual misconduct allegations, but clarified that in this case she was suing for libel.

I couldn't quite let it rest...yet. I stated my belief that situations like this one with Governor Schwarzenegger, and other cases like O.J. Simpson and Lacey Peterson, distract the country from more important issues. I added that I wasn't demeaning the cases, they're of course important, but that we'd lost our focus on important issues of the country. Like, for example, "They could nuke the world!" I sensed that this argument could consume the rest of the show, particularly since I had mentioned the Lacey Peterson case (Gloria was representing Amber Frey), so I said, "Yeah, right, I'm gonna win an argument against Gloria Allred!" And we moved on.

I brought up the "Hooters case." Gloria was representing 55 applicants for positions at the restaurant Hooters. According to Gloria, the women were told that they needed to change into a Hooters uniform for a photo, which would be placed on the wall, and then after a short time the company would decide whether they'd be hired. The women were also told that they shouldn't have panty lines showing in the picture, suggesting they shouldn't wear underwear. But the women were being secretly videotaped while changing clothes! Gloria said that it was "outrageous" that a company could do this. She said she's very proud of the young women that they're standing up and fighting back.

I mentioned my amazement at how busy Gloria stays, wondering how much stress she must be under all the time. I asked, "Do you sleep well at night?" Gloria responded, "Yes, because I have a clear conscience. I do what I have to do."

As I watched the tape of this show with Gloria, I was pleased to see that we were discussing same-sex marriage way back in 2004. Gloria was the first in California to file a lawsuit on behalf of a same-sex couple. The suit was challenging the constitutionality of California's marriage law, which defined marriage as between a man and a woman.

Gloria compared this case to the Perez case of 1948, which challenged prevention of interracial marriage. She was clearly passionate in her conviction that gay couples should have the same rights that others have. She said that having equal marriage rights was particularly important for same-sex parents.

And, OK, we got into another little argument about this. I brought up the religious issues. I observed that there are so many dysfunctional relationships, and stated my belief that you need a mother and a father, a female and a male, to raise children. Gloria said that "this is about the law," implying that it's not a value judgment about what types of parenting situations are better for children. She said, "It's time for them to have equal rights; it's long overdue."

I couldn't let Gloria, a respected women's rights attorney, leave my show without stating again, as I had on previous shows with her, that I had always thought I was against equal rights for women because we'd have to "go down five levels" to be equal to men. As I closed the show and thanked Gloria, I said, "If nothing else, I'm exhausted!" I added that not very much intimidates me but that Gloria had today!

Unfortunately, our friendship hit a snag in the road. Nothing special, except I'm the kind of person for whom, once I consider someone a friend, it's a lifetime thing. Unlike the come-and-go "friends" that people seem to make in "LaLa Land," mine are for a lifetime. Not so in Gloria's case. Over a short period of time she suddenly became "too busy" to go out with me. And after being fairly close for ten or twelve years, I never understood how or why our friendship was dropped like that.

I wonder, though. Gloria was always an interesting interview, but a tough one. After we had known each other for a number of years, I lost the awe I once had for Gloria and was a little vocal about the types of cases she was taking on. I said earlier that I had disagreed with her opinion of Arnold Schwarzenegger when she was representing a woman who was suing him. And, in the Tiger Woods case, in which she was also involved, I didn't think he was a good guy, but to defend one of the women who was attacking him as a victim who had lost her livelihood when she became involved with Tiger and could no longer work as a PORN star... I mean, come on! I got to the point sometimes when I would give my opinion more. And, maybe it wasn't always welcome?

Peter Falk...Just One More Thing

Peter Falk was adorable. He appeared twice on my show, in 2006 and 2007, and I loved having him as a guest. But it wasn't easy to get him there! On his first appearance, I told my viewers that I have interviewed prime ministers and presidents and religious figures, and I had "less aggravation" getting them on the damn set than I did with Peter. But the funny thing is that Peter (or at least his representative) eventually called *me* after I had called him so many times!

I put "Actor/Artist/Icon" under his name when it appeared on the screen. He did so many things! We started by talking about his book which had just come out, *Just One More Thing: Stories from My Life.* I commented what an easy read his book is, compared to a lot of things I get that I don't have the energy to get through. Peter said he wrote it for people like himself—who want to get in bed, read for 12 minutes, and fall asleep with a smile on their face. He added that the stories in the book are short, which he likes. There are so many wonderful stories in this book, and he told several of them on my show.

Peter was born in New York in 1927. He couldn't get into the Army because he had a glass eye and was designated 4F. He was able to join the Merchant Marine, but said that if you're 4F you couldn't be on the crew or in the Engine department, so he became a cook. His specialty was pork chops.

Peter told us a hilarious story of his first night on the ship. When he went into his cabin his cabin mate was lying on the other bunk. Peter had a bridge with some false teeth, which he took out and placed on a table next to his bunk. Then he took his glass eye out and put it next to the teeth. By this point he could tell that his cabin mate was watching him closely. So Peter reached down and started to act like he was going to unscrew his leg, and the guy jumped down from his bunk and said, "I think I'll go get a little air."

Peter said he came back from the Merchant Marine after about a year and a half and attended college for about a semester. But he wanted more excitement. So he tried to join the Israeli Defense Force (IDF). It was against the law to sign up to fight for a foreign army, but he found out that you could go to the Roosevelt Hotel in Manhattan and sign up for the IDF. Peter said that he wasn't really passionate about Israel or Egypt, who Israel was fighting at the time. He just wanted excitement. But the war with Egypt was over in eight days before his ship sailed. So that was the end of that.

Peter was 29 when he first decided to become an actor. He described telling his father about it. Peter said, "Pop, I've made a decision. I'm gonna be an actor." His father responded, "You're gonna paint your face and make an ass of yourself for the rest of your life?" And Peter responded, "Uh, yeah." His father put out his hand and said good luck. Peter concluded this great story by saying, "He was great, my father."

Peter said that his first acting appearance was in a summer theater production of *The Pirates of Penzance*. Another of his early roles was in the Eugene O'Neill play *The Ice Man Cometh* with Jason Robards. Peter described this one as "a play about drunks."

As an off-Broadway actor, Peter was getting paid $10 a week during rehearsal and $30 a week when the play opened. But then he got his first movie role in *Murder, Inc.* And it was quite the part—he was so good in the role, in fact, that he got an Academy Award nomination for Best Supporting Actor!

With Peter Falk on my set, 2006

Peter told us a wonderful story about the Academy ceremony. He said he was sitting there expectantly as the Best Supporting Actor award presenter introduced the nominees. When the presenter said, "And the winner is, Peter..." he stood up out of his seat. But then he heard "Ustinov!" Peter was embarrassed: "So I'm sitting down now. And when I hit the seat I turned to the press agent and said, 'You're fired.'"

Of course we had to talk about Peter's best-known, and what I termed "fabulous," character, Columbo. Peter confirmed that it was true that he got temporarily barred from the Universal Studios lot for being a troublemaker before shooting even started. He said that he liked Columbo because he "did not wear his brains on his sleeve. He was a very ordinary guy."

I laughed about how "well-dressed" he was on *Columbo*. He told us how he didn't like the original wardrobe selected for the character (winter suits, summer suits, driving jacket, etc.) He said everybody wore that kind of stuff and he wanted something unique for the character. So, he told them to dye one of the suits brown, and then he went home and got his raincoat. And that became the distinctive Columbo look!

I asked Peter what characteristics he shares with Columbo, and he responded that they both have an obsessive quality. Like Columbo, Peter won't give up until he finds the answer. He also said that he used to talk to his character and tell him what a great detective he was.

Peter had a few other stories about movies and acting. He told us why he wasn't in *The Godfather*. He said he had trouble finding his part when he read the script. He even joked to the producer that he was having a P.I. come in to help him find it. The part only had two lines! When I asked Peter why they didn't change the script for him, just because it was *him*, he said, "Maybe you should have been my agent." Great sense of humor this man had! Peter also told my viewers that they had to read his book to find out why Marlon Brando wore a plug in his ear when acting.

Peter was also a wonderful artist, and he brought some of his work to the show. Most of the pictures were drawings of women. They were gorgeous! I told him that his work reminded me of a cross between Degas and Toulouse-Lautrec, but when I said "Degas" I pronounced it as if it rhymed with "Vegas." We got a chuckle about that, and he told us a story about Degas. He was paid a million francs for a single painting, an astronomical sum in his day. Degas was asked what it felt like, and he responded that he felt like the horse who's won the Kentucky Derby and they feed him the same old bag of oats.

Peter said he didn't start seriously drawing until he was grown. He said he had always liked drawing but thought that it was "cheating" to look at the subject. He thought you had to do it all in your imagination.

He then told the great story about how he found out it was "OK to look." He was in Serbia with Burt Lancaster shooting *Castle Keep*. A Yugoslavian architect/sculptor came to his room for coffee and saw a picture he had drawn of his leather valise, which Peter had worked on at night after each day's shooting. He told Peter that it was pretty good, and Peter said "Thanks, but I cheated." When the Yugoslavian asked Peter what he meant, Peter responded that he had needed to look at the valise while drawing it, and he thought that was cheating. So this guy corrected his misperception and told him it was all right to look! "Maybe I'm just stupid," Peter said to me. I quickly corrected another misperception of this clearly brilliant man and said, "No, maybe just a bit naïve."

The year after shooting *Castle Keep* Peter was doing a stage play in New York. His hotel was on 56th Street. He was out walking one night and saw The Art Students' League on 57th Street, and for some reason decided to go inside. Nobody was there it seemed. Peter quietly opened a door, and, as he put it, "There she was." Peter saw a beautiful naked model posing on a pedestal. The art students were drawing her. Peter said to himself, "This is where I'm gonna be tomorrow morning!" And that's when he started taking drawing classes.

I was absolutely delighted when he sent me of his paintings. The inscription said "To Arlene, My Thanks, Peter Falk."

Peter was also very proud of his wife, Shera; they were married for over 30 years. I quoted his dedication in the book: "To my lovely wife, light of my life, and all the dogs." He included a picture of her; she looked gorgeous in a bikini, and it was a recent picture!

Peter told us a great story that showed Shera's love for dogs. Their dog had gotten a thorn in his paw out in the yard, and she was trying to get it out. A tour bus came by, and the tour director said, "How's Peter?" She was so concerned trying to help the dog and didn't want to be bothered that she responded, "He died this morning."

He told another story about the time he came home and his Emmy statues were missing, which was odd because they had been sitting in the same place for years. So he yelled out, "Shera, where are the Emmies?" and she responded "Upstairs in Aunt Linnie's room!" Peter went upstairs and discovered that Shera was using them for wig stands! I didn't ask who "Aunt Linnie" was...

"Just one more" with Peter

Peter was also arrested several times internationally, but never in the U.S. He said that the first time he was arrested was in Havana, Cuba. One day he was walking a few blocks from his hotel and a car screeched up. Two guys got out, threw him down and pinned him to the ground, and then tossed him into the car. Peter said he was actually relieved when the car pulled up in front of a police station, because that hopefully meant they weren't going to kill him. The officers couldn't speak English and he couldn't speak Spanish. They took his wallet and passport and drove him back to the hotel, where they talked to the concierge, who could speak some English. He explained to Peter that they thought he might have been one of Castro's men. In those days Peter had a big black beard and a mass of black hair. Castro and his men were up in the hills at the time. And three days later they invaded and took over the country.

At one point in our first interview, Peter leaned back in his chair and the table between us, on which his book was sitting, fell over. And we just kept on going!

I was so disappointed when we ran out of time on the first show that I said he had to come back, and he said "OK." And he did, and I was thrilled! Peter was a brilliant actor and artist, a true icon. I wish by some miracle he could come back just one more time!

Arlene Peck...I Am My Own Celebrity

Occasionally someone horrible cancels their guest appearance on my show at the last minute. As you can imagine, it isn't easy to get a celebrity at the last second. So, one time when this happened, who did I decide to book? Me! And Readers, it is not easy being in front of a camera for 30 minutes when you are not prepared. I sat there like a deer in headlights when the cameras started. I introduced myself saying, "Today we have someone fabulous and flawless who has a television show, has been in movies— but never any good ones." As I continued bragging about myself I sat there thinking, "Oh my G-d, what am I going to talk about?"

I said, "This is my favorite guest in the whole world. She is someone I love the best—except maybe G-d. She never disappoints." I continued with a description of myself. "I was married, had 3 children. For several years of marriage I was 'a pot roast' and today I am a chateaubriand. I was born in the South, but G-d knows, I never did fit in. I never spoke Southern, and I grew up in the shadow of Laura Ashley. So I ended up in Los Angeles. Here, I like the weather and I like the people."

After my self-introduction I began to talk about men and relationships. I introduced my topic saying, "As I think about men and relationships, I have to say that men have the attention span of a gnat. I think finding a good man is like finding a parking spot at the mall. You drive around and around and all the ones that are left are handicapped spaces. All the men I met in Atlanta were gay, married, or dead...and sometimes they were all three."

I continued on. "I personally feel men would be one of our national resources if they could just get their act

221

together. I think we have emasculated them in our efforts to make them sensitive by wanting them to go shopping with us. I, personally, don't want a man to go shopping with me, because I think a man will only be looking for a chair in the store."

I added, "We also want men to talk to us, but they don't have a woman's support system or a woman's curiosity. Women go the bathroom to put on lipstick and leave knowing the whole life story of the other women who were applying lipstick beside her." I told a story about when my "then husband" and I were at a holiday party, and I mentioned to him his secretary's sad situation, with her husband leaving her and her burden of dealing with her sick mother. He looked at me, mouth open, and said, "When did you hear all that?" I replied, "She told me as we were going through the buffet line." He said, "She's been my secretary three years and I didn't know she had a husband or a mother." Men!

I also questioned why men do the things they do. For instance, they will take you out, show you a wonderful time, but won't call after the date, even though they had said they would. I told my viewers that in these situations I want to believe my date had been kidnapped by al Qaeda bandits and as a result lost my number.

Whether in L.A. or Atlanta, finding a good man is truly like putting a saddle on a cow. You work and work and finally get it on the creature. You then look and say, "What's the use?" Women in L.A. are 45 years old and think they want to have a child. To which I say, "Why have both of you in diapers at the same time?" In the South, it seems that everyone has grandchildren no matter what their age! I have noticed another difference between L. A. and Southern women: every L.A. woman is so "nipped and tucked" that pool parties have more plastic in the pool than at a Tupperware party. In Atlanta, the plastic is used at Target and Macy's.

When women in L.A. and Atlanta ask me where to travel to meet men, I say, "Never go on cruises, because there are only senior citizens and travel agents. Go to Italy and Israel where men look at women as a national treasure."

I ended this show with a quote from my mother, Queen Molly, who said, "It's better to be a 'has been' than a 'never was'."

Do I look like a celebrity?

Arnold...Need I Say More?

Arnold Schwarzenegger and I sat next to each other an entire evening during the Milton Berle Celebrity Golf Tournament at La Costa. I had been invited as Milton Berle's guest.

We were at this fund-raising event because Milton's wife had recently died of breast cancer. This tournament was held in honor of his wife to raise money for the Breast Cancer Foundation. So, with that in mind, I thought it very tacky when Milton brought a woman with him as his date. He introduced her to the crowd as his "interior designer." For heaven's sake, his wife had just died, all her friends were there, and he brought in his designer/date? I don't remember too much of the evening, but I do recall that she was tall and a little zaftig, about forty-five years his junior. I believe she was blonde, very blonde and wore a low-cut red dress, red stockings and red shoes...so out of style. Anyway, it wasn't long after that I read he had married her.

A few years later, I invited Milton to be a guest on my television show. He accepted and gave me his home number to call and schedule a time. When I called, I got his wife, the "debutante," on the phone. She quizzed me on why I was calling. She became hostile and said something about not allowing him to go on cable shows. She was really terrible; she reminded me of something out of a Jackie Collins novel—one of those Hollywood wives who have no life or identity unless they are "Mrs. Somebody."

Milton had always been polite and very nice to me when we met, but I had seen him act lewdly to casual strangers. He was the epitome of the dirty old man. Once, I was meeting Patricia Marciano for lunch. She had recently been divorced from Armand Marciano of GUESS jeans.

Patricia is French and very refined. Milton was sitting next to us, so I introduced Patricia to him. For some unknown reason, Milton kept mentioning during his conversation with Patricia his reputation for having the biggest sexual organ in Hollywood. She told him she thought he was a disgusting, dirty old man. Milton thought that very funny; we didn't. Anyway, since she was so French and totally oblivious to the nuances that were being directed at her, it didn't go any further. But, to tell the truth, that experience shattered my image of the "Uncle Miltie" I remembered from childhood, staying up late to watch him on television.

Somehow, Miltie's older brother took a liking to me and invited me to join their table for the dinner the evening of the tournament. Since he was long past driving age—at that time, I believe, he was one year younger than G-d—he picked me up in a golf cart and we headed towards the dinner. That is where I first saw Arnold Schwarzenegger. What a force! The man doesn't walk into a room, he swaggers. Truly. Anyway, that was in the early nineties and I'm sure that memorable moment for me is less than a blur for him.

With Arnold Schwarzenegger at Milton Berle's celebrity golf tournament, La Costa, 1992

Since those years, Arnold and I crossed paths several times; these occasions were completely unmemorable for him, but, oh, they lingered in my memory! I always enjoyed our chance encounters at a restaurant, Café Roma in Beverly Hills, where he was often dining with Ralf Moeller. I always thought of each of these guys as a "Mountain of a Man." Ralf, like Arnold, was Mr. Universe a few times, and let me tell you, neither had lost his looks or sex appeal. It took me a year of trying, but I was finally able to get Ralf as a guest on my show. It was shortly after he filmed "The Gladiator." Remember the big guy who was the friend of Russell Crowe? That was him. On my show that day, I remember my introduction of Ralf quite well. I looked across the set at this gorgeous man and said, "I know the reason I do this show. In fact, if I forget to ask questions, you women... and men, (if you live in West Hollywood), can just look."

Anyway, back to Arnold...

At "our" restaurant, Café Roma, I always sat at my usual table, and Arnold sat in the corner at the "power table" with his industry friends. Our tables were within 10 feet of each other. One beautiful day, we were sitting at our respective tables and were facing each other. I couldn't resist; Arnold's buddies couldn't see me because I was sitting behind them, so I winked at Arnold. He winked back at me with a smile. I threw him an air kiss across the room. He blew back three more to me. After that I mouthed the words, "I love you." He mouthed back, "I love you more." After that there were more mouth kisses blown back and forth through the air between the both of us, all in good fun. However, eventually it captured the attention of one of his tablemates, who turned to me and asked, "What in the hell are you doing?" Arnold smiled and said, within my hearing distance, "That woman is coming on to me. They all do. They don't let me breathe." Then he leaned back, laughed and said, "I can't help it. It's a curse."

Listening to this, I caught the eye of his buddy and mouthed the words, "It's in his head." And I circled my head with my finger and shook my head, "No." His buddy then said, "You're really after *me*, aren't you?" And I said, "Yeah, I just love men with beards." Then everybody laughed.

I remember a couple of times while Arnold was governor of California I was in my back yard in Marina Del Rey and Arnold would cut through the yard on his bike, which was right on the path. He had one body guard in front and one in the back; I recognized them from Café Roma. I would raise my arm and yell, "Hi Arnold!" Arnold always raised his hand and responded "Hi."

Arnold never knew that I defended him in conversation with my friend Gloria Allred when she came out of the woodwork to sue him. He also never knew the lingering memories I have of him—and it's probably a good thing he didn't! On the other hand, this story might get to him soon!

The Who...Who Knew?

It was in the fall of 1982, and I believe at the time it was being billed as The Who's last concert tour. However, back then, I didn't know or care "who" they were. All I cared about at the time was making sure that two fifteen-year-old girls had a good time on their school vacation at Disney World. You see, I had schlepped my daughter, Dana, and her best friend, Julie, to every ride, concession, and food stand at the "happiest place on earth." Finally, after a long, busy day, we went back to the Hyatt where we were staying. I was exhausted and had every intention of sleeping until the next day. However, Dana and Julie had no intention of resting or letting me rest. So I sent them away to the game room in the hotel with orders not to go anywhere else.

Shortly thereafter, I woke to them shaking me excitedly saying, "The Who are here! The Who are here!" To which I replied groggily, "Who in the hell are The Who?" They pulled me out of bed and filled me in, not only on the history of The Who but also what the two of them had been doing the last hour. It seems the rock group was appearing in concert the following day at the Tangerine Bowl. It seemed that no one knew that they were at the hotel, except, of course, my child and her friend. The girls had passed by the bar and had seen several of the band members heading inside. However, since my girls were most definitely under age, they rushed back to the room to get me.

The girls informed me that if everything went according to plan, I would go downstairs and into the bar to talk to The Who with the intention of luring them into extending an invitation for their upcoming concert. Their first task was to get me up and dressed. There was a little disagreement about which outfit would be the "sexiest." I swear to G-d, I felt as though I was being pimped out by two 15-year-old nymphets. I think I ended up wearing a sweater that was much too tight and a skirt that was much too short. After my girls selected some tacky earrings, they decided that I was ready to be viewed by The Who, and I was soon heading down to the elevator with the girls right behind me.

While my girls were hyperventilating, I entered an almost empty bar trying not to act like the hooker I felt I looked like. A few minutes later, a man walked over, introduced himself as the manager of the group, and asked if I'd like to join their table. I glanced at the door, where the girls were hiding, smiled and asked, "How can I refuse?"

After sitting at their table a short time, one of the members of The Who asked if I was a "working girl." Readers, the moron that I was, and dressed as I was, I still had no idea what that meant! So, I smiled brightly and said, "Yes, I work for syndicated newspapers." That got a laugh and they said, "Great. We'll arrange for you to sit in the press box at the stadium tomorrow to see our concert." I knew my girls would be pleased; as for me, the only other concerts that I had attended, at that time, were Little Richard and Elvis Presley.

So, I accepted the invitation on behalf of my girls who, by this time, thought they had died and gone to heaven. Since it was my first "rock" concert, I had absolutely no idea what to expect. Dana and Julie began to pick outfits two hours before show time. I had a feeling that it wouldn't really matter what they were wearing. I was sooo right.

This concert was probably one of the scariest things I've ever attended. Truly, there were 70,000 crazed teenagers there, and some of them were peeing in the aisles. Thankfully, we were able to watch the show from the press box at the Tangerine Bowl. I was amazed at the thousands of arms waving below. I briefly wondered if that was how Hitler got his start. Oh, and I have to mention…my eardrums were almost bleeding from the noise.

We did go backstage to say good-bye and, actually, all the members of The Who were very nice. I learned that they were playing the following day at the U.S. Women's Soccer team match. This concert was to be a surprise appearance by The Who and had not been publicized. I said I'd meet them at the field, and we did! But frankly, they were so English I couldn't understand half of what they said. Remember, I'm a "Southern Girl"! On the cover of this book you can see a picture of me with The Who's lead singer Roger Daltrey. I think it was taken before or after the band's show at the soccer match.

A couple of nights later my phone rang in Atlanta and my daughter came into my room shouting, "Mom, a guy from The Who is on the phone, calling for *you!!*" Not wanting to embarrass myself too much, I found myself asking the gentleman on the line, "Were you the one in the red polyester suit who kept jumping up and down, or were you the one with the white pants, messy hair and torn shirt that was such a fashion statement, who kept shouting into the microphone?" Not understanding that funny English accent, I looked questioningly at my daughter, who explained to me that he was the drummer who was inviting me to come and see him in Dallas where they were playing next. Readers, I do keep a packed suitcase, but when it comes to men, I also have a rule I try not to break. I never want to become involved with any man who wears more make-up, has longer hair, or has a smaller tushie than me. This drummer had all three.

As a footnote to this story, I want to give you an idea of what a moron I still am when it comes to The Who. When I sent my synopsis about The Who over to the famous author, Mark Bego, to give me his opinion of my proposed book, he wrote back with his suggestions. One of them concerned my alleged "sort of" involvement with The Who's drummer Keith Moon. Mark loved the content of my story; however, he informed me that, in the 1980s, it would have been difficult to meet Keith Moon, as he had died in 1978. So, I called my daughter Dana, all grown up now, and relayed to her his comment. There was a pause while I think she was suppressing laughter, and Dana said, "He's right...you never met Keith Moon...it was Kenny Jones who was calling you."

G-d knows...it's not easy being a sex goddess.

Jonathan and Annie Pollard...
Unjustly Imprisoned

Jonathan Pollard was a civilian intelligence analyst for the U.S. Navy when he was arrested in 1985 for passing classified documents to Israel. He was charged, in other words, with being a spy for Israel. As evidence in the trial showed, for over a year in 1984-85, and as Pollard ultimately admitted, he had removed large amounts of classified information from his office, made copies of the documents, and passed them on to Israeli representatives. Pollard eventually pleaded guilty and was sentenced to life in prison. In November 2015, when Pollard became eligible for parole according to the sentencing guidelines in place at the time of his conviction, he was finally released.

Many in Israel had always considered Pollard's punishment to be too harsh. Pollard was, and still is, the only American to be given a life sentence for spying for an ally. Negotiations between Israel and the U.S. for his early release occurred on several occasions during his 30 years in prison. But the U.S. negotiators, strongly influenced by present and past officials at the CIA, the FBI, and the Justice Department, eventually backed down every time. At the time of his sentencing, Caspar Weinberger had warned of the great harm to national security that had been caused by Pollard's actions, and Weinberger's unjustifiable opinions remained influential over the years.

After a time, though, many powerful people in the U.S., including many members of Congress, began to advocate for Pollard's release. Their influence, and perhaps the desire on the part of the U.S. to ease its frostier relations with

Israel following the signing of the nuclear deal with Iran, surely contributed to his being granted parole.

I even got involved in trying to secure Jonathan's release. In 2002 I sent a letter to "Bibi" Netanyahu, who I had met on several occasions and had interviewed for one of my newspaper articles. In the letter I encouraged Netanyahu to continue his efforts on Pollard's behalf and offered to provide any additional support I could.

Pollard always cited a love of Israel as his justification for his actions. He also continually maintained that he had only passed on information that was essential for Israel's own security and that the U.S. was withholding from Israel. Pollard was paid many thousands of dollars for providing the documents. Since his arrest Israel has admitted to its role in Pollard's espionage and apologized to the U.S.

But Jonathan was not the only Pollard imprisoned. His wife, Anne, was also sentenced to five years in prison for possession of classified documents that her husband had brought to their apartment. She served a term of about three and a half years when she was released to serve the remainder of her term on parole because of a stomach condition and other health problems.

The Pollard case received much more extensive coverage in Israel than in the U.S. over the years, and I always followed the news closely. But I didn't fully appreciate the human tragedy of their situation until Anne came into my life. In 1990, when Anne had just been released from her prison term and subsequent parole, she became friends with my daughter Dana, who was living in Israel at the time. They were taking Hebrew classes together. I remember when Dana would call me and would mention her new friend Anne whose husband was in jail. Anne came back to Los

Angeles with Dana soon afterwards, and over a period of several years she was my houseguest on several occasions.

During this period I got to know Anne, and she opened up with me about her period of incarceration. In 1992 I wrote an article about Annie, as I had come to call her, in which I relayed some of her prison difficulties. Annie was transferred *eight* times to different federal prisons, including three times to the all-male facility in Rochester, MN. She was particularly vocal about the treatment she received at Rochester. Annie recalled that when she arrived there the warden said, "We're gonna fix your ass, Pollard." She told me that she was constantly watched, with someone sitting outside her cell 24 hours a day, making notes about her every move. And she long maintained that her health problems were a direct result of the treatment she received while in prison.

I also mentioned good old Caspar Weinberger in this article. In his attacks on the Pollards, Weinberger raised the issue of dual loyalty—that any American Jew loyal to the Pollards would be considered disloyal to this country. At the time of the article, Weinberger had recently been indicted for his role in the Iran/Contra affair. When I mentioned this to Annie, she said, "What goes around, comes around. I hope that justice will prevail this time around."

Annie said that she was advised by the prosecutors and her own attorney to testify against Jonathan, but she refused. She also said that she could have gotten an earlier release if she had agreed to divorce Jonathan and agreed to condemn Israel, as the U.S. Parole Board asked her to do when she came up for parole.

Ironically and sadly, soon after Annie's release Jonathan divorced her. She was in the emergency room at Mt. Sinai in New York, getting treatment for her stomach condition, and a man dressed as a hospital orderly came and dropped divorce papers in her lap. Annie couldn't believe that after refusing to divorce Jonathan under pressure, she ultimately found herself divorced.

With Annie Pollard at my house in Marina Del Rey, 1992

At that time Annie speculated that members of Jonathan's immediate family were involved in encouraging Jonathan to divorce her. She showed me many beautiful and sensitive love letters Jonathan had sent her from prison. She said that the only people allowed to visit him in prison were his father, mother, and sister, along with a rabbi. Annie felt that the rabbi in particular influenced Jonathan in the direction of divorce and suggested that his family members also had a part in his decision.

In 2003 I wrote another article, "The Truth About Pollard," soon after I saw a play in Los Angeles called *The 11th Hour* starring my friend Ed Asner. In the article I told how I had learned through my relationship with Annie the deplorable conditions under which her husband was being held. And I said that our government had for years "promised his release and never kept their word." I told of my recent dinner with Jonathan's father, Dr. Morris Pollard, who had understood that Bill Clinton had reached an agreement with Bibi Netanyahu to release Jonathan at the Wye Accords meetings, yet didn't follow through. Clinton instead pardoned Marc Rich, a million-dollar donor to the Clinton Foundation.

I understood that for years the world had apathetically condoned Jonathan's imprisonment. Yes, I knew all that and more, as I told my readers. But *The 11ᵗʰ Hour* opened my eyes about the role that Israel had played in Pollard's arrest. For this play didn't cast aspersions on the usual suspects such as Caspar Weinberger, but suggested that Israel itself was the culprit. For the Israeli government, represented by Rafi Eitan, betrayed Jonathan's trust and turned the Pollards over to the American authorities. Jonathan began dealing with Eitan and others at the Israeli Embassy when he knew the U.S. Federal government was after him. Jonathan had been told, "Israel takes care of our own. We will bring you and Anne to Israel." It had been suggested to him that certain "Laws of Return" might apply and that "We'll work some sort of deal." Yet, when Jonathan and Annie were followed by federal agents to the gates of the Israeli Embassy in Washington, Israel turned their backs on them.

At the time of that article Jonathan had been in jail for years. I asked readers why Israel wasn't doing more to protest Pollard's inhuman incarceration. For how many years had he been in solitary confinement? And I also said, "Those who did far more, those who gave secrets, which he never did, and things that were injurious to America received far better treatment and were released many years earlier." The culpability for Pollard's poor treatment lay with both the U.S. and Israel.

In the article I argued that some of the documents Jonathan passed along to Israel concerned Saddam Hussein's plans to kill Israelis, information that the U.S. should have already been providing to Israel. If he hadn't done so, how many Jews would have been killed?

Around the year 2000 or so, I pitched a movie about the Pollard case to Hollywood producers but was told "the time isn't right." I remember thinking, "When is the time right?"

Even though Jonathan has finally been released, as I look back on the Pollard story I am still sad. I remember one of the meetings I had with Dr. Morris Pollard. He told me that, soon after Jonathan married his second wife, Esther Zeitz, she made him cut all ties with his family. Dr. Pollard told me that from the day she came into the prison to meet his son, she was able to pull him away from his family, and they hadn't been able to speak with him since. Dr. Pollard continued by saying how his wife had died broken-hearted because she was never able to see or contact Jonathan after that. And he still mourned the loss of his wife—and son.

I believe that Jonathan Pollard served over 30 years in prison unjustly. It was a travesty that he was put in jail to begin with, especially for such a long period. Many of the documents that he provided to Israel, an ally of the U.S., contained information we should have already been providing anyway. Jonathan was a young man in his thirties when he entered prison and an old man in his sixties when he got out.

In my years of knowing Annie Pollard I came to believe that her only crimes were refusing to testify against Jonathan, to whom she was a loyal and devoted wife, and her love of Israel. Like her husband, she suffered unjustly for doing what she thought was right.

Monty Hall...Humanitarian

Monty Hall, real name, Monte Halparin, is originally from Canada. When he was on my show, I described him as "not just another pretty face from Canada who crossed the border years ago." He told us that he had come to the States from Canada about 50 years earlier. He added that he still considers himself to be a Canadian in many respects.

I commented, "Canadians don't seem to get mad; they are always so nice. They don't even have an army." I added that if a Canadian man sees that a woman has left her jacket in a restaurant, he'd run outside with it and say, "Hey lady, you left your jacket." Monty laughed and responded, "Not me, I'd probably sell it on e-Bay."

Under Monty's name on the screen credits we described him as a "Game Show Host/Humanitarian." The man is not only an amazing game show host and humanitarian, he's also an author. He wrote a book in the early seventies called *Emcee Monty Hall*. He told us that his publisher had recently contacted him to ask if he wanted to update it. Monty replied, "You can add one chapter with one sentence: 'More of the same.'"

Monty has over <u>500</u> plaques that were given to him for his charity work. I suggested that those 500 stories could be content for a book. Monty replied that he had in fact spoken with a publisher seven or eight years previously regarding the possibility of doing a book about his charity work. Monty had talked with the publisher about some of his experiences, relating tales such as the royalty he'd met over the years (including Prince Charles and Prince Phillip) and other stories he thought might be interesting for readers. But it became clear to Monty that the publisher wanted a kiss-and-tell book, with insider stuff on Hollywood. Monty said,

"You're not gonna get that from me." As to the plaques, we joked that anytime he did a benefit after that he could give *them* a plaque!

Monty is still the international chairman for Variety, the Children's Charity. He told us the story of how he got involved with Variety. The night he got married, his wife's father, who was a charter member of the Toronto chapter of Variety, said to him, "You take care of my daughter, and join the Variety Club." "Why?" Monty asked (meaning, of course, why join the charity, not why take care of his daughter!) His new father-in-law responded, "Because it deals with children and people in the entertainment business. You love children and you're in the entertainment business." And, Monty said, "I've spent the next 59 years doing it."

That's right, at the time of this interview, Monty had been married for 59 years, and they are now approaching their 70th anniversary! His wife, Marilyn, was a producer. Monty told a great story about when she was working on *A Woman Called Golda*, with Ingrid Bergman starring as Golda Meir. Monty was flipping through the script and said, "Hey there's a part here for me; there's an American senator who goes to visit Golda in Jerusalem. I could play the American senator." Marilyn said "Did you read the whole script? There's a line where Golda says to him, 'Senator, Let's make a deal.'" Monty realized that if he played the role, when the audience heard those words from him they would become distracted. So Monty let it drop.

It was clear on the show that Monty is a very proud father. All of his children are in the entertainment business. His son, Richard, is a reality show producer for shows such as *The Amazing Race*. His daughter, Joanna Gleason, acts on Broadway and received a Tony Award for her role in *Into the Woods*. Monty mentioned that her most recent performance had been in *Dirty Rotten Scoundrels*. His other daughter is a Senior Vice President at Sony.

With Monty Hall on my set, 2007

But this proud father also has a great sense of humor. He said that his kids are "all in the business, all doing great, and none of them send money home. I always say, I've got writers, actors, producers, so on...I didn't get one dentist! I could have used a dentist." I told him that I, too, wanted one of my children to be a dentist; but none chose this profession.

We talked about what was happening in television, with shows like *Desperate Housewives* in which everybody is jumping in and out of each other's bed. We both concluded it was just a reflection of society. I asked Monty what current shows he watched, and he mentioned *Brothers and Sisters*, particularly because he likes Sally Field. But, he added, "All they do is whine." He said he was getting tired of shows about dysfunctional families that you're supposed to identify with and enjoy. "Where are the great dramas that we enjoy and love?" he asked.

We talked about a few of the successful "talent" shows like *American Idol*. Monty said that they used to have amateur hour shows, but they were never really successes. But, with *American Idol*, they let the audience at home pick the winner. That was the key to its success.

I said that I go to the theater a lot, but nobody in the audience is ever under 60 years old. Monty said that they're probably watching TV, noting that the TV executives program for younger people. I commented that it's like they're designed for people with the IQ of an eggplant.

We discussed the challenges of hosting a television show. I commented, "You have to be careful what you say. When I say, I don't give a 'diddlysquat,' producers tell me I can't use the word 'diddlysquat' on air, and I ask, 'Why not?'"

When I asked Monty if he still travels a lot, he said he had been doing so until recently, when Marilyn put her foot down. Monty was the host of *Let's Make a Deal* on TV for 27 years. In recent years they had been doing the show in casinos and hotels around the country. Monty said people were coming by the thousands, many dressed in costumes, just like the audience members did on the show. Monty's agent called him one day to talk about the next three casinos they'd be doing. Marilyn was standing beside the phone, shaking her head and running her finger across her neck, as if she were saying "cut it." Monty said to his agent, "You'd better talk to the boss."

Monty talked about the tennis tournament for diabetes that he hosts, which at the time was in its 35th year. The three-day tournament has raised millions of dollars. He has been bestowed with The Office of the Order of Canada by the Canadian Prime Minister for his humanitarian work in Canada and other nations of the world. Four children's wings or floors of hospitals have Monty's name on them: in

Toronto and Philadelphia, and at Johns Hopkins and UCLA. Monty said that he did children's telethons and benefits for so many years and they repaid him with this honor, which, he said is "just wonderful."

Monty had discussed all of these accolades with such grace and humility. So I commented on how humble he is, and he responded, "Not that humble." I said, "But you're gracious, generous, and professional." He said that charities have been his life. He added that his priorities have always been family first, charities second, and career third.

I asked Monty to give us some closing words in 10 seconds are less. He thought for a moment and said, "My grandchildren are brilliant!" What a great way to close the show; I hope those lucky grandchildren were watching!

With Monty at a Hugh Hefner party, 1991

Stan Lee...Stan the Man!

I introduced Stan Lee as an "amazing icon who's been called a prince among men." I added, "I didn't even like comic books, but Stan Lee, how could you not? The man is wonderful, an absolutely adorable person." Stan created Marvel Comics, with wonderful characters such as the Incredible Hulk, Spider-Man, and the Fantastic Four. I held up Stan's book, *Stan Lee and the Rise and Fall of the American Comic Book*, and said that for me to read a whole book—or at least most of it—really said something about the author!

Stan said, "You were so complimentary with those things you were saying, I couldn't wait to see who you had as your guest! I couldn't believe it was me." Yes, Stan is amazing, but he's also very humble and sarcastically self-effacing. When I said how good he looks, he said "I know, that's my stock-in-trade, the secret to my success. I look so incredibly good! The only thing is, it's awful, but that Brad Pitt is so jealous!" With the talent and personality that still oozes out of this man at his age, I wouldn't doubt it.

Stan appeared on my show in 2008. I knew that he had been married forever, like our friend Peter Mark Richman, but when I said that Peter Mark had been married 50-something years, Stan replied, "I beat him: 60." Amazing! Stan added, "We're going to stay with it until we get it right." Readers, I believe he and his wife have it right! I'm having a flashback to my grandfather, who was married for over 50 years. He once said to me that the 50th anniversary should be the iron anniversary instead of gold, because any man who can stay married to the same woman for that many years is made of iron not gold.

Stan Lee was born as Stanley Lieber to immigrant parents. His father was a dress-cutter during the Depression, and because there wasn't enough work for him Stan had to start earning money as a kid. He got his start with a news service writing obituaries for famous or at least well-known people—who were still alive! Stan said maybe you've wondered how it is that when some famous people die, a two-page write-up about them is available almost immediately. He added, "The only way you know you're famous is if your obituary is already written. I'd like to think that my obituary is already written and is ready at the Associated Press and everywhere else." But in the end he found it was too depressing to write about living people in the past tense!

Stanley Lieber "created" Stan Lee with the same wonderful imagination that created all of his wonderful stories and characters. He's been Stan Lee a lot longer than Stanley Lieber. His career as a comic book genius got its start when he took a job as an assistant with his cousin's publishing company, performing tasks such as filling ink wells and getting the writers their lunch. Eventually he became one of the writers. One day, he said, "Everybody had quit for some reason, and I was the only one there, so I was writing all the stories. It was a very strange situation."

I asked Stan how they created the comics. Stan said it was very simple: he would come up with an idea and write it, and the artist would draw it. He humbly added, "I was so lucky, they way they drew the characters was so wonderful that it drew people to them. Otherwise it would have been just a lot of words, and nobody would have been interested."

Knowing that a lot of the entertainment industry was Jewish back in the early days, I asked if that was the case with comic books. He said it was, at least for the publishers and founders of the companies, but added that a lot of the artists were Italian back then.

I commented that Stan seems to really love his work. He said, "It's not work. When you're working with people who are creative, excited, energetic—someone like you! You love doing the show, you're as big a ham as I am—it energizes you when you're with people like that."

I was thrilled with this compliment! I replied, "I know, if you can get paid for what you enjoy doing, what's better than that! I love what I'm doing; the people I meet are so interesting. And if they're not, I don't have them on the show!"

Regarding the beginnings of Marvel Comics, Stan said, "I treated the whole thing like an advertising campaign. Even in the beginning, I made up slogans like 'Make Mine Marvel,' 'Marvel Marches On,' 'Welcome to the Marvel Age of Comics.'"

Stan's partner in the creation of Spider-Man was Steve Ditko. When I commented that I had heard that Ditko doesn't like the spotlight, Stan agreed. He said that Steve "doesn't like publicity, doesn't do interviews, nobody could get him on their shows. But it's OK, I make up for all of them!"

So Stan has been a promoter for Marvel since its inception. Movies depicting Stan's characters have generated over $15 billion in worldwide box office sales. I've noticed Stan in the background or doing a "cameo" in several of his movies. He'll pop up on a street scene or in a place where you least expect to see him. In fact, in *Iron Man*, the movie based on another of his creations, I briefly caught a glimpse of him in a Hugh Hefner spot surrounded by a bevy of showgirls. Incidentally, that scene is totally different from his lifestyle.

Stan told us about a technique he used for naming some of his characters. He said he has "no memory for what he's done" (which I have a hard time believing!) so he gave them names like Bruce Banner, Peter Parker, and Reed Richards (Mr. Fantastic), with the same first letter for the first and last name. He said if he can remember one name it would give him a clue as to what the other name might be.

On my set with Stan Lee, 2008

Stan's favorite character was the Silver Surfer. He said that was his only character through which he could express his own bits of philosophy, because the Silver Surfer was a philosopher. As Stan said, "He was always commenting about the foibles of the human race." Stan explained that the Silver Surfer believed that we have heaven here on earth, with clean air, all the food we could ever want, and beautiful oceans and mountains. Yet the Surfer worried why we don't enjoy our paradise, why we fight each other, why we hate each other. But then Stan explained, "Well, not as corny as that; I spent more time crafting the words when writing it, but that was his general attitude. I was able to get across a lot of ideas that are a little deeper than you find in most comics through the Silver Surfer."

At one point we began talking about the general perception of "Hollywood People." Stan said that when he moved to L.A. from New York, everyone in New York was asking him how he could live "out there" with the "wolves" and "backstabbers." But in L.A., he said, "I have met the greatest people." And I agree!

Then he told a story about meeting one particular "Hollywood person." Stan and his wife were having dinner with Lou Ferrigno and his wife. Lou, of course, played The Incredible Hulk in the TV show based on Stan's comic, and it so happens that he was also a guest on my show. Charles Bronson walked in to the restaurant, and Stan said to his dinner guests, "Man I think he's great; I am some fan of Charles Bronson." But Bronson must have overheard Stan, because when the picture-taking girl came by (yes, they have those in L.A. restaurants) and asked if they wanted a picture taken, Stan felt a tap on his shoulder. It was Bronson asking if Stan wanted him to be in the picture. So Bronson stood behind them and they got the picture. Stan said, "I thought that was the nicest thing that a guy could do."

On the topic of pictures of famous people and my previous guests such as Lou Ferrigno, we talked a bit about Steve Allen, who was on my show many times. Stan was at an event with Steve, and had his picture taken with him, the night before Steve died. Stan still has both pictures.

Stan's comics sometimes address serious issues. He said he once got a letter from the Department of Health, Education, and Welfare in D.C. (Washington, not DC Comics!) saying that, considering how popular he was, it would be great if he could do an anti-drug story. Stan agreed, and created a three-issue series with an anti-drug message. He said that in those days you had to send your comic books to the Comic Association so they could give their "approval"; they basically censored all the comics because they're considered to be reading for children. When he sent his series to the Association, they sent it back "rejected" because the stories mentioned drugs. Stan replied, "We're not telling kids to take drugs; it's an anti-drug story!" But the censors said that you couldn't even mention drugs in comics according to "The Code."

Stan said that he was very proud of his publisher Martin Goodman, because they published all three issues without the "Code Seal," which is the seal of approval from the Association. The issues sold well, and Stan received letters of commendation from teachers and religious leaders. Also, because of those issues, the Association loosened up a little bit with the code. Or, as Stan put it, "They became a little more sane and rational."

Stan said he's always running into people who love comic books, including many famous ones. He told a funny story about sitting next to Gene Simmons of KISS on the plane. Stan said Simmons seemed to have a photographic memory; for example, he would recall a specific page and panel of "Spiderman 16." Stan said Simmons was rattling off old comic book stuff from years ago like he was reading from the comics themselves; he could remember the dialogue, the issue, the page it was on, etc. And Stan had recently been at the Jules Verne Awards when some guy had come up to him and begun quoting lined after line from the Silver Surfer, stuff that Stan had written years ago. "Some people are just incredible," Stan concluded.

I asked Stan about comic book conventions. He said he used to go to all the conventions, but not so much anymore. He said he still goes to the big San Diego convention every year. When I commented that he seems to love the spotlight, he said he's "getting used to it." Stan is always willing to sign autographs, at conventions or anywhere. I commented that some famous people don't like doing that. Stan replied, "I don't understand why people get annoyed. I think it's so flattering, and what could be easier than signing your name?"

Incidentally, Stan had a new book coming out at the time of our interview, and I showed a copy of the cover. The book, called *Election Daze*, is about the 2008 Presidential campaign.

I had referred to Stan as an icon several times, and he said "You know I'm gonna look up the word 'icon' one of these days. I have no idea what it means, but it sounds wonderful!" At another point, he said, "Wait a minute . . . this is going to be on cable? Can we start over so I can have a little more dignity?" This man and his humorous humility!

I asked Stan about children. He said that he and his wife have one daughter, and they lost one. He added that his wife couldn't have any more kids, so they spoiled their daughter rotten! Stan's daughter is an artist, jewelry designer, and, as he described her, a "real dilettante." Stan said she paints beautifully but doesn't like to sell her paintings. The same with her jewelry; she doesn't like to sell it even though a lot of people want to buy it. He said she loves the stuff she creates and wants to keep it.

As we were nearing the end of our time, Stan said that he had to go. He explained that he still has responsibilities with Marvel even though he's "only Chairman Emeritus." I said, "Just five more minutes?" and he responded, "OK, but if I'm late with this thing for Marvel, I'll tell them to call you." I said, "What, are they gonna fire you?" He shot back jokingly, "No, they'll fire you!"

I asked Stan for some final words of wisdom. He said, "I sign my name at the end of comics with the word 'Excelsior!', which means upward and onward to greater glory." He said that this word is also on the seal of the State of New York. And Stan closed our wonderful interview by saying, "Excelsior!" How can you top that?!

Sometime in the winter of 2016 I received a Costco magazine, one of the few places I get mail from other than Bed Bath & Beyond, but I digress. On the cover of the magazine was a picture of Stan entitled "Marvel Man: A Graphic Journey with Comic Stan Lee." The first thing I noticed when I opened the magazine was a picture of Stan arriving on a motorcycle at a premiere of *The Avengers* in L.A., which is unusual for a 90-year-old man! It reminded me of when he arrived at my studio wearing a brown leather bomber jacket, which he had worn when riding his motorcycle to the interview. He accidentally left the jacket at the studio. I told him I'd return it to him if he'd put me on his party list. I said, "Don't worry about leaving the jacket, that sort of thing happens when you get older."

Readers, I hope you now understand my reference to "Stan the Man"— which he will always be to me!

Joe Bologna...The Italian Stallion

Joe Bologna was on my show a couple of times, one of which was with the baseball player José Canseco. As I mentioned in my story about José, I was almost hyperventilating looking at this gorgeous man sitting across from me. I described Joe as "an oldie but goodie, like me, who I've always had a crush on, one of the reasons I've always liked Italian men." As we started the interview, he said, "Damn," and then asked, "Can I say 'damn' on your show?" He then commented that he hoped that we could keep the show clean, and I responded, "I hope not."

Joe has been married for over 50 years to Renée Taylor, who played Sylvia Fine, the mother of Fran Drescher's character, on the TV series *The Nanny*. Together, they have written numerous screenplays. They received an Emmy for *Acts of Love and Other Comedies* and an Oscar nomination for the movie adaptation of their Broadway play *Lovers and Other Strangers*. He made light of these accomplishments, saying, "If you have been in the business as long as me and don't have a few awards, something is wrong." I responded, "Well, I know a lot of people who've been in the business as long as you, and nobody knows who they are today."

Joe and Renée co-wrote and starred in a play called *The Bermuda Avenue Triangle*. I had recently seen the play and thought it was hysterical. Lainie Kazan, who I've written about elsewhere in this book, was also in the play. I had also seen the play when it premiered ten years previously, with Bea Arthur starring as the character played by Lainie in the current production.

I observed to Joe that he has a lot of movies to be proud of, and added that he "doesn't do crappy stuff." Joe said that there's a bottom line for him that has nothing to do with morality, because everybody's morality is different. He has to decide what he can do that will allow him to sleep at night. As an actor, Joe said, you don't want to perform something bad, where you're not connected or you're unreal, where you have to do something you don't believe in. But he added that actors are also professionals. He said sometimes he'll review a script, and think that it's not the greatest thing but also not the worst, and it pays well, so he takes the part. But then "every now and then you get something to do and it's a joy."

He said that, with Renée, as playwrights, "it's the best of us; that's it, it's the best we can write; like you say in sports, we leave nothing in the locker room."

Perhaps to contrast some of the movies I'd seen recently with the high-quality films Joe is usually involved with, I had to mention that every movie I see now has a peeing scene and someone throwing up. I added that the horror scenes used to be the car crashes, but now there's a movie with Kathy Bates and Jack Nicholson butt naked! Talking about nude shots in movies, I said if I ever did one, they would tell me to put it back on! Joe told a funny story about Renée in the 1960's. After she was asked to do a partially nude scene, she responded, "Absolutely not; I go totally nude or no nudity at all."

Joe has performed in dozens of movie and television roles since the 1970s; he's one of those actors who you'll see in something, and you know they've been in a lot of things, but you can't remember from where. For the life of me I watched him for years and never knew his name.

While we were discussing José's book about steroid use in major league baseball, Joe joked, "I take steroids before every performance. Isn't it obvious? That's why I have such a nice tush." I said it's because he's Italian.

Backstage at my studio with Joe Bologna, 2006

Joe made a few more comments about drug use in sports, Hollywood, and the world at large. He said he loves baseball and wants it to be a level playing field. But he added that in the entertainment business actors and actresses are taking all kinds of drugs, and it doesn't affect their careers whatsoever. And the same is true with lawyers, doctors, and other people in important and respected professions. Joe commented, "I'd rather have baseball players taking drugs than some doctor who's getting ready to operate on me. But you never hear about that. In the limelight as an athlete you're much more harshly judged than other people."

I asked Joe if he preferred acting in theater or the movies, and he responded that he prefers whichever one allows him to be the freest to create. He said that he had recently finished a movie called *Boynton Beach Club*, directed by Susan Seidelman. Joe said that he had a good working relationship with her; he was able to develop the character with her and "do a piece of work." He added that in the theater it's easier to do that. And, obviously, when he and

Renée write their own stuff, they're free to create from the beginning.

I asked Joe about what it was like doing a voice character in *Ice Age*. He said that when he's doing live acting, if a director says to do something he doesn't agree with and doesn't think is going to work, he doesn't do it, because he has a good sense of what works and what doesn't. But in animation, it's totally different. It's the animator's characters, or "actors," and the voice person is just an effect. If the animator tells him to raise his voice, to do it faster, or whatever, he does it. He said that with animation you have to remember that you're not the character; you've got to work to the animator's vision.

I commented that you are not allowed to get old in L.A. Joe told me, "The trick is to always have the camera above you so the folds in your chin and neck can't be seen." This reminded me of the time I had a brain tumor and needed surgery. I asked the surgeon if he could do a little "nip and tuck" while I was "under." He replied haughtily, "I am not a plastic surgeon, I am a neurologist." My daughter assured me that, at that moment, I did not want to piss him off. Later, I had this same neurologist on my show. I thanked him for saving my life, but I did ask, "Couldn't you have pulled it up a little while you were there?" pointing to my face. Since my brain surgery was over, I felt it was safe to tell him what I had really wanted!

Joe responded with a story about coming to California as a young kid from Brooklyn. He said he went to the pool soon after he arrived, and the first dialogue he heard, really the first California conversation he ever heard, was at that pool between two women. One woman said, "I like your eyes," and added, "Rubenstein?" The other women answered, "No, Schwartz." Joe said his wife jokes that she is forever being stalked by plastic surgeons in L.A.

I know Joe is Italian, but I asked him if he ever played any Jewish characters other than the rabbi in an episode of the TV series based on the book *Chicken Soup for the Soul.* Joe said that he and Renée had played Holocaust survivors in a show called *Everwood.* On the Italian-Jewish connection, I said, "Jewish and Catholic mothers are the same: Italian shame, Jewish guilt. I think Italian and Israeli men are the last men in the world who truly like women!" But on a more serious note, I mentioned that I had been to Auschwitz, how powerful it was, and how important it had been for me for my children to see it.

Lainie Kazan...Sexy Lady

I started my show with Lainie Kazan by saying that I usually don't introduce my women guests as sexy, but today my guest is a woman who is *so* sexy, and she has charisma. I reminded Lainie that I had first met her about 15 years earlier when she was singing at CineGrill. I was there with Gloria Allred, and Lainie came and sat at our table. Theo Bikel also joined us that evening. I mentioned that he doesn't like me anymore because I'm too politically incorrect.

I had recently seen Lainie in the Joe Bologna/Renée Taylor play *Bermuda Avenue Triangle*. She said that it was one of the funniest plays she'd ever read, been in, or heard. She said that up on stage she felt like she was "on a surfboard riding the waves of laughter."

I told our audience just a few of Lainie's accolades. She received a Golden Globe nomination for her role in *My Favorite Year*, an Emmy nomination for *St. Elsewhere*, and an ACE award for the TV series *The Paper Chase*. I played a clip from *Beaches*, in which Lainie plays the mother of Bette Midler's character.

After I played a clip from *Lust in the Dust*, she recalled that when Tab Hunter called and asked her to read the script she couldn't believe it was him. Along with the script he gave her a VHS tape with a scratch-n-sniff accompaniment. The tape contained a John Waters movie starring Divine, who was going to star in *Lust*. Lainie found the script hilarious and signed on for the picture. She enjoyed filming in Santa Fe and is still friends with the people from the movie.

Menahem Golan had been on my show, and we talked about Golan's film *Delta Force*, in which Lainie starred with Chuck Norris, Joey Bishop, Shelley Winters, and George

Kennedy. Lainie was in Israel for three months during filming. We shared our fond memories of Tel Aviv.

Lainie is perhaps most well-known for her role in *My Big Fat Greek Wedding*. She said the film was made on a very low budget in Canada, and at the beginning nobody had any idea of the spectacular success it would become, eventually making hundreds of millions of dollars. The movie was shown at Cannes. Before opening weekend in the U.S. and Canada, Nia Vardalos, the screenwriter and star, called Lainie to ask her to contact the synagogues and ask people to come out and see the film! Lainie felt that they had "genius marketing"; they went to many little towns to do TV promos and create other publicity.

Lainie said that she knew Frank Sinatra very well. She appeared in *Lady in Cement* with him and Raquel Welch. She was in Miami, staying at the Fontainebleau, and was supposed to meet Frank to read for the film. Sinatra asked her to come see his show one night, but she said she had to do hers. Sinatra said he'd wait. After her show Sinatra's associate Jilly Rizzo picked Lainie up and drove her to Sinatra's show. Not only had he waited for her, he had waited to *start his show* until she got there. And she got the part!

The Adam Sandler movie *Don't Mess With the Zohan* had just come out. Although I hadn't seen this one yet, I had never been a big fan of his movies, so I asked Lainie what it was like working with him. She described him as a "nice Jewish boy."

I described Lainie as "the epitome of an entertainer" because she is such an accomplished singer as well as actress. She told our audience that her latest album was produced by David Benoit, the accomplished jazz musician who was her conductor for 10 years.

Somehow we got on the topic of old hotels in the Catskills, like the Shawanga Lodge. I used to go there when I was young; in fact, I was once named Miss Shawanga Lodge! Lainie said that she sang up in those mountains one time, at The Concord Hotel. She reminded me that they didn't applaud with their hands; they had these sticks with little balls on them that they would shake. Lainie speculated that they used these because they were too tired from eating and playing shuffleboard!

Lainie's parents were born in Jerusalem, and she has done a lot of work for Israel. She was once Woman of the Year for B'nai Brith.

She was also on the Board of the Young Musicians Foundation. Lainie told a funny story about how she got started with this group. She was singing at one of their events, and Carl Reiner tripped over one of her monitors and broke his leg. When he has written about that event, Carl calls that speaker "Lainie's box."

With such a wonderful singer as my guest, I decided to close out my show by playing Lainie singing "The Man That Got Away" from her smoldering album *Body and Soul*.

On my set with sexy Lainie Kazan

Billy Carter...Brother Wanted Dead

In the late 1970s, when Jimmy Carter was President, his "infamous" brother, Billy, was starting his own beer business. Billy, a high school graduate, had made a trip to Libya with some Georgia legislators and businessmen, and he was now hosting a Libyan delegation in my hometown of Atlanta. I had heard, via the grapevine, that Billy was calling a press conference. Here, he would introduce his newfound Arab friends to a small contingent of the Atlanta press corps that had been invited for the event. Coincidentally, it just happened to be at the time that the Georgia Legislature was meeting to vote on a law that would prevent any foreign entity from owning more than 5% of Georgia property.

So, the following day, like a good reporter, I took my notebook over to the hotel where Billy and his group were speaking and stood outside the press conference room. I wonder if my status as a member of the Jewish Press was a reason I was left off of this select list of the press invitees. Amazingly, I saw an acquaintance, a reporter from Associated Press, and greeted him like a long-lost friend. I walked in with him.

Seated at the front table were three Libyan representatives, and also, I believe, a delegate from Jordan. Oh, and of course, the high school graduate turned statesman, Billy Carter, was there. I made myself available to this table—knowing that Arabs love blondes and redheads. It was obvious that the head guy at the table was giving me lingering looks. At the time, it meant nothing; but, later in the story, I will tell you how his remembrance of me came in handy.

Brother Billy was no longer the court jester; he was highly dangerous. He opened the session with glowing reports of his warm and wonderful friendship with Colonel Gadaffi of Libya. According to Billy, Colonel Gadaffi was a misunderstood, loving human being. I wondered, at the time, how much Billy and the rest of the family would profit financially from this friendship. When asked about President Carter's involvement with the invitation of the Libyans, Billy replied, "Jimmy knew that I invited them and had no objections whatsoever to the Libyans coming." He introduced his good friend the Libyan Ambassador, who spoke about how "the Americans are victims of the Zionists in this country." Later, he related how the Libyans are not anti-Semitic but are Semites themselves. He spoke about how close the Jews were to them. "It is the Zionists who are a problem, who we don't care about." At that point, I expected him to refer to some of my best friends.

On the subject of the PLO, the Ambassador stated, "We are not only supporting the PLO, we are a member of the PLO. We support them with money, with guns, and with everything in our hands. We cannot deal with a people of three million (Israel) who seek to improve their lives by doing bad things and having enemies all over the world." During this press conference I listened to an hour-long tirade about the "infidel Jews" and the "Zionist entity" and what must be done to both. I heard enough to curl the hairs on the back of my neck. We've heard it all before, but I found it chilling to listen to the brother of our President and his Arab friends tell their plans for developing more cooperation between our two countries. I had the feeling that his claim to provide the PLO with "whatever they desire" had the underlying meaning of the destruction of Israel.

With Jimmy Carter, 1990

I was alarmed by the plans that these Arabs had. When I left, I called the Anti-Defamation League (ADL) and asked, "Are you aware that Billy Carter is in Atlanta with a pack of Arabs? Tomorrow night they are giving a party for the entire Georgia Legislature in the hopes of convincing them to raise the limit of Georgia land that can be purchased by outside countries." The ADL did what they usually do and said, in essence, "Don't make waves. We're looking into it." Yeah, right. So, my next call was to Rabbi Meir Kahane's group, the Jewish Defense League (JDL), in New York.

When I explained the situation to the JDL, they immediately asked me if I could get them invited to the party. I replied, "Give me a few minutes." I then called the hotel where the Libyans were staying and talked to the same Arab gentleman whose eyes had lingered on me. He did remember me, and within the hour he delivered five invitations to the party. Of course he did not know I was turning over the invitations to the JDL members who were flying in for the event.

I gave the engraved invitations to the JDL guys and went to the event alone. I thought it would be best that these visitors did not have a direct connection with me. I stood chatting with one typical guest in attendance, Mr. Tito Howard. (He made 17 pro-Arab documentaries; many were paid for by the UN.) At this point Carter and his boys were lined up in full regalia. Carter's mother, Miss Lillian, was standing nearby; I surmised she was officially giving the Carter family sanction.

**With "Miss Lillian"
Carter, 1979**

I knew that at precisely 10:00 when the Libyans were going to welcome the Legislature members, the JDL guys were going to cause a ruckus which would hopefully make national news. Sure enough, while most of the press was fawning over Miss Lillian, and while Billy and the Libyans were signing a charter establishing a "friendship society" between the peoples of Libya and Georgia, the two JDL men pulled their yarmulkes from their pockets. They then began shouting that these Libyans were the hijackers and also murderers of children and Israeli athletes.

The outburst was completely non-violent but highly effective. Coincidentally, I just happened to be standing next to Billy Carter when they were carried out because of the scene they created. I drawled my best southern drawl and said, "My goodness weren't they just awful?" With that, Billy Carter looked at me and said, "Well, them damn Jews better learn there's a hell of a lot more A-rabs than there are Jews!" Readers, fortunately, I have that quote on tape. Just let me say, "The rest is history."

The following day, every major magazine and television station picked up the story; even Walter Cronkite took notice. When the Jewish reaction was brought to Billy's attention, his comment, which was allowed to be printed in a family newspaper was, "The Jews can go to hell!"

The following day, the JDL called its own press conference. The press was asking questions about "outside agitators" being called. At that point, I chimed in and said, "Hey, this isn't an Atlanta problem. It's not even a Jewish problem." They responded with "Lady, don't you know these people are here to buy up your city?" Then I continued, "Frankly, I don't know why Billy Carter isn't listed as a government agent working for the Libyans. That's what he appears to be to me."

It was interesting how several months later, I happened to open the evening newspaper and noticed the headline, "Billy Carter being investigated by the Justice Department as a foreign agent." This incident significantly harmed his brother's presidency.

And, speaking of the Carter family, I am reminded of a conversation I had with the former President and his wife, Rosalynn. It was a few years later when we both happened to be at a party Ted Turner gave for his new movie starring Billy Crystal, *City Slickers.* We were standing by each other at the buffet table and I couldn't resist. Since I knew Rosalynn's plastic surgeon was Dr. John Louis, the king of Atlanta "nip and tuck," I casually mentioned to her, "Did you ever wonder, now that Dr. Louis is getting older, what's going to happen to all those 'before and after' pictures in his office?" I continued, "Can't you see one of his assistants at an office Christmas party calling everybody over and saying, 'Hey, look what I found in the files today!'"

A look of shock came over Rosalynn's face and she began to wave at her husband, "Jim-mey, Jim-mey, come over here! I want you to meet this lady and listen to what she's got to say about Dr. Louis." So, for the next twenty minutes, we stood there and talked about privacy issues and what could happen when your plastic surgeon dies.

It's a good thing President Carter didn't remember having this conversation when a few months later, I questioned him at a press conference about his partiality for the Arabs and the double standard he held for Israel.

That family caused President Carter nothing but trouble and grief. Each had their special talents: his sister, with her evangelist lifestyle, trying to convert everyone; his brother, Billy, an alcoholic peeing behind cars and hanging out with Libyans, which caused trouble for the United States; and his mother, Lillian, who gave a press conference whenever she had the chance. His mother even appeared on Johnny Carson without a bra, in a white t-shirt and sneakers. She stated that she had a sign in her front yard that read, "My son is President."

What a group, Readers! That family reminds me of an old joke from the time when Carter was running for re-election:

What does Ted Kennedy have that Jimmy Carter wished he did? A Dead Brother. Amen.

With Jimmy and Rosalynn Carter

Billy Crystal and I are Soooo Close...Not!

I remember Billy Crystal...when. That is, when he wasn't so famous, so important, or so noticeably funny. How could this happen? Well, Billy Crystal and I have the same aunt and uncle. I have an uncle (my father's brother) named Uncle Greenie. Now, this man, Uncle Greenie, married a woman, my Aunt Jean, who happens to have a sister who is the mother of Billy Crystal. I know somewhere in his psyche he has to remember when he was a struggling young comedian and appearing at comedy clubs in places like the Playboy Club in Atlanta, where members of the audience included such notables as our mutual aunt and uncle. I even remember being at their house with the Crystal family in years gone past for Passover Seders, breaking matzo together. Except, somehow, when Billy has seen me over the years, he never quite remembers it.

**With Billy Crystal,
around 1994**

When I moved out to California, I was sure that I'd call "cousin Billy" and right away be put on his "favored family" list. The problem was, I could never find the right person to tell me where to contact him. Eventually though, I found myself invited, as a journalist, to an opening of one of his movies in Los Angeles. I waited for a few minutes while he talked to some of the "industry" people. Then, when I saw an opening, I walked over to where he was standing and introduced myself by saying, "You know, we have the same aunt and uncle." He looked at me as though I came from outer space and said, "Oh really? And how is that?" I responded, "Well, your aunt Jean married my Uncle Greenie." About that time, the PR guy, on the alert for pesky fans, came over to whisk the star away. But by now a look of recognition was dawning on Billy's face, and he said, "Oh yeah, I have an Uncle and Aunt with those names." So I went through the family genealogy for Billy. I gave my card to him and said, "Well, at least put me on your press list." Right.

Our paths didn't cross again until one night when I was out at Spago with Gloria Allred. Gloria stopped to introduce me to Billy, who was in the valet line with us. I stopped her and said, "Yes, I know. We have the same aunt and uncle." I don't think he was terribly impressed or had any memory of our conversation at the movie opening. Doesn't matter. I gave him my card again and said, "Hope to see you at family functions." I don't think so. But, in Hollywood, could that be a claim to fame?

Casey Kasem..."The Voice"
With Many Voices

One of my more colorful guests was Casey Kasem. Of all the many celebrities on my show, Casey was the only one who would arrive an hour early, and who brought his own stylist and make-up girl to get him ready for the show. He always dressed immaculately. I remember that before we started taping he was concerned how his outfit would look on camera.

Casey was the son of Lebanese Druze immigrants, who were grocers in Detroit, where Casey was born in 1932. His birth name was Kemal Amin Kasem. In high school, Casey played baseball and was also in the radio club. He said he created "a little sports show" that he broadcast at the school, and that's how he got the name Casey. This was the beginning of an incredible radio career.

Casey was in Korea during the war there and described himself as "fortunate enough" to be stationed at the headquarters where Armed Forces Radio was broadcast. He got a gig as a DJ for a show that started at 6 A.M. Casey played bebop and called himself Crazy Kasey. After a short time, a number of the soldiers who had been listening to Casey's show while eating breakfast in the officer's mess signed a petition to get him off the air. So his show only lasted two weeks! Casey figured that bebop must have been a little too much to take while you were having your morning coffee in Korea.

Casey started out in show business as a voice actor on the Lone Ranger radio show. He played several characters aged 12 to 22. He voiced characters on The Green Hornet too. About radio, Casey said, "Radio is the best medium for

On my set with Casey Kasem, 1997

using your imagination. You can create million-dollar sets in the mind. You can paint any picture you want to paint. That's what I do on my show with the human interest stories and the requests and dedications." Of course we all remember American Top 40! Casey was the youngest person to be inducted into the Radio Hall of Fame.

On the subject of doing voices for characters, I mentioned *Scooby Doo*. Casey was the voice of Shaggy on this show, which he said was the longest-running Saturday morning network TV show, lasting for 22 years. Casey told us that he borrowed the voice from a Richard Crenna character in a popular radio and TV show called *Our Miss Brooks*. Also, he added, "With a little Dave Hull thrown in," explaining that Dave Hull was another disk jockey.

When I made the comment that there was "no more music anymore," Casey responded, "You're probably referring to rap." He said that rap music does have a purpose for people who like it and that the music delivers a powerful message. I commented, "Hostility and hate!"

Casey responded that he had seen music come and go, adding that he'd never been identified with any particular style of music. But, he said, he learned to never give himself a "Van Gogh ear— to cut one off and pre-judge the music." He explained that you had to listen with both ears to really hear what is going on. Surprisingly, he said that he had initially pre-judged Elvis, but people learned to love Elvis; that he had pre-judged the Beatles, and people learned to love them. Casey added, "People don't like change. But young people don't have Van Gogh ears; they listen with both. If they like something they gravitate towards it and embrace it. And a lot of young people are doing that with rap."

Since I had been in Beirut in 1982, I asked Casey if he had ever been to Lebanon. He hadn't, but he had tried. He was invited to the country as part of the American Task Force for Lebanon. He went through Canada and got to London but had forgotten his passport. So he had to go back.

With Casey and his wife Jean

I knew Casey had worked with Julio Iglesias, so I asked about him. Casey said that Julio was a soccer player in Spain until he was in an auto accident and couldn't play anymore. A friend suggested to him that he play guitar and sing to pass the time. Julio and others discovered that he was great at both! Casey said that he found Julio to be "very genuine," adding that he was also "very critical of himself." I told Casey that I had interviewed Julio, describing it as a "weekend interview, but not in the biblical sense." Then I told Casey my "Julio story," which you can read elsewhere in this book!

We also had each crossed paths with Elvis. Casey said that he got into an Elvis show in Vegas with a date but without tickets. He slipped the doorman a few bucks, and he and his date somehow got at one of the high roller tables. Elvis came out, saw Casey's date, and leaned over and kissed her. Then ten minutes later, he did it again! And yes, you can read about my own encounter with Elvis in this book.

I had heard Casey was a vegetarian, like my daughter. I told Casey that I was trying vegetarianism, at least on occasion, and he was interested. I responded that I feel better when I eat vegetarian and know it's better for me. Casey said that he tries to encourage others to embrace vegetarianism. He told us about a comment from a famous vegetarian, Paul McCartney, who once said that if slaughterhouses were made of glass and people could look into them, half the world would be vegetarian.

Still on the subject of health, Casey said that he was a four-pack-a-day smoker for seventeen years. I was shocked. But he stopped in 1964 after the surgeon general's announcement came out. I told my own story of quitting smoking. I was writing for Health Spa magazine and went to a spa for a few weeks to do a story. We couldn't have any cigarettes in the spa, so that helped me quit.

Casey said that he had been inspired by Gandhi, who once said that the only way to break a bad habit is if the habit is standing in the way of something you want more.

About smoking, he realized that what he wanted and had worked so hard for was to get to Hollywood. So, once the surgeon general's warning about smoking came out, he asked himself, "Why would I want to kill myself now that I'm on my way?" And he quit.

Casey's final years were tragic before he died in 2014. He suffered from dementia, and there were significant conflicts between his wife Jean and Casey's kids from his previous marriage. The stories are sad to read. I'm just glad that Casey appeared on my show when he could still smoothly and eloquently relate stories from his life in that beautiful, golden, unmistakable voice, the same one I had heard on the radio for so many years. I prefer to remember him that way.

Sally Kirkland...Outrageous Lady

I first met Sally in the early to mid-nineties when my daughter, Dana, was General Manager of The Laugh Factory, a comedy club. Every year, the owner, Jamie Masada, gave a Thanksgiving dinner for homeless comedians. Sally and I met at this event, while spooning mashed potatoes for the homeless.

I asked Sally if she would be a guest on my show. She accepted my invitation, and a few days later came to the station for the taping.

Sally arrived looking gorgeous. My show was in its early years, and I was excited she was there; when I introduced Sally I said, "Today we've got a big-time, big-time star; no more grabbing my friends off the street." I mentioned that she was a stage actress and a star in over seventy films, including *Anna,* for which she received an Academy Award nomination. And Sally returned the compliment, saying that she had a particular interest in coming on my show because she knew of all the good work I had done for Israel and making sure there is a bridge between Israel and America. How nice of her, and what a great start for the show!

Sally had traveled to Egypt and Israel at the beginning of the first Iraq war with the group Movement of Spiritual Inner Awareness (MSIA). The group's purpose there was to bring the spirit of peace. She remembered sitting in the Jerusalem Hyatt while the bombs were going off in Kuwait. She said that her experience during that time was the "most alive I've ever felt."

I asked her about her connection with Judaism. She said that she "grew up high church Episcopalian." I responded, "Tell me how to spell that!" She laughed and said that when she was young her nurse was a black Jew. She had converted to Judaism, and she was "black and beautiful and sang the gospel." How unusual! We talked about going to the wall in Jerusalem and putting our wishes in the wall. Sally said that when you did that, you "felt like you're connected to something bigger." I've felt the same thing at the wall. Sally went on, saying, "If I can do anything as a human being, I want to go to places like Israel and tell people, 'I don't know what you've read in the papers, but I myself want us to be peaceful in each others' houses.'"

We talked about Menahem Golem, the Israeli director and producer. I described him as a pussycat, and she agreed; in fact, Sally actually looked straight into the camera and told him he's a pussycat; I hope he was watching! She talked about shooting a movie with him called *Hit the Dutchman*. The movie was filmed in Russia, the same month that Gorbachev was on his way out. While there Sally took films of the Russian Guard outside Lenin's tomb, as well as the fuel and food lines, and she "lived on borscht." She said that Golem turned Moscow into 1929 Yonkers New York. Sally played Dutch Schultz's mother, with a German Jewish accent. I shared my experiences from the late seventies, when I was briefly detained by the KGB for smuggling prayer books.

Sally had recently completed *In the Heat of Passion*, with executive producer Roger Corman. She said that Golem got his start with Corman. Sally said she considers Golem and Corman to be two of her biggest role models.

We stayed for awhile longer on the topic of Communist countries. Sally had just come back from China. I've been there, too. She showed us pictures of her at the top of the Great Wall. Sally had been there representing the Academy of Motion Pictures at a film festival; the Academy was reaching out in an effort to build a bridge between the countries' film industries. At the festival she had seen "five great films, four of them about women." She mentioned one in particular in which a taxi driver finds an abandoned baby girl in the back of his cab. The child had been abandoned because of China's one-child policy. The taxi driver brings up the baby.

On my set with Sally Kirkland

Switching to a perhaps more famous subject, Sally said that she "brought Bobby De Niro to Lee Strasberg." Among other things, Strasberg was a world-renowned acting teacher. Sally remembered watching De Niro play "about 14 parts" in a Strasberg play. She said that De Niro is very shy, but after the play she went backstage and told him that he's "gonna be the hottest thing since Brando." He started calling her a lot after that! She worked with him on stage, too, in a Shelley Winters play.

De Niro, of course, starred in *The Godfather Part II,* and Sally told us how that film's director Francis Ford Coppola was instrumental in the success of *Anna.* Coppola's assistant Susan Landau (Martin's daughter) was assistant director to Yurek Bogayevicz, the director of *Anna.* The film didn't have a distributor. Coppola helped place the movie at the

San Francisco Film Festival; from there it got picked up by Cannes. And, as Sally said, "the rest is history."

I loved to hear Sally tell her stories of all the men she's known—some in the biblical sense and some not. Sally told us that Rip Torn was a "catalyst" for her, that he "was her first true love." She acknowledged the big age difference but thought that he was sexy. She was at The Actor's Studio with Torn and Brando and James Dean. Brando and Dean left, but Torn was still there, and he, Sally said, "had their vibe." She did *Richard III* with him, and when they were in the film *Coming Apart* together they fell in love. Torn was separated from his wife Geraldine Page at the time, but he eventually went back to her. Geraldine got pregnant and had twins. Sally tried to kill herself; her heart had even stopped before she was revived. She found her spiritual path after that. So that's what she meant when she described Torn as a catalyst for her, because he pushed her into another consciousness.

The famous people Sally has worked with, wow! She was in *The Sting* with Paul Newman and Robert Redford and *The Way We Were* with Redford and Barbra Streisand. I asked Sally to try to identify a favorite out of all of her theater and film experiences, and whether she preferred one medium over the other. She said her favorite was her role as Anna because "it was theater in film." She talked about the "long five-minute scenes, not cut cut cut, edit edit edit." Sally described one particular scene where she's comforting the character played by Paulina Porizkova. The camera started high, and during the course of the scene came closer and closer until Sally's face filled the screen. She said she had to do a three-page monologue in the course of five minutes. Sally said that the theater is her favorite medium in terms of being in control, but appreciates TV because it reaches so many people. And TV and movies are preserved, so they last.

On the lasting nature of TV and films, Sally, who by the way is also an ordained minister, had just done a funeral for an actor who had accidentally shot himself. She went back to his mother's house after the service and watched him on one of his TV shows. While watching, Sally said, "He's in heaven now, but there he is still (pointing to the screen)."

Sally could be an outrageous guest with her unique demeanor and provocative style of dressing. Let me tell you, her dress code did not go along with her role as minister. A few times she had me go to her church meetings. I didn't really get into the service. Chanting, and the like, had never interested me much. I really didn't want to hurt her feelings, but I told her that I called her church "The Church of the Weird People Who Hummed." I have to say, though, that the people I met there were usually genuine.

For one of her other appearances on my show, Sally arrived at the studio in a state of flurry. Let me just say, Sally is a wild woman. She was wearing a red dress cut to the navel and looking sexy. She had also brought a recent magazine with pictures of herself in various poses, wearing dresses cut so low she could have nursed Zimbabwe. I asked if they were putting her boobs on milk cartons! And yes, I got a picture.

Sally tried to take control of my show. This was my first lesson in being nice, but firm, as I reminded her whose show it actually was. I'm not saying she was not nice; it's just that she was so totally overpowering. I had my agenda and Sally had hers.

I have to say that Sally was charming, witty, and fun as long as we talked about what Sally wanted to talk about. When she wasn't steering the conversation to religious issues, most of her topics were fun and always interesting. She was into world peace and helping the women of Afghanistan. I realized that Sally thrived on causes.

I'm trying to look at the camera instead of, well, elsewhere . . .

I learned that Sally wants what she wants, when she wants it. She once appeared on my show with Kent McCord (of *Adam 12*) and Peter Mark Richman (Reverend Snow on *Three's Company* and many other roles). Sally saw Kent and Peter Mark already on the set, and she didn't want them to go on. I swear, she flounced in like Bette Davis in some A&E movie and asked me, "What are they doing here?" I replied, "They're guests, just like you." Sally gave me one of her looks of astonishment and said, "I thought it was just going to be us; just us girls." And I said, "No, actually it's going to be Peter Mark and Kent first, and on the second part of the show, you will join Peter Mark." By now her theatrics were going to my head, and I think I said something to that effect. In her best display of cajoling, bordering on temper tantrum, she sighed and said something like, "What do I have to do...throw myself on the floor? Beg? Okay, go tell them that it's just going to be us on the show."

Embarrassed in front of my director, I looked at her, tried not to laugh, and said, "Now Sally, you don't want me to be rude to them. I can't go out there and tell these men that they can't go on because Sally has decided she doesn't want them to." Amazingly, they knew her and didn't seem to take offense. They shrugged and said, "That's Sally." Lesson learned: I had to keep control of my own show! Once taping began, Sally was wonderful. The show was like one big happy family, with all four of us—thankfully.

Sally was also on my show with Tom Bower. You might know Tom from *Die Hard 2* or *Crazy Heart*, or perhaps from *Law & Order* or *The Practice*, but he has played over 200 TV, film, and stage roles. Our topic was "Good Union, Bad Union." Unions, my favorite subject!?! After I introduced Sally and Tom I cracked, "God willing, I'll keep control of this show."

For this particular show we identified Sally as "Actress/ SAG activist" on the screen credits. I had just joined the Screen Actors Guild (SAG), after doing a commercial for Walgreen's. Yes, folks, I had been discovered...in the parking lot at Costco! That's right. I was talking to some casting person there and was asked to come do a screen test, which I did. A few days later, when I was back in Atlanta, they called me to ask if I could come shoot a commercial. I said I couldn't because I lived in Atlanta. Then a few days after that they called me back to say that the management of Walgreen's would pay me to come out and shoot it. I was floored! I told this story on my show with Sally and Tom, and added, "G-d, they pay a lot of money for those things!" Sally and Tom nodded and said that's because of the union. And that got us started on our topic for the day!

At the time there was yet another pending merger of SAG and the American Federation of Television and Radio Artists (AFTRA) on the table. Sally had been involved with the merger situation for a number of years. She told us a story from the late nineties, when Ron Howard let her out of a "looping session" for EDTv to go to a meeting where the pending merger was being discussed. She took some papers that Ron had given her. At the time, Tom was in the board room, and he said he was one of eight people voting against it. They had the strength of the "Minority Report" behind them, and they defeated the merger.

This time around, Sally and Tom felt they were getting muzzled by the SAG leadership, which was not allowing the Minority Report to be sent to SAG members and had spent $2 million of dues money promoting the merger. They felt they were being told that they have to merge with what they felt was a "weaker union." We posted www.savesag.com on the screen several times during the show. Sally and Tom said Save SAG was formed so members could get information about all of the relevant issues related to the merger. They talked about the difference in guaranteed contract rates per week between SAG and AFTRA. They and other SAG people were afraid that if the unions merged they were going to end up with a rate that's less than they'd been getting for years and years. They said AFTRA had already been stealing SAG contracts and lowering rates.

Sally and Tom mentioned a number of names of people who were against the merger, including several past SAG presidents. They felt that SAG was spending $2 million of dues money to give one side of the story, providing no opposing point of view. Members were getting "brainwash mail" with the message, "Empower yourself, consolidate." But Sally and Tom felt that even if the merger was good for the organization it was bad for the individuals.

I asked them what concerned members could do to fight the merger. They said to get the truth out. In addition to their concerns over lower guaranteed contract rates, they were concerned that the members' pensions and benefits might be less with the merger. By merging with a weaker union, they said, the new union would provide for more people but give them less.

I had to chime in, stating that I'm usually against unions, which seemed to irk Sally a bit. But I added that I also didn't like the idea of making a union an even bigger union, stating that I believed in what the individual wants.

Sally agreed, saying that we need to stand up for the individuals, stand up for the artists who fear they're being turned into a machine like all the corporate conglomerates. She told a story about David O. Selznick, who told her, when she was only 17, that she may not make it as an ingénue, as a young leading actress, but that she would make it as a character actress when she was older because she was so independent, with a mind of her own. Selznick told her that she was going to want to do her own contracts, to get involved in the negotiating process. Sally said that she's always held that in the back of her mind.

But that's enough about unions. Back to the topic of the famous men Sally has known. I never asked how she and Elliott Gould became so friendly, but they were. I remember meeting Elliott at the Four Seasons Hotel one night a few years ago. We were sitting next to each other. It was almost impossible not to have a conversation. Mr. Gould, however, managed to do just that.

Shortly after that awkward time, I was with Theodore Bikel at the Playboy Mansion, where he introduced me to Elliott. Somehow, even though I was standing directly in front of him and next to Theo, I seemed to be an invisible person to Elliott. During one summer, Sally invited me to her birthday party. I even took a picture with Sally and me standing next to Elliott. We all looked like we were having tons of fun. When I got the pictures back from being

developed, I couldn't wait to see if he (or I?) were invisible...
like Count Dracula.

**With Elliott Gould
and Sally at her
birthday party,
circa 2005**

Another time, I remember Elaine Young, Sally, and I were
taping one of my shows regarding who could out-horror
the other with their personal implant story. The taping was
called, "Implants from Hell!" Elaine, the real estate lady
to the stars, was once married to actor Gig Young and
about a half-dozen others. And Elaine, like so many others
in the seventies, had cheek implants. Sally made no bones
about the fact that her cleavage, one of her trademarks,
did not come by way of nature. In fact, a couple of years
after her first visit on my show, she had serious medical
problems caused by those damn breast implants. As for
Elaine, she said that one day she woke up and looked like
a chipmunk because the silicone had begun to separate.
That led to one operation, and then another. In the end,
that poor woman had over forty operations because the
silicone would wander and move near her optic nerve. As
you can imagine, this made for quite an interesting show.
And, Elaine, although about as outrageous as Sally, was a

good guest. Both of them were pretty passionate about the dangers of silicone implants.

A few years later I received a call that Elaine had died from <u>face</u> cancer. I had never heard of such a thing, but obviously she had had so many surgeries that her face and system had reached the point of exhaustion. Anyway, I was invited to her funeral…both of them! Only in L.A. does craziness, like having multiple funerals, seem…well, normal. My mind wanders to the fact that "normal," or what passes for normal, is a rare commodity in Beverly Hills and the entertainment industry. In Atlanta, where I come from, if you wanted to fix a friend up, the friend would ask, "Who is his family? What does he do? Where does he live? How's his personality? Who are his friends?" In L.A., the first and foremost question was, "Is he normal?"

So I dressed appropriately in black and headed to the first funeral. I was told that the reason there were two funerals was because her daughter didn't like the friends that had planned the "big funeral," so she wanted to have another one at Café Roma. This was a popular Beverly Hills hang-out of the "older" entertainers where you never quite knew who would be there to see and be seen. Café Roma was Elaine's "claim to fame," as she always seemed to be occupying the table in front, in the middle, on the patio right as you entered. Elaine sat, held court, and had her own entourage in that specific space. Once, Elaine invited me to join her there for lunch. Let me tell you, lunch consisted of sitting there while her cell phone rang non-stop. She carried on conversations with everyone but me. But, despite all that, she had a good heart, and since she married actor Gig Young, and had seven husbands following that marriage, she always had a good story to tell!

Elaine's second funeral was a couple of days later at the Wilshire Theatre, and she would have loved the ruckus. The crowd was large and even filled most of the balcony. Her publicist, Edward Lozzi (yes, the same guy who represents Shirley Jones and a host of Hollywood stars and wannabes) conducted the event. Let me tell you, it was quite the show!

Sally has been a sporadic friend over the years. I wouldn't hear from her for months; then, out of the blue she'd call, sounding lonely and wanting to talk...at almost midnight! Then, another month or two would pass, and she would call excitedly and say, "Quick, turn on Lifetime Television; my part is about to come on." Other times, she would do something very nice, like invite me to something that she knew I would enjoy—forgetting, of course, that the previous two or three times that I had called her, she had blown me away with total rudeness. She can be sweet, so genuinely sweet. Her birth sign is Scorpio and she was born on Halloween; perhaps this explains a lot!

George Takei...Activist Trekkie

George Takei is probably best-known for his portrayal of Mr. Sulu in *Star Trek*, but he has also appeared in more than thirty feature films and has had a multitude of television roles. George's career has spanned over five decades. He first starred in *Ice Palace* with Richard Burton in 1960. George has appeared as Sulu in six *Star Trek* motion pictures.

This man received his star on the Hollywood Walk of Fame in 1986, and in 1991 he placed his signature and handprint on the landmark in the courtyard of Grumman's Chinese Theater in Hollywood.

At the time George first appeared on my show he was starring as a recurring character on NBC's *Heroes* playing Kaito Nakamura, the father of time-traveler Hiro Nakamura. He started his career with a voice role in a film called *Rodan*, a Japanese science-fiction classic about a prehistoric creature terrorizing Tokyo. George was one of the voice actors dubbing English dialogue into the film. He talked about the difficulty of finding English words to sync with the Japanese lip movements.

George got his Screen Actors Guild (SAG) card in 1958. He said that he "was still a star-struck theater student in college" when he did *Ice Palace*. George said he and Burton were a perfect match, because he was full of questions, and Burton loved talking about himself!

George told us about the correct pronunciation of "Takei," which is "Ta-Kay," rather than "Ta-Kie" as most people usually say his name. He said that the Japanese word *Takai* translates as "expensive." Once, after a movie producer mispronounced his name, George told the producer the translation. The producer said something like, "Oh, well, you're definitely 'Takay' then." George laughed as he told us that William Shatner couldn't ever get his name right. He was at a "Shatner roast" one time and said, in front of an audience, "Bill, it's pronounced Takay; rhymes with Toupee." Hilarious!

George told a great story about the beginning of Star Trek. In the first pilot, which Leonard Nimoy was in but George wasn't, the producers weren't pleased that the second-in-command on the Enterprise was a woman. So Gene Roddenberry did another pilot in which Spock, as an alien (!), was first officer. Roddenberry also brought in George and Shatner for the second pilot. We talked about the diversity of the characters on Star Trek— not just the aliens, but the human characters. This was very progressive for its time.

Am I a Trekkie? With William Shatner, 2002

George and I talked a *lot* of politics. George announced that he is a proud lifelong Democrat. I said that I was an independent. We were both very disappointed in George Bush and discussed our mutual disillusionment with the Iraq War.

George was advocating at the time for the repeal of "Don't Ask Don't Tell" in the military. The Iraq war was still raging, and George commented how ridiculous it was that during a time when the military had such a great need for personnel that it had lowered its standards as to someone's criminal background, gay and lesbian people were being discharged from or not accepted into the armed services if they disobeyed the "don't tell" policy. He felt that this was hurting our nation's security.

We continued discussing George's activism. He is very involved with the Human Rights Campaign, the country's largest organization devoted to fighting for gay, lesbian, bisexual, and transgender equality. George is also very passionate about Asian-American rights. He said that most of the Alien Land Laws in our country have targeted Asians. George was in a Japanese interment camp during World War II. He was five years old when he was taken to the camp and eight when he came out.

George has an absolutely wonderful voice, which explains his success as a voice actor. We talked a bit about his role in the Disney film *Mulan*. He has even been the "narrator" for several theatrical musical productions, particularly in England, where he did *Snow White* and provided the voice for the genie in *Aladdin* at the Hexagon Theatre in Reading.

George appeared for a second time on my show with Peter Mark Richman. These guys have appeared in literally hundreds of television shows! Because Peter Mark was there with Mr. Sulu, we felt we had to show a clip of Peter Mark in *Star Trek: The Next Generation*.

Peter Mark's first film was *Friendly Persuasion,* and we showed a clip from this film as well. I showed viewers copies of Peter Mark's two books, *Hollander's Deal* and *The Rebirth of Ira Masters.* I told him that I'd read them both and found them to be fast-moving and very interesting. And then Peter Mark added, "sexy." And I responded, "Yes, hot, hot!" I also showed a few examples of his amazing artwork.

Peter Mark worked with Sophia Loren in *Black Orchid* when she was 23 years old. He said that when she walked onto the lot at the studio he thought that she was the most fantastic-looking woman he had ever seen. He told us that when they were sitting around reading the script she used to bat her eyes at him. Peter Mark's wife was pregnant at the time, and he recalls she wasn't too thrilled about him working with Ms. Loren! But you know what, their marriage survived it—at the time of our taping, the Richmans had been married for 54 years!

We briefly discussed the phenomenon of Star Trek conventions. George said that Senator Patrick Leahy from Vermont and Paul Allen of Microsoft are huge fans, so they're not all weirdos!

On my set with George Takei

Theo Bikel...The Fiddler

Here was a guest dressed in a red sweater and brown pants, with a white beard and white head; boy, was I was excited! My guest was Theo Bikel, an actor, singer, composer, and activist. Not only had he played Tevye in the musical *Fiddler On the Roof* over 2,000 times, he also starred as "Mitch" in a London stage production of *A Streetcar Named Desire* with Vivien Leigh. He played Captain Von Trapp in the original Broadway production of *The Sound of Music*. Theo could speak—and sing!—German, Yiddish, Russian, and Spanish, all with varying accents. He also had parts in the films *Guess Who's Coming to Dinner* and *My Fair Lady*.

We talked about our mutual friend, Nobel Prize winner Elie Wiesel. Theo said, "Elie was a calmer person than I am or ever was. There are two things I have to tell you about Elie—first, he walked with a distinct limp, and secondly, he has been dead for 11 years!" I had no clue what Theo meant by this comment, since Elie was at the time not only still very alive but also more active than ever, so I changed the subject by asking, "How do you manage 50-60 live shows a year?" He answered, "I take many red-eyes when I travel." I asked him, "Who are your favorite people to work with?" He replied that he had the most fun working with Peter Houston in London. "We are a kindred spirit—we both know many languages, and he is funny and intelligent." He continued, "My appeal today is not visual, it is sexual, and I can say it now because of my age."

I was with Theo many times, and it was always an adventure, especially the times he took me to the Playboy Mansion. It's a good thing that I am a confident and fabulous person, because I needed that confidence at the Playboy Mansion surrounded by all the bunnies! One time when we were there, when he introduced me to Larry David, the creator of Seinfeld. I didn't know who he was, and Theo was astounded.

I never considered Theo one to brag or drop names, but he did mention a time or two that he had been to the White House. He was active politically; however, he always turned down the offer to run for Congress because, as he said, "I am not rich enough to win."

Theo was born in Vienna. His father was a lifelong Zionist. Back then, visas were given to those who had seniority within the Zionist movement. However, when the Nazis arrived Theo's family did have to escape, because his father had only a few visas. Acting on his feeling that "we always have to have an Israel someplace that will open doors for Jews," he moved to the United States in 1954. Theo commented, "If you cannot remember the bitter times, you can't face the good times of peace." We discussed events with Sadat. I told him that I still wonder what would have happened if he had not been shot. I told Theo that I was lucky to be in the same place when Anwar Sadat and Menachem Begin signed the peace treaty in 1979.

As this show ended, I asked him if he had any "words of wisdom." Theo said, "Money isn't everything. It can't buy you everything. It can't buy poverty." And I agree.

Theo also appeared on my show in 2004. I had just been to see Ed Asner do a reading from the play The Gathering. Theo had starred in the play off-Broadway in 1999. He was currently doing a play set in the Middle Ages called The Disputation, in which he starred as a rabbi debating a Christian monk who happened to be a former Jew. Unfortunately, although I saw both of these plays, I never saw a production in which Theo starred.

Out and about with Theo Bikel

Since Theo had extensive experience on both stage and screen, I asked him whether he preferred theater or films, and he quickly answered "theater." Theo said that he likes the fact that a play has a beginning, a middle, and an end, and that it's done when it's done, not produced "in bits and pieces" as films are. He loved the "immediacy" of the theater. He said he appreciated performing in front of a live audience, where you can hear the reaction, "the laughter when they laugh and the intake of breath when they're moved." When I asked him to name his favorite play of all the ones that he'd done, he replied that "it's a toss-up between *Fiddler on the Roof* and *Zorba*." Theo said that he loved the character of Zorba.

When I commented that he seemed to usually play these very powerful, strong roles, he said, "Well, a mouse I'm not." Later I said that he often seems to play "earthy" characters, and he responded that he did play the owner of a dude ranch once but pointed out that he'd also done university professors, doctors, and more "cerebral people." And he received an Oscar nomination for playing a southern sheriff in *The Defiant Ones*. The man had some versatility!

As I do with many actors who have been in the business for awhile, I asked about the changes he'd seen in Hollywood. He said the producers today "don't look for actors, they look for personalities." He added, "They want you to *be* what you play instead of *play* what you play." He then described the difference between "personality acting" and "acting acting." For Theo, a personality actor was one who "always looks the same, walks the same, talks the same," regardless of the role. A real actor, though, "changes faces, walks, and accents." He added that "there are very few of those left because people don't trust them, trust in the power of acting." He described Robin Williams as an "actor actor" and said that Alec Guinness was also one. Theo lamented, "It's a shame that people don't trust them enough to play the roles." As an example, he said, "If you want a prostitute, do you go out in the street and fine one to play one? No, you take an actress."

Another of Theo's frustrations at the time was that "people want you to repeat what you did yesterday, to play a formula." He added that the same thing happens with scripts. He found many of them to be formulaic; that is, they would find something that works and then change the story a bit the next time but not really very much.

On the topic of business and marketing in Hollywood, Theo said, "I don't sell bread, I bake bread. I'm not concerned with how what I do is marketed. That's not my job." I segued into how hard it would be to market him since he did so many things, and he replied, "People don't really want that either; they want to pigeonhole you." I mentioned his being an entertainer, actor, singer, and activist, and then he added, offhandedly, "Actor's Association President," and

I said "What?" Then I learned that Theo was the President of the Associated Actors and Artistes of America (4As), which he described as the "umbrella organization" for SAG-AFTRA, Actors' Equity Association (AEA), etc. He was president of AEA at one point, too, at the same time that Ed Asner was president of SAG, and they used to attend international actors' meetings together. I also learned on this show that Theo was one of the founders of the Newport Folk Festival. Wow!

Somehow we got on the topic of long words that are supposedly intelligent-sounding. I said I'm hesitant to use words longer than three syllables because I was afraid my readers wouldn't know what they meant, and I might not either! Theo told a funny story about a dinner party hosted by Sonny Bono, who Theo said was a very good cook. But unfortunately there were some people at the party, from Texas he thought, and it was a "football night." Theo said, "It was dire." About an hour into the night Theo commented, "I hope you appreciate the fact that I'm being properly monosyllabic," and the response he got was, "Yeah, far out." Theo said he realized that they had no idea what monosyllabic meant. I admitted, "Would you believe I don't either?" He said that it means talking with words of one syllable, and I said "Oh, yeah, I knew that." Not! I asked him how the dinner was, and he said wonderful but "the conversation sucked."

When I commented that Theo seemed to be everywhere, he responded that he's constantly traveling and on the move. He joked that a flight attendant once asked him where his permanent home was and he answered, "4B."

I asked Theo if he still travelled to Israel a lot. He said that when his mother was alive he used to go to Israel about four to five times per year to visit her. She had died a few years earlier at age 97, so now he "only" went about once a year. I commented that it's sad how so many Jewish people have never even been.

We didn't talk politics much on this show, although I acknowledged that Theo and I are pretty much political polar opposites. I said, "I'm to the right of Attila the Hun," and he quickly responded, "Well, I'm not necessarily to the left of Lenin. I can't stand totalitarianism of any type."

Theo also commented, "Your bedfellows say a lot about who you are. If you associate with people who are unsavory, dirt rubs off." We talked about the influence of the fundamentalist Christian right in the Republican Party. Theo shook his head and asked, "Would you want to be at a dinner and somebody gets up and says 'Jews are cursed, God doesn't want to hear the prayers of the Jews.'?" He continued on, asking "How often have you heard a legislator say 'This is a Christian country.'? Since when? This is supposed to be a country where all religions are equal and accepted and divorced from the running of the country."

When I told him how I was singled out in school for refusing to sing the Christmas songs, he noted that this is one of the points of not having religion in schools, because of the peer pressure that kids experience. Children don't understand religious reasons for engaging or not engaging in an activity and then point their fingers at those who don't participate. Then he noted that the Jews promoted Hanukkah, a minor Jewish holiday, into a major holiday so as not to make the Jewish children feel bad that they didn't have Christmas like all the other kids did.

We didn't have time to discuss all the causes Theo was involved in, but I can tell you it was a lot. Theo said that one time at an event he was standing with a famous person he had met at many other charitable functions. Someone asked

Theo if he knew this famous person, trying to introduce them, and Theo responded, "We met several causes ago."

As we were winding up, I asked Theo about his future goals. "My plan for the future is surviving. That's my plan." I said that sounded a bit negative, and he replied that at his age survival is a very positive thing! I noted that he's not getting older, he's getting better, and he joked, "Yes, so does the wine that I drink." But then he clarified that he was talking about creative survival; that his life and what he does with the rest of it has to mean something. Finally, I was so disappointed that our time had gone so fast I said that I was going to kidnap Theo, and he replied with a smile, "Allright redhead, you can kidnap me anytime you want." What a great finish!

As I indicated earlier, Theo and I did not always share the same political viewpoints. Theo would occasionally read my columns prior to publication and give me feedback via email. One time I wrote an article on Muslim terrorism and sent the article to Theo. He responded with an email saying that he could no longer be friends with me because of my Nazi thinking. I, in turn, decided to write another article on the liberalism of Hollywood, using Theo Bikel as my prime example. I included the email he had sent to me and stated how "off the wall" Mr. Bikel's thinking was. Needless to say, Theo was furious, and he did not speak to me for quite awhile. But eventually we made peace.

I was sad when Theo died in 2015. When I was watching the 2016 Academy Awards I was pleased to see his picture on screen during the "In Memoriam" portion of the show. It was a well-deserved honor.

Dinner with Theo

Martin Landau...Mr. Debonair

I first met Martin Landau at a party following the Cannes Film Festival. It was about 4:00 AM; they always had parties in the middle of the night! I was at a celebrity's house with a mob of people. I was having a nice conversation with Martin when some young, Asian hooker came over and tried to take him away to dance with her. I told him, "Don't think about going with her, she will put you in traction."

"Marty," as I call him, appeared on my last show in its final year. He was looking debonair in a black suit, red cashmere scarf, and a royal blue sweater. I started the show by saying "Today is a special day, and I have the *man* here. And when I say the man—all of his contemporaries have gotten older, and this man has only gotten better." I noted that not only is he a great actor but also an entrepreneur, producer, and director, who has to his credit "Golden Globes, Emmys, Oscar nominations..." "Oscar winner," he corrected me, and I apologized and said I had lost my head for a minute! I mentioned that he had worked with Sharon Stone, Carol Burnett, and Patricia Arquette, and added, "You do well with the sexy ladies." At the time he had *six* movies coming out.

We discussed Marty's early career as a cartoonist. At age 17, he started working at the *New York Daily News*. He said he lied to them and told them he was 18; he's not sure why he did that because they hadn't said anything about having to be 18 to work there. He liked the comics and could draw, so he became a cartoonist. He also did cartoon work for Billy Rose's syndicated "Pitching Horseshoes" column three times a week. Marty would read the piece and do a thumbnail sketch to accompany the article.

On my set with Martin Landau on my last show, 2008

Marty said that he was really good at caricatures and that he did a lot of those. He said his job was maybe the most "cushy" job at the newspaper, not to mention one of the highest-paid art jobs at any newspaper. So when he had a chance to move up to a more prestigious cartoonist position at the paper, he realized that if he took the job he would never leave. So he quit to become an actor.

Marty is still drawing cartoons, which he calls doodles. He brought some of them on my show. He said that he has thousands of these and has even had some interest from publishers for a book. As he showed the pictures he noted, "I like women, so there's a bunch of women." That's always good to confirm! Marty told me that he can draw straight lines without a ruler and that he often doodles while on the telephone. He commented that the pictures have a sort of Deco look, and I agreed. After he showed me his artwork, I showed him my book that had just been published, *Prison Cheerleader: How a Nice Jewish Girl Went Wrong Doing Right*. Marty was very nice about my book. He joked that I'd have to shorten the title for the movie!

Early in his acting career, Marty was one of 2,000 auditioning for the Actor's Studio, and he and Steve McQueen were the only two to be accepted that year. Marty noted that he is still involved with the Actor's Studio, running the West Coast studio with Mark Rydell.

For such a sweet guy, he played many "heavies": Mafia guys, cowboys, and even Indians and Mexicans. He did some humorous mobster and cowboy accents on the show. Honestly, I didn't know they had Jewish Indians, but I guess if Sammy Davis, Jr., could carry it off, so could Martin Landau!

Marty of course has a star on the Hollywood Walk of Fame. On a related note, Marty, a native of Brooklyn, had been named the "King of Brooklyn" about 15 years earlier. He said he even wore a crown for this role! He's in the Brooklyn Hall of Fame as well.

We talked about his early theater days. He replaced Franchot Tone at the Fourth Street Playhouse in a production of *Uncle Vanya*. Marty, in his twenties at the time, played a character in his fifties. He said when he looks back on that now, he sometimes wishes he could get another shot at it!

He also starred in *Middle of the Night* on Broadway with Edward G. Robinson and Gena Rowlands. After seeing Marty in this play, Alfred Hitchcock called him and asked him to come to his office. There he showed Marty the storyboard for *North by Northwest*. He said he and Hitchcock "got along amazingly well," and Hitchcock cast him in the film.

We reminisced about the early days of television. Marty reminded me that the first three networks were CBS, NBC, and Dumont, which was eventually replaced by ABC. I'm glad that has changed so now everyone can watch my show!

Martin won his Academy Award, along with a Golden Globe and SAG award, for his role as Bela Lugosi in Tim

Burton's *Ed Wood*. He had been nominated for an Oscar twice previously, for his roles in *Crimes and Misdemeanors* and the Coppola movie *Tucker*. Marty won a Golden Globe for the latter movie. Marty was very knowledgeable about the life of the "real" Tucker upon whom the film was based.

At one point during our conversation I admitted that I had been banned from Google for being "politically incorrect." Marty didn't believe that and said he would verify it through his Blackberry before the show ended.

Since this was my last live show, I asked Marty for a closing comment, some words of wisdom to pass on to my viewers. He said, "Follow your dream. If it's possible, do it. It's one time around." I answered, "I'm not sure about that. I want to come back as a tall, blonde, skinny shiksa, married to a Jewish man for the second time. Named Whitney." And no shopping at Marshall's or Loehmann's. Because second wives get everything.

At Peter Mark Richman's birthday party, 2007